CICERO
Philippics I & II

Edited with Introduction and Notes by
J.D. Denniston

Bristol Classical Press
(by arrangement with Oxford University Press)

This impression 2003
This edition published in 1978 by
Bristol Classical Press
an imprint of
Gerald Duckworth & Co. Ltd.
61 Frith Street, London W1D 3JL
Tel: 020 7434 4242
Fax: 020 7434 4420
inquiries@duckworth-publishers.co.uk
www.ducknet.co.uk

First published in 1926 by Oxford University Press
This reprint has been authorised by Oxford University Press

A catalogue record for this book is available
from the British Library

ISBN 0 906515 08 4

Printed and bound in Great Britain by
Antony Rowe Ltd, Eastbourne

PREFACE

CICERO's first two Philippics have often been edited, the Second perhaps as often as any of his speeches. But many of the formidable historical and antiquarian problems which they suggest have been inadequately discussed, or entirely ignored[1]. My main object in the present work has been to state the difficulties clearly, and to present the reader with the materials available for their solution. Recent historical research has cleared up many points, but much remains obscure: and I conceive it to be an editor's business to formulate such problems as occur to him, and, where he cannot solve them, to admit his inability with frankness. Apart from actual *cruces*, I have thought it worth while to present these speeches against a tolerably detailed historical background, and to investigate with some care how far Cicero's statements regarding himself, Antony, and other persons are reconcilable with statements made by himself elsewhere, and with what we learn from other sources. I have further thought it not irrelevant to discuss fully certain features of Roman life and institutions to which allusion is made in these speeches. All this has involved the writing of some rather long notes, though I hope I have not wasted words. In compensation, I have cut down the grammatical notes to the barest minimum.

The task would have been more suitably undertaken by some one possessing a far wider and deeper knowledge of Roman history than any I can claim. I started upon it accidentally, when lecturing on the speeches to Hertford Passmen before the war, and was led by growing interest in the

[1] e.g. i. 3, 6, 8, 13, 19-20; ii. 16, 26, 31, 49, 71, 81-4, 99, 110.

subject to complete it. My mistakes would certainly have been more numerous and more serious had it not been for the kindness of several Oxford colleagues. The whole work has been read in manuscript by Mr. G. H. Stevenson of University College, and in proof by Mr. C. Hignett of Hertford (who dissents strongly from my estimate of Cicero): both have made many valuable suggestions and discussed many details with me. Mr. H. M. D. Parker of Keble has helped me on several points, particularly in connexion with the Roman army, and has written me a note on ii. 58. Finally, Mr. J. G. C. Anderson read the Introduction in an early stage. My thanks are due to all these, and to the staff of the Clarendon Press for the great care with which the proofs have been corrected.

As to editions, I have constantly used K. Halm's *First and Second Philippics*, (8th ed., revised by G. Laubmann, 1905); J. R. King's *First and Second Philippics* (2nd ed., revised by A. C. Clark, 1908); J. E. B. Mayor's translation of Halm's edition, with large additions, 1884; and A. G. Peskett's *Second Philippic*, 1887. I have also referred frequently to H. de la Ville de Mirmont's *First Philippic*, 1902, and to E. G. Sihler's *Second Philippic*, 1901. I may add that F. Schoell's text of the *Philippics* (1916) contains a convenient resumé of passages in ancient authors bearing on the speeches. On historical points I have used W. Drumann's *Geschichte Roms*, 2nd ed., revised by P. Groebe, 1899–; T. Rice Holmes's *Roman Republic*, 1923; W. E. Heitland's *Roman Republic*, 1909; G. Ferrero's *Grandezza e Decadenza di Roma*, 1901, Eng. Trans. by A. E. Zimmern and H. J. Chaytor; E. Meyer's *Caesars Monarchie*, 2nd ed., 1919; E. Becht's *Regeste über die Zeit von Cäsars Ermordung bis zum Umschwung in der Politik des Antonius*, 1911; and W. Sternkopf's articles in *Hermes*: on constitutional and legal points, Th. Mommsen's *Römisches Staatsrecht*, 3rd ed., 1887–8; A. H. J. Greenidge's *Roman Public Life*, 1901, and *Legal Procedure in Cicero's time*, 1901; and J. L. Strachan-Davidson's *Problems of the Roman Criminal*

Law, 1912: on religious points, G. Wissowa's *Religion und Kultus der Römer*, 2nd ed., 1912; W. Warde Fowler's *Roman Festivals*, 1899, *Roman Ideas of Deity*, 1914, and *Religious Experience of the Roman People*, 1911; and I. M. J. Valeton's articles in *Mnemosyne*: on Roman private antiquities, H. Blümner's *Die römischen Privataltertümer*, 1911. I have drawn freely on Pauly-Wissowa, *Real-Encyclopädie*, and, to a less degree, on Daremberg et Saglio, *Dictionnaire des Antiquités*, and W. Smith's *Dictionary of Antiquities*. Other obligations are noticed as they occur.

Some readers will think that I have done less than justice to Cicero, as a man and as a statesman. I admit that he was in many respects an attractive person, a pure liver in a licentious age, and an unusually honest provincial governor: and in certain great crises, as in the Catilinarian conspiracy and the closing scene of his life, he showed coolness and resolution. But throughout the greater part of his career he lacked, in my opinion, both a definite policy and the courage to carry one out. His character was well summed up by a friend who had ample opportunities for judging him correctly (Brutus, quoted on p. 111). He has been unfortunate, no doubt, in bequeathing to posterity a correspondence which has furnished so much of the evidence against him. But the plea, freely urged, that other ancient statesmen were no better, but had the good luck to remain undetected, seems to me an inadequate one. Opinions have differed, and always will differ, as to Cicero's merits. I have not wilfully set out to traduce my author, and, where I have criticized him, I think I have always brought evidence to support my judgement.

J. D. D

23 *March*, 1926

CONTENTS

NOTE ON ABBREVIATIONS

(1) References to ancient authors are by books and sections (to Asconius by marginal pages): references to modern authors are by volumes and pages.

Where no author is given, Latin references are to Cicero.

References to the Philippics, in the Commentary, give number of speech and section only, except where ambiguity would be caused by the omission of 'Phil.'

(2) References to Becht, Blümner, Ferrero, Groebe-Drumann, Heitland, Meyer, and Wissowa are to the works mentioned in the Preface.

(3) A. = Epistulae ad Atticum.
F. = Epistulae ad Familiares.
App. = Appian, Bellum Civile (unless otherwise stated).
Nic. Dam. = Nicolas of Damascus, Vita Caesaris.

All other abbreviations will, I hope, explain themselves.

INTRODUCTION

THE indecision shown by the conspirators after Caesar's murder on the 15th March 44 B.C. is sufficient proof that they had thought out no plan for future action. Possibly, as Mr. Heitland suggests,[1] they had been reluctant to imperil the unity of their enterprise by discussing details in advance. Cicero afterwards bitterly regretted their lack of foresight. 'Acta enim illa res est animo virili, consilio puerili' was his comment.[2] However this may be, they could think of no better expedient for dealing with the situation than an appeal to the populace to rise and assert their newly won freedom.[3] Finding little response, they retired to the Capitol, and there began deliberations which, in a reasonably well-organized conspiracy, would have been completed in advance. Antony meanwhile had fled to his house and fortified it,[4] not knowing what fate might be in store for him, or what the extent of the conspiracy. Here he was joined by Lepidus, Caesar's Master of Horse, who may at first have hoped to lead the Caesarians, but in fact played only a subordinate role. The conspirators now received some encouragement from the attitude of Dolabella, who had been elected to succeed as *consul suffectus* when Caesar should leave Rome for the Parthian campaign,[5] and now appeared publicly in his robes of office, and declared his hostility to the Dictator's memory.[6] Brutus and Cassius

[1] iii. 372.
[2] A. xiv. 21, 3.
[3] Nic. Dam. 25; App. ii. 119; Dio xliv. 20-1.
[4] Phil. ii. 88; Plut. Brut. 18; Ant. 14; Caes. 67; App. ii. 118; Dio xliv. 22, 2.
[5] Phil. ii. 80-4.
[6] Vell. ii. 58, 3; Dio xliv. 22.

ventured to descend into the Forum and make another speech.[1] But the second demonstration fell as flat as the first, and returning to the Capitol they resumed their debate. They were now joined by Cicero and other persons who, though in sympathy with the plot, had not been privy to it.[2] Cicero urged that the praetors, M. Brutus and C. Cassius, should assume command of the state and convene the senate.[3] But this bold advice was rejected, and it was decided to open negotiations with Antony, who, towards evening, after an interchange of emissaries in which Cicero refused to participate, promised a definite answer on the following day.[4]

During the night of the 15th/16th Lepidus occupied the Forum with such soldiers as he could muster,[5] and Antony obtained from Caesar's widow, Calpurnia, the dead man's papers and ready money, amounting to 100,000,000 sesterces.[6] We may conjecture that Antony had recovered from the first shock of surprise, and that his prospects were improving every moment. The conspirators had failed in their attempt to carry the people away on a wave of republican enthusiasm. Already, probably, discharged veterans were streaming into the city, and Antony was sending round to the newly founded military colonies and urging the settlers to hasten to Rome and vindicate their claims.[7] On the following day, the 16th, the Caesarians held a council of war. Lepidus was for massacring the conspirators: but Hirtius advocated a milder policy, and Antony supported him.[8] The negotiations were

[1] Nic. Dam. 26a; Plut. Caes. 67; Brut. 18; App. ii. 122; Dio xliv. 21.

[2] Phil. ii. 25-34; App. ii. 119; Dio xliv. 21, 3-4.

[3] A. xiv. 10, 1.

[4] Phil. ii. 89; Nic. Dam. 27.

[5] Nic. Dam. 27; App. ii. 126; Dio xliv. 22, 2. (The first the most accurate of the three: στρατιὰν ἐπικούρων, not a formed body of troops. See Ferrero iii. 315.)

[6] App. ii. 125; iii. 17. Plutarch (Ant. 15), no doubt erroneously, puts the occurrence after Caesar's funeral. Antony did not plunder the temple of Ops during the night of 15th/16th, as is often asserted. See i. 17 and note.

[7] Nic. Dam. 27.

[8] Nic. Dam. 27, in spite of App. ii. 124.

concluded by an agreement to hand over outstanding problems to the senate for solution. Order was restored in the city, and messages were sent round to the senators, requesting their attendance in the temple of Tellus before dawn on the following day, the 17th March.[1]

Cicero was present at the meeting,[2] but none of the conspirators ventured to attend. The debate was long and wandering, but Antony brought it to the point by reminding the senators that, if Caesar was to be regarded as a tyrant, his acts must be held null and void.[3] The argument produced considerable effect on the many persons who owed preferments and emoluments to Caesar's benefaction, especially Dolabella, who, being under the legal age, could not normally expect to retain his consulship. A compromise was accordingly adopted, by which an amnesty was granted to Caesar's murderers, but his *acta* were declared valid, including his unpublished decisions, as contained in the memoranda now in Antony's possession.[4] The conspirators thereupon left the Capitol, after receiving the sons of Antony and Lepidus as hostages,[5] and a semblance of peace was established between the two parties.

Soon afterwards Antony's position was strengthened by the opening of Caesar's will, in which he left his gardens beyond the Tiber to the people, and a sum of 300 sesterces to each citizen individually:[6] and the funeral, which ended in riots and incendiarism, gave Antony an opportunity of enlisting popular sympathy.[7] Nevertheless he proceeded at first with caution, and took pains to reassure the republicans.[8] He used but sparingly, and apparently honestly, the power accorded him of

[1] App. ii. 124-6; Dio xliv. 22, 3.
[2] Phil. i. 1. Dio xliv. 23-33 gives what purports to have been his speech on this occasion.
[3] App. ii. 127-9.
[4] Phil. i. 31; Plut. Brut. 19; Cic. 42; App. ii. 135; Dio xliv. 34, 3.
[5] Phil. i. 2; i. 31; ii. 90; Liv. Ep. 116; Vell. ii. 58, 3; Dio. xliv. 36, 4.
[6] Suet. Iul. 83; App. ii. 143; Dio xliv. 35, 2-3.
[7] Phil. ii. 90-1; A. xiv. 10, 1; Plut. Caes. 68; Ant. 14; Brut. 20; App. ii. 148; Dio xliv. 35-51.
[8] Phil. i. 2-5; ii. 91 (with notes).

giving effect to Caesar's acts ; he was careful to consult leading senators on important matters ; he restored but one single exile ; he agreed to the curtailment, perhaps for a time to the total abolition, of his power to make use of the *Acta Caesaris*; he himself proposed the perpetual abolition of the dictatorship : a few days later (perhaps on the 13th April) he executed without trial a certain Amatius, who posed as the grandson of Marius, and was exciting popular opinion against Caesar's murderers. Many thought that the republic was 'on its feet again'.[1] It was not long, however, before the cloven hoof appeared. From about the 18th April Antony began to publish palpably forged *Acta Caesaris*, for which he was well paid by the beneficiaries.[2] At about the same time, it began to be rumoured that he intended to obtain, either by a decree of the senate or by a law of the people, the command of Cisalpine and Transalpine Gaul for an extraordinary period of five years, on vacating his consulship, in exchange for Macedonia, to which he had already been appointed, probably early in April.[3] The support of Dolabella, to whom Syria had been assigned at the same time, was won by promising the extension of his command for a similar period. Suspicion was heightened by Antony's leaving Rome towards the end of April for a tour in Campania,[4] where he was to administer the settlement of discharged soldiers in the colonies recently founded by Caesar. On the 11th May Cicero heard from Balbus that Antony was systematically canvassing and organizing Caesar's veterans, with the intention of using them to overawe the senate.[5] Thus he, on his side, was carrying out a carefully conceived plan. He meant to base his power, as Caesar had done, on a long provincial command, and he was methodically collecting the money and men necessary to ensure success. The republicans, on

[1] Phil. ii. 92.
[2] Phil. ii. 92, 97, 100; A. xiv. 12, 1; 13, 6; F. xii. 1, 1.
[3] A. xiv. 14, 4. See Appendix I.
[4] Phil. ii. 100–7 (with notes).
[5] A. xiv. 21, 2.

the other hand, had no plan and no leader. For one thing, they were scattered. Cicero had left Rome probably on the 7th April,[1] and about the same time Decimus Brutus and Trebonius had departed for their provinces, Cisalpine Gaul and Asia.[2] M. Brutus and Cassius had been compelled, in consequence of the riots provoked by Amatius, to leave the capital on about the 13th April.[3] Intellectually the republicans looked to Cicero, by far the most experienced statesman on their side, or indeed in Rome: morally both he and they looked to Brutus. We find this feeling everywhere in his letters. 'The Republic hangs on Brutus.' 'If Brutus can live safely in Rome, we have won.'[4] And so on. But neither Brutus nor Cicero had the vestige of a constructive policy. Cicero kept a careful watch on public opinion, as manifested by such signs as demonstrations in the theatre;[5] he kept an eye on Sextus Pompeius, who was still maintaining some show of resistance in Spain;[6] he nursed a vague hope that things would be better next year, when Hirtius and Pansa entered office as consuls, Caesarians, it was true, but not such bad men; he even, with indifferent success, attempted to encourage Hirtius in the way he should go.[7] When Dolabella, in Antony's absence, suppressed some rioters who had erected a monumental column on the site of Caesar's pyre, Cicero acclaimed him with almost hysterical enthusiasm as the long-awaited leader of the constitutionalists.[8] But in all this there is no sign of even an attempt to deal with a situation which was every day growing more serious: nothing but useless regrets for the past, and self-centred brooding over his personal prospects.

[1] The exact date is uncertain. Groebe (Drumann i². 420) and Merrill (Class. Phil. x. 255) give 7th April; Ferrero, 6th or 7th; Becht, between 5th and 11th.

[2] A. xiv. 10, 1; 13, 2; App. iii. 2.

[3] Phil. i. 6, note on *patriae liberatores*.

[4] A. xiv. 20, 3.

[5] A. xiv. 2, 1.

[6] A. xiv. 1, 2; 4, 1; 13, 2.

[7] Phil. i. 6, note on *consules designati*.

[8] Phil. i. 5, note on *afuisset*.

Returning to Rome on about the 20th May [1] Antony found the situation complicated by the arrival of Octavius, Caesar's heir and adopted son. He had been at Apollonia, completing his military training with the legions destined for the Parthian expedition, when the news of the Dictator's murder reached him. Landing at the port of Lupiae, near Brundisium, early in April, he proceeded to sound opinion among the troops there, found it favourable, and decided to accept the inheritance, against the advice of his father-in-law, Philippus.[2] He passed through Campania, declining, with a level-headedness remarkable in a boy of eighteen, the offers of allegiance which the veterans showered upon him. On the 18th April he reached Naples, and soon after went to stay with Philippus at Puteoli, where he met Cicero, whom he treated with great respect.[3] Cicero evidently liked him well enough personally, but mistrusted his entourage, and, with Philippus, pointedly refrained from addressing him as 'Caesar'. He reached Rome late in April or early in May, and presented himself to the Praetor Urbanus, C. Antonius, to whom he announced his acceptance of the inheritance and adoption.[4] Introduced to the people by L. Antonius, the tribune, he made his first public speech. Cicero found its tone unsatisfactory, and was displeased with the preparations the young man was making, in collaboration with prominent Caesarians, for the forthcoming celebration of games instituted by Caesar in honour of his victory at Pharsalus.[5] On Antony's arrival in Rome, Octavius called upon him and asked for the payment of Caesar's legacy.[6] The request was rudely brushed aside, and there sprang up between the two men a coolness which the republicans did their best

[1] Phil. ii. 108, note.
[2] A. xiv. 10. 3; Nic. Dam. 17-18; Suet. Aug. 8; Vell. ii. 59-60; App. iii. 9-13; Dio xlv. 3-4.
[3] A. xiv. 11, 2; 12, 2.
[4] App. iii. 14.
[5] A. xiv. 20, 5; xv. 2, 3; Dio xlv. 6, 3.
[6] Nic. Dam. 28; Liv. Ep. 117; Plut. Ant. 16; Vell. ii. 60, 3; App. iii. 14.

to increase. As a possible counterpoise to Antony, Octavius, with the prestige of his adoptive name (he now styled himself Gaius Iulius Caesar Octavianus), and the popularity which he subsequently gained by paying part of Caesar's legacy to the people out of his own pocket, was clearly 'worth nursing' (*alendus*).[1]

In the course of his Campanian journey Antony had collected arms and veterans in considerable numbers, and brought a large body of them to Rome.[2] These intimidatory measures evoked a protest from Brutus and Cassius, and even Hirtius was indignant.[3] Speculation was rife as to what Antony intended. It was uncertain whether he would bring his proposal for an exchange of provinces before the senate or before the people:[4] the latter, Cicero hoped, so that the senate might be spared the ignominy of compliance. Moreover, it was rumoured that he would not be content with a mere exchange, but would precipitate war by attempting to expel D. Brutus from Cisalpine Gaul by force instantly, without waiting for the expiry of his term of office, while his own friends in Rome set upon the conspirators' party.[5] It was known that he would use soldiers on the 1st June to overawe the senate:[6] the leading republicans, Cicero among them, could not make up their minds whether to attend this meeting or not, but carried on a feverish and vacillating correspondence with one another.[7] However, when the 1st June arrived, expectations were upset, for no important measure was proposed. The Senate House was virtually empty, none of the principal senators daring to appear.[8] Encouraged apparently by this symptom, Antony carried through the comitia on the following day, before a packed and cowed assembly, without legal notice, and in the midst of a violent thunderstorm, a law giving himself the command of Gallia Cisalpina and Gallia Transalpina for five years,

[1] A. xv. 12. 2.
[2] Phil. ii. 108.
[3] F. xi. 2; A. xv. 6; 8.
[4] A. xv 4, 1.
[5] A. xv. 4, 1; 5, 3; Sternkopf, Hermes, xlvii. (1912) 370.
[6] A. xiv. 22; xv. 4, 1.
[7] A. xv. 1, 5; 5, 1; 8, 1.
[8] Phil. ii. 108.

and prolonging Dolabella's tenure of Syria from one year to five.[1] Simultaneously a land-law was rushed through, providing for the distribution of allotments on a large scale. On the 5th June Antony persuaded the senate to pass a decree conferring on M. Brutus and Cassius the task of organizing the corn supply in Asia and Sicily respectively:[2] they were to enter forthwith upon these duties, which would keep them out of the way until the end of their year of office: they would then proceed to their provinces (which had not yet been assigned to them). The 'heroes' were furious at this ingenious euphemism for banishment, and Cicero was reduced to despair. He regarded the commission as an insult, but strongly recommended its acceptance. Brutus, after the first excitement was over, seemed disposed to accept, and began to collect ships.[3] The situation looked very black. Brutus's removal would be an incalculable blow to the republican cause. There was no quarter from which aid could be expected. Octavianus, like Hirtius and Pansa, seemed on the whole well disposed, but unreliable.[4] An embarrassing success added a new peril. By mid-June news arrived that Sextus Pompeius had occupied Carteia, near the Straits of Gibraltar. With a port at his disposal, it was rumoured that he was on the point of sailing for Italy.[5] War seemed inevitable, a war, Antony said, in which there would be no room for neutrals.[6] In preparation for it, he was further securing the allegiance of the veterans by means of a land-law, promulgated by himself and Dolabella, and carried out by a commission consisting entirely of his relatives and adherents.[7]

Cicero had long thought of leaving Italy,[8] and the design now took definite shape in his mind. Dolabella had appointed him legate on the 2nd June,[9] and he was consequently free to

[1] Phil. v. 7; Appendix I.
[2] A. xv. 9.
[3] A. xv. 10; 11; 12; 24
[4] A. xv. 12; 22.
[5] A. xv. 20; 21.
[6] A. xv. 20, 3; 22.
[7] Phil. ii. 6 (note on *et de te*); vi. 14; xi. 13.
[8] A. xiv. 7; 10; 13; 16; 18; 21.
[9] A. xv. 11,4; 20, 1.

quit the country when he wished. But he could not actually make up his mind to start. He had an uneasy feeling that people might think he was running away in the hour of danger.[1] Early in July, it is true, one source of danger was removed. Sextus Pompeius had lain down his arms, and for the moment it seemed that 'servitude, rather than civil war, was in prospect'.[2] One day full of alarm, the next day convinced that all was quiet, and that the real trouble would begin with the new year, when he was back in Rome,[3] Cicero finally, on the 17th July, actually did embark at Pompeii.[4] Travelling by Velia, Vibo, and Rhegium, he arrived at Syracuse on the 1st August, and embarked again the following day.[5] A storm drove him to Leucopetra, where he stayed a few days. Leaving again on the 6th, another storm drove him back to the same spot. On the following day some Rhegians lately arrived from Rome gave him news of recent events: they brought with them a speech of Antony's, couched in moderate terms, and a manifesto of Brutus and Cassius asking to be relieved of the odious corn-commission.[6] Things were looking much better, they assured Cicero; Antony would probably relinquish his pretensions to Cisalpine and Transalpine Gaul, and recognize the authority of the senate; a compromise would be reached, and Brutus and Cassius would be able to return to Rome; there was to be a full meeting of the senate on the 1st August, and Brutus and Cassius were beating up their supporters: people were asking why Cicero was absent from Rome at so critical a time.[7] On hearing this report Cicero at once abandoned his journey and started back for Rome. He met Brutus at Velia on the 17th August, and heard from him news which dashed all his new-born hopes to the ground. The meeting on the 1st August had proved a complete fiasco. Piso, speaking against Antony, had stood alone, and had not ventured to appear in the senate

[1] A. xiv. 13, 4; xv. 25; xvi. 7.
[2] A. xv. 29, 1; xvi. 1, 4.
[3] A. xvi. 3, 4; 7, 2.
[4] A. xvi. 3, 6.
[5] Phil. i. 7; F. vii. 20; A. xvi. 6
[6] Phil. i. 8, note.
[7] Phil. i. 8; A. xvi, 7.

on the following day.[1] Cicero could now avail nothing by returning. But his reputation, which had suffered severely by his departure, demanded that he should return. He arrived back in Rome on the 31st August. The senate was to meet in the temple of Concord on the following day, to discuss a proposal for adding to all public thanksgivings a day in honour of Caesar's memory.[2] Cicero dared not oppose such a measure, but could scarcely have sat silent while it was being discussed. He therefore decided to absent himself from the senate, and sent a message to Antony, couched in friendly terms, that he was tired after his journey. (Attendance in the senate was theoretically compulsory, but in practice the rule was usually not enforced when the motion before the house was of a purely complimentary nature.) The senate met, and all resistance was overawed by Antony's soldiery, which thronged the temple. The gates were shut, to prevent any attempt at succour from outside. Antony censured Cicero's absence in violent language, and threatened to fetch him from his house by force. The cowed senate obediently carried the proposal in Caesar's honour. On the following day, the 2nd September, Antony, pleading indisposition, was himself absent from the senate, but Cicero attended and delivered the First Philippic, a restrained and temperate speech,[3] in which he remonstrates with Antony for his violent language, and contrasts the excellence of his earlier conduct with his subsequent political excesses. Antony kept silence for seventeen days. He spent this period, according to Cicero, in the villa of Q. Metellus Scipio, Pompey's father-in-law, composing a violent invective against Cicero's whole career, which he delivered at a meeting of the senate on the 19th September. Again the temple of Concord was packed with soldiers.

[1] Phil. i. 1–10; A. xvi. 7.
[2] Phil. i. 11–13; v. 18–20 (and for the whole history of events from 1st to 19th September).
[3] Phil. ii. 6; v. 19

Antony had challenged Cicero to be present, and Cicero says he would have accepted the invitation, though it meant certain assassination, had his friends allowed him. The two men were now open and declared enemies. Cicero forthwith began the composition of the Second Philippic, an elaborate defence of his own political career and attack on Antony's. The speech purports to be a reply delivered on the 19th September to Antony's invective, and, although never actually spoken, it contains several touches of local colour, introduced for the sake of verisimilitude.[1] Cicero took great pains over its composition, and obviously intended it to be, as indeed it is, a most elaborate production. He sent a rough copy to Atticus in October 44, and carefully discussed with him minute points of diction.[2] The finished speech was published perhaps in December,[3] soon after Antony's departure from Rome for his campaign against Decimus Brutus. Twelve further speeches were composed by Cicero against Antony. The title 'Philippics', after the speeches delivered by Demosthenes against Philip of Macedon, was first suggested half jokingly by Cicero in a letter to M. Brutus.[4] Brutus was pleased with the name, which was then adopted by Cicero as a serious title, and has held the field ever since, though Aulus Gellius refers to the speeches as 'Antonianae'.[5] It must be admitted that the title 'Philippics' is not a very happy one. If we are to look for a Demosthenic parallel, the De Corona, in spite of many differences, resembles at any rate the Second Philippic more closely. Both speeches contain an elaborate defence of the author's whole political career, delivered near its close: and both combine this defence with a fierce and virulent attack on the career of a political opponent. A comparison of the two speeches gives a fair measure of the distance between the two men, as statesmen and as orators.

[1] Phil. ii. 8; 15; 19; 36; 46; 76; 84; 104; 110–12.
[2] A. xvi. 11, 1–3.
[3] Halm, Introd., p. 38.
[4] Ad Brut. ii. 3, 4; 4, 2; Plut. Cic. 24; 48.
[5] vii. 11; xiii. 1; 21.

ANALYSIS

I

1–5. Before discussing politics I will explain the reason of my departure and sudden return. After Caesar's death Antony's conduct was at first constitutional and conciliatory.

6. But from 1st June he began to employ terrorism. I therefore decided to absent myself until 1st January, when there was a hope that orderly government would be restored under the new consuls.

7–8. Adverse winds interfered with my journey: and the news that Antony was reverting to constitutional methods induced me to return.

9–10. The news proved false, but I abode by my decision.

11–12. Antony hotly resented my absence from the senate on 1st September. But, as the motion before the house was of a complimentary nature, attendance was, by tradition, optional.

13. Had I been present I could not have voted in favour of the motion to decree public thanksgivings in memory of Caesar.

14–15. I shall in future boldly express my political opinions. I wish I had been in the senate on 1st August, and regret that responsible politicians failed to support Piso on that occasion.

16. Turning now to the general political situation: I believe in upholding Caesar's *Acta*, but refuse to include in that category casual memoranda produced on Antony's sole authority.

17–20. A politician's legislative measures form the most important part of his *Acta*: and Antony has flouted Caesar's legislative measures by such enactments as the *lex de provinciis* and the recently promulgated *lex iudiciaria*. The latter is simply an attempt to interfere with the impartial administration of justice.

21–22. Another law has been promulgated, allowing appeal against condemnation for violence and high-treason. The object is to make it impossible for any one to be prosecuted for these offences.

23. This law, again, controverts Caesar's legislation.

24. Even if we approve Antony's use of the *Acta Caesaris* in other respects, we cannot approve such violation of Caesar's laws.

25. The traditional checks on pernicious legislation are overridden by force.

26. Laws so passed do not deserve the name.

27–28. Of the two consuls, Dolabella will, I am sure, not resent my frankness. Antony ought not to resent it, if I refrain from personalities.

29–32. I know that the aims of both consuls are honourable. Both have experienced the true glory which is won by disinterested patriotism.

33–35. If Antony adopts the motto *oderint dum metuant* he will make a great mistake.

36–37. The demonstrations of sympathy with Brutus and Hirtius show the state of public opinion.

38. I have set my opinions on record, and you have heard me with attention. I hope that it may be possible for me to continue speaking to you.

II

1. You,[1] Antony, are the first enemy of Rome wantonly to challenge my enmity.

2. Presumably you think this the only way to prove yourself an enemy of Rome.

3–5. You accuse me of betraying friendship by acting against you in a certain case. I had every right to act as I did. You also falsely claim to have been a pupil of mine, to have withdrawn your candidature for the augurship in deference to me, and to have saved my life at Brundisium in the Civil War. You could not have killed me on that occasion: and in any case the benefaction would have been a negative one.

[1] In the Second Philippic Cicero usually addresses Antony in the second person, though he frequently refers to him in the third. For the sake of clearness I have used the second person throughout the analysis of the speech.

6. The tone of the First Philippic was remarkably moderate and free from personalities.

7. You read out in the senate a letter which you said I had written you. In the first place, this was a breach of etiquette: in the second, I might deny authorship: in the third, the letter was a most friendly one. And if your point is that it *was* friendly, so too was *your* letter, and disingenuous as well.

10. I have got to defend myself and attack you. I shall not treat you as a consul, because you do not deserve it.

11–14. You have taken occasion to attack my consulship. Every one else has approved of it.

15. What company you keep!

16–17. You accuse me of suppressing the Catilinarian conspiracy by force of arms. What about your own use of arms? And how loyal was the response to my appeal for armed assistance!

18. The story that I refused to give up Lentulus' body for burial is a lie.

19. It is, I repeat, ridiculous for you to blame me for using arms, when you are blockading the Senate House with foreign soldiers.

20. Your attempts at humour are feeble.

21–22. You say I planned the assassination of Clodius. You once tried to kill him yourself. I never knew Milo meant to kill him. And at the time no one threw suspicion on me.

23–24. You say I caused the Civil War by alienating Pompey from Caesar. At first, it is true, I tried to keep the two apart. But after Pompey had committed himself irrevocably to Caesar, and immeasurably strengthened Caesar's position, I tried to compose their differences and so maintain peace.

25–27. You charge me with complicity in the assassination of Caesar, a flattering accusation. But my complicity could not have remained secret, and the assassins did not need my encouragement.

28. That Brutus called out my name proves nothing.

29. If I wished for Caesar's death, so did all good citizens.

30–31. What is your real attitude to the conspirators? Are they heroes or criminals? They must be one or the other. You have often enough honoured them, in word and deed.

32–33. They are, as a matter of fact, heroes, on your own showing. And I am glad to be numbered among them.

34. If I had been in the plot I should have killed you too. Incidentally, you once thought of assassinating Caesar yourself.

35-36. You stood to gain much by his death.

37. You reproach me with my behaviour in Pompey's camp. I confess I was gloomy, foreseeing the disastrous future.

38-39. But, as a matter of fact, I was on the best of terms with Pompey. Inconsistently enough, you also blame me for my occasional flippancy, which was perfectly natural.

40-41. You say I have inherited no legacies. I have inherited large legacies; but from friends, not, like you, from total strangers.

42-43. So much for your speech, the result of careful preparation and expensive professional assistance.

44-46. Now let me turn to your career. You started life as a bankrupt. Your boyhood was spent in debauchery.

47. I will pass rapidly over the following years, reserving my detailed attention for your conduct during and after the Civil War.

48. You enjoyed the intimacy of Clodius, and accompanied Gabinius in his Egyptian adventure. Then you joined Caesar in Gaul.

49. Next you stood for the quaestorship, cultivating my friendship assiduously.

50. Elected quaestor, you returned to Caesar.

51-55. On 1st January 49, as tribune, you precipitated the outbreak of the Civil War, and must be regarded as the cause of all its miseries.

56. You reinstated scoundrels like Lenticula, but refused to recall your uncle Gaius.

57. When Caesar left for Spain he handed over the command of Italy to you.

58. In this capacity you behaved most disgracefully.

59-61. You then fought in the Thessalian campaign, and, returning to Italy, claim to have saved my life at Brundisium, where your mistress awaited you.

62. On reaching Rome you were appointed Magister Equitum.

63. You were sick at an assembly of the people, having got drunk at a wedding the day before.

64-70. After Caesar's return from Alexandria you bought Pompey's confiscated property at an auction. But it did not last you long. You polluted the dwelling of that upright man with your debaucheries.

71–72. You did not follow Caesar to Africa. On his return he prosecuted you for the money owing to him on account of Pompey's property.

73–74. In desperation you attempted to hold a sale of your effects, but were prevented. Caesar gave you a few days' grace, and left for Spain. Again you stayed behind.

75. At last you started after him, but got no further than Narbo.

76–77. You returned from Narbo in disguise and enjoyed an affecting reconciliation with Fulvia.

78. You went to meet Caesar on his return, and were restored to favour.

79. He even nominated you as his colleague in the consulship, throwing over Dolabella.

80. When Caesar announced that he would nominate Dolabella as *consul suffectus* during his own absence in Parthia, you declared that you would, as augur, invalidate his election.

81. This threat was a sign both of stupidity and of shamelessness.

82–84. In the event, you interposed at the last moment, when the election was almost over.

84–87. At the Lupercalia you attempted to crown Caesar with a diadem.

88. After Caesar's assassination you fled in terror.

89. I refused to take part in the negotiations with you.

90. At the meeting of 17th March you behaved well.

91. And so you continued to do for a little while, in spite of your disgraceful speech at the funeral.

92. But, as I expected, your true nature soon showed itself.

92–96. You forged *Acta Caesaris* wholesale. The decree about Deiotarus was a grotesque instance. But he had already taken the law into his own hands.

97. The decree about Crete contained an incredible anachronism.

98–99. You restored exiles indiscriminately. In this connexion I must again mention your treatment of your uncle.

100. You never convened the Commission for investigating the *Acta Caesaris*.

101. In April and May you distributed Campanian land among your boon-companions.

102. By founding a new colony at Casilinum you infringed upon the rights of the existing colony at Capua.

103–105. At Casinum you seized Varro's house, and made it the scene of your customary debaucheries.

106–107. On your return journey you behaved with gross rudeness to the inhabitants of the country towns.

108–109. Arriving in Rome, you used armed force without the slightest concealment. We dared not attend the senate on 1st June. But you did not care: you obtained the extension of your provincial command from the assembly instead.

110–111. You pretend to be loyal to Caesar's memory. Why, then, have you made no preparations for celebrating to-day, which on your own proposal was dedicated to him? You are not even consistent in your blasphemy.

112–114. Arms will not save you from the fate you deserve. The liberators may be far away, but they will return. And, at any rate, their example will inspire others.

115. Remember your better days, Antony, and compare them with the present. Fear should move you, if honour cannot.

116–117. Caesar's friends and talents did not save him; and you are not to be compared with Caesar.

118–119. Once again, I beg you to remember the common weal and your own ancestry. But, whatever you do, I am ready to die for the state.

SIGLA

V = cod. tabularii Basilicae Vaticanae H. 25, saecl. ix
Cus. = cod. Nicolai Cusani, saecl. xii, excerpta quaedam continens, ab I. Klein collatus
D = codd. (*b*) *cnst* consensus
b = cod. Bernensis 104, saecl. xiii
c = familia Colotiana, i.e. codd. Paris. 5802, 6602, et Berol. Philipp. 201 consensus
n = cod. Vossianus, Lat. O. 2, saecl. x
s = cod. Vaticanus 3228, saecl. x (codex Scalae)
t = cod. Tegernseensis, saecl. xi
v = cod. Vaticanus 3227, saecl. xii (codex Langobardicus Ferrarii)

---

h = cod. Harleianus 2682, saecl. xi
l = cod. Regius 15 A. xiv, saecl. xi
o = cod. CCLII Collegii Novi Oxon., saecl. xii
π = cod. Parcensis, nunc Bruxellensis 14492, saecl. xiv
cod. Amst. = codex Amstelodamensis Univ. 77, saecl. xiii, ex quo lectiones aliquot exscripsit Deiterus
cod. P. Laeti = cod. Vaticanus 3229, saecl. xv
δ = codd. deteriores

Poggii emendationes in cod. Laur. xlviii. 22 inveniuntur

M. TVLLI CICERONIS

IN M. ANTONIVM

ORATIO PHILIPPICA PRIMA

ANTE quam de re publica, patres conscripti, dicam ea **1**
quae dicenda hoc tempore arbitror, exponam vobis breviter
consilium et profectionis et reversionis meae. Ego cum
sperarem aliquando ad vestrum consilium auctoritatemque
5 rem publicam esse revocatam, manendum mihi statuebam
quasi in vigilia quadam consulari ac senatoria. Nec vero
usquam discedebam nec a re publica deiciebam oculos ex
eo die quo in aedem Telluris convocati sumus. In quo
templo, quantum in me fuit, ieci fundamenta pacis Atheni-
10 ensiumque renovavi vetus exemplum; Graecum etiam verbum usurpavi quo tum in sedandis discordiis usa erat civitas
illa, atque omnem memoriam discordiarum oblivione sempi-
terna delendam censui. Praeclara tum oratio M. Antoni, **2**
egregia etiam voluntas; pax denique per eum et per liberos
15 eius cum praestantissimis civibus confirmata est. Atque his
principiis reliqua consentiebant. Ad deliberationes eas quas
habebat domi de re publica principes civitatis adhibebat;
ad hunc ordinem res optimas deferebat; nihil tum nisi quod

10 renovavi *Vns* : revocavi *ct*   11 discordiis usa erat *V* : discordaverat *c* : discordiis erat *t* : discors erat *ns*   18 referebat *Reid*   nisi . . . omnibus *om.* *D*

erat notum omnibus in C. Caesaris commentariis reperiebatur; summa constantia ad ea quae quaesita erant re-
3 spondebat. Num qui exsules restituti? Unum aiebat, praeterea neminem. Num immunitates datae? 'Nullae' respondebat. Adsentiri etiam nos Ser. Sulpicio, clarissimo viro, voluit, ne 5
qua tabula post Idus Martias ullius decreti Caesaris aut benefici figeretur. Multa praetereo eaque praeclara; ad singulare enim M. Antoni factum festinat oratio. Dictaturam, quae iam vim regiae potestatis obsederat, funditus ex re publica sustulit; de qua ne sententias quidem diximus. Scri- 10
ptum senatus consultum quod fieri vellet attulit, quo recitato auctoritatem eius summo studio secuti sumus eique amplis-
2 simis verbis per senatus consultum gratias egimus. Lux
4 quaedam videbatur oblata non modo regno, quod pertuleramus, sed etiam regni timore sublato, magnumque pignus 15
ab eo rei publicae datum, se liberam civitatem esse velle, cum dictatoris nomen, quod saepe iustum fuisset, propter perpetuae dictaturae recentem memoriam funditus ex re
5 publica sustulisset. Liberatus periculo caedis paucis post diebus senatus; uncus impactus est fugitivo illi qui in 20
Mari nomen invaserat. Atque haec omnia communiter cum conlega; alia porro propria Dolabellae quae, nisi conlega afuisset, credo eis futura fuisse communia. Nam cum serperet in urbe infinitum malum idque manaret in dies latius, idemque bustum in foro facerent qui illam insepultam sepul- 25
turam effecerant, et cotidie magis magisque perditi homines cum sui similibus servis tectis ac templis urbis minarentur, talis animadversio fuit Dolabellae cum in audacis sceleratosque servos, tum in impuros et nefarios liberos, talisque eversio illius exsecratae columnae ut mihi mirum videatur tam 30

1 reperiebat *Kraffert* 2 summa cum dignitate constantia *D* 4 nullae respondebat *om. D*: nullas respondebat *Wesenberg* 7 ea quae clara sunt *D* 9 iam vim *Vt*: vim iam *cns* possederat *Hirschfelder* 10 qua *VD*: qua re *cod. Amst* · *ut voluit Klussmann*: quo *Stangl* 24 urbem *Vns* 27 suis *codd.* (*cf.* ii. 2; iii 18): *corr. Angelius* minitarentur *V* (*cf. Zielinski, Philol.* 1906, *p.* 614)

valde reliquum tempus ab illo uno die dissensisse. Ecce 6
enim Kalendis Iuniis, quibus ut adessemus edixerant, mutata omnia: nihil per senatum, multa et magna per populum
et absente populo et invito. Consules designati negabant se
5 audere in senatum venire; patriae liberatores urbe carebant
ea cuius a cervicibus iugum servile deiecerant, quos tamen
ipsi consules in contionibus et in omni sermone laudabant.
Veterani qui appellabantur, quibus hic ordo diligentissime
caverat, non ad conservationem earum rerum quas habe-
10 bant, sed ad spem novarum praedarum incitabantur. Quae
cum audire mallem quam videre haberemque ius legationis
liberum, ea mente discessi ut adessem Kalendis Ianuariis,
quod initium senatus cogendi fore videbatur. Exposui, **3**
patres conscripti, profectionis consilium: nunc reversionis, 7
15 quae plus admirationis habet, breviter exponam. Cum
Brundisium iterque illud quod tritum in Graeciam est non
sine causa vitavissem, Kalendis Sextilibus veni Syracusas,
quod ab ea urbe transmissio in Graeciam laudabatur: quae
tamen urbs mihi coniunctissima plus una me nocte cupiens
20 retinere non potuit. Veritus sum ne meus repentinus ad
meos necessarios adventus suspicionis aliquid adferret, si
essem commoratus. Cum autem me ex Sicilia ad Leucope-
tram, quod est promunturium agri Regini, venti detulissent,
ab eo loco conscendi ut transmitterem; nec ita multum
25 provectus reiectus Austro sum in eum ipsum locum unde
conscenderam. Cumque intempesta nox esset mansissemque 8
in villa P. Valeri, comitis et familiaris mei, postridieque
apud eundem ventum exspectans manerem, municipes
Regini complures ad me venerunt, ex eis quidam Roma
30 recentes: a quibus primum accipio M. Antoni contionem,

2 edixerat *t* 7 in cont. *V*: et in cont. *D* 8 qui appellabantur *Vns*: qui appellantur *ct*: *om. Arusianus K.* vii. *p.* 488: *del. Jordan*: appellabantur *transponit post* habebant *Hirschfelder* (*del.* qui) 9 caverant (*sup. l.* timebant) *V*: timebat, caverat *t* 18 ab urbe ea *D* 24 transmitteremus austro *V*[1] *med. omissis*: nec ita multum si coniuctus proiectus *add.* *V*[2] 30 M. *om.* *V*

quae mihi ita placuit ut ea lecta de reversione primum coeperim cogitare. Nec ita multo post edictum Bruti adfertur et Cassi, quod quidem mihi, fortasse quod eos plus etiam rei publicae quam familiaritatis gratia diligo, plenum aequitatis videbatur. Addebant praeterea—fit enim plerum- 5 que ut ei qui boni quid volunt adferre adfingant aliquid quo faciant id quod nuntiant laetius—rem conventuram: Kalendis senatum frequentem fore; Antonium, repudiatis malis suasoribus, remissis provinciis Galliis, ad auctoritatem 4 senatus esse rediturum. 9 Tum vero tanta sum cupiditate 10 incensus ad reditum ut mihi nulli neque remi neque venti satis facerent, non quo me ad tempus occursurum non putarem, sed ne tardius quam cuperem rei publicae gratularer. Atque ego celeriter Veliam devectus Brutum vidi: quanto meo dolore non dico. Turpe mihi ipsi videbatur in 15 eam urbem me audere reverti ex qua Brutus cederet, et ibi velle tuto esse ubi ille non posset. Neque vero illum similiter atque ipse eram commotum esse vidi. Erectus enim maximi ac pulcherrimi facti sui conscientia nihil de suo 10 casu, multa de vestro querebatur. Exque eo primum cog- 20 novi quae Kalendis Sextilibus in senatu fuisset L. Pisonis oratio: qui quamquam parum erat—id enim ipsum a Bruto audieram—a quibus debuerat adiutus, tamen et Bruti testimonio—quo quid potest esse gravius?—et omnium praedicatione quos postea vidi magnam mihi videbatur gloriam 25 consecutus. Hunc igitur ut sequerer properavi quem praesentes non sunt secuti, non ut proficerem aliquid—nec enim sperabam id nec praestare poteram— sed ut, si quid mihi humanitus accidisset — multa autem impendere videntur praeter naturam etiam praeterque fatum— huius tamen diei 30

7 quo *cs*: quod *Vnt* 8 Kalendis] Sextilibus (Sex. *V*) *add. codd.*, *del. Madvig*: Kal. Sept. *Halm* senatum frequentem *om.* V^1 12 non *ante* putarem *om. D*: *del. Bake* 17 non posset *om.* V^1: non esset *coni. Halm* 19 ac *V*: atque *ns*: et *ct* 20 ex quo *D* 26 quem *om.* V^1: q. V^2 27 neque enim *D, et Gellius* xiii. 1 29 videntur *V et Gellius*: videbantur *D* 30 etiam *V et Gellius*: *om. D* tamen *V*: *om. D et Gellius*

vocem testem rei publicae relinquerem meae perpetuae erga se voluntatis.

11 Quoniam utriusque consili causam, patres conscripti, probatam vobis esse confido, prius quam de re publica dicere incipio, pauca querar de hesterna M. Antoni iniuria: cui sum amicus, idque me non nullo eius officio debere esse prae me semper tuli. 5 Quid tandem erat causae cur die hesterno in senatum tam acerbe cogerer? Solusne aberam, an non saepe minus frequentes fuistis, an ea res agebatur ut etiam aegrotos deferri oporteret? Hannibal, credo, erat ad portas aut de Pyrrhi pace agebatur, ad quam causam etiam Appium illum et caecum et senem delatum esse memoriae proditum est. 12 De supplicationibus referebatur, quo in genere senatores deesse non solent. Coguntur enim non pignoribus, sed eorum de quorum honore agitur gratia; quod idem fit, cum de triumpho refertur. Ita sine cura consules sunt ut paene liberum sit senatori non adesse. Qui cum mihi mos notus esset cumque e via languerem et mihimet displicerem, misi pro amicitia qui hoc ei diceret. At ille vobis audientibus cum fabris se domum meam venturum esse dixit. Nimis iracunde hoc quidem et valde intemperanter. Cuius enim malefici tanta ista poena est ut dicere in hoc ordine auderet se publicis operis disturbaturum publice ex senatus sententia aedificatam domum? Quis autem umquam tanto damno senatorem coegit? aut quid est ultra pignus aut multam? Quod si scisset quam sententiam dicturus essem, remisisset aliquid profecto de severitate cogendi. 6 13 An me censetis, patres conscripti, quod vos inviti secuti estis, decreturum fuisse, ut parentalia cum supplicationibus miscerentur, ut inexpiabiles religiones in rem publicam inducerentur, ut decernerentur supplicationes mortuo? Nihil dico cui.

4 confido etiam *V* 5-8 quaerar hs (= *hic supple*) de hesterna in senatum tam acerbe V^1 *med. omissis* 5 M. *om.* V^2 7 die hesterno in sen. *Halm* (*e vestigiis cod. V*): in sen. hesterno die *D* 10 deferre *V* 15 quorum de *D* 19 hoc ediceret *D* audientibus . . . se *om.* V^1 22 tanta *om.* *D* 31 mortuorum *D* cui *c*: cui' *n*: qui *Vst*

Fuerit ille L. Brutus qui et ipse dominatu regio rem publicam liberavit et ad similem virtutem et simile factum stirpem iam prope in quingentesimum annum propagavit: adduci tamen non possem ut quemquam mortuum coniungerem cum deorum immortalium religione; ut, cuius sepulcrum usquam 5 exstet ubi parentetur, ei publice supplicetur. Ego vero eam sententiam dixissem ut me adversus populum Romanum, si qui accidisset gravior rei publicae casus, si bellum, si morbus, si fames, facile possem defendere; quae partim iam sunt, partim timeo ne impendeant. Sed hoc ignoscant di immor- 10 tales velim et populo Romano qui id non probat, et huic 14 ordini qui decrevit invitus. Quid? de reliquis rei publicae malis licetne dicere? Mihi vero licet et semper licebit dignitatem tueri, mortem contemnere. Potestas modo veniendi in hunc locum sit: dicendi periculum non recuso. 15 Atque utinam, patres conscripti, Kalendis Sextilibus adesse potuissem! non quo profici potuerit aliquid, sed ne unus modo consularis, quod tum accidit, dignus illo honore, dignus re publica inveniretur. Qua quidem ex re magnum accipio dolorem, homines amplissimis populi Romani bene- 20 ficiis usos L. Pisonem ducem optimae sententiae non secutos. Idcircone nos populus Romanus consules fecit ut in altissimo gradu dignitatis locati rem publicam pro nihilo haberemus? Non modo voce nemo L. Pisoni consulari sed ne voltu 15 quidem adsensus est. Quae, malum, est ista voluntaria 25 servitus? Fuerit quaedam necessaria; neque ego hoc ab omnibus eis desidero qui sententiam consulari loco dicunt. Alia causa est eorum quorum silentio ignosco; alia eorum, quorum vocem requiro. Quos quidem doleo in suspicionem

1 L. Brutus] Bru(ui)tus *V* (ui = Lu.) 2 iam prope in *V*: in prope *ns*: prope in *c*: in *t* 4 deorum *om.* *V* 5 usquam *h*: nusquam *cett.* 7 dixissem P. C. *D* si qui *Vns*: si quis *c*: si quid *t* 13 dicere mihi. Verum *cns*: mihi dicere verum *t* 18 accidit *V* 22 altissimo amplissimoque *V*[2] 24 Pisoni *Vn*[2]*s*: Pisonis *cett.* consulari *V* *cn*[2]*s*[2], *ed. R*: consularis *n*[1]*s*[1]*t*

populo Romano venire non metu, quod ipsum esset turpe,
sed alium alia de causa deesse dignitati suae. Qua re 7
primum maximas gratias et ago et habeo Pisoni, qui non
quid efficere posset in re publica cogitavit, sed quid facere
5 ipse deberet. Deinde a vobis, patres conscripti, peto ut,
etiam si sequi minus audebitis orationem atque auctoritatem
meam, benigne me tamen, ut fecistis adhuc, audiatis.

Primum igitur acta Caesaris servanda censeo, non quo 16
probem—quis enim id quidem potest?—sed quia rationem
10 habendam maxime arbitror pacis atque oti. Vellem adesset
M. Antonius, modo sine advocatis—sed, ut opinor, licet ei
minus valere, quod mihi heri per illum non licuit—doceret
me vel potius vos, patres conscripti, quem ad modum ipse
Caesaris acta defenderet. An in commentariolis et chiro-
15 graphis et libellis se uno auctore prolatis, ne prolatis quidem
sed tantum modo dictis, acta Caesaris firma erunt: quae ille
in aes incidit, in quo populi iussa perpetuasque leges esse
voluit, pro nihilo habebuntur? Equidem existimo nihil tam 17
esse in actis Caesaris quam leges Caesaris. An, si cui quid
20 ille promisit, id erit fixum quod idem facere non potuit? ut
multis multa promissa non fecit: quae tamen multo plura
illo mortuo reperta sunt quam a vivo beneficia per omnis
annos tributa et data. Sed ea non muto, non moveo:
summo studio illius praeclara acta defendo. Pecunia utinam
25 ad Opis maneret! cruenta illa quidem, sed his temporibus,
quoniam eis quorum est non redditur, necessaria. Quamquam ea quoque sit effusa, si ita in actis fuit. Ecquid est 18
quod tam proprie dici possit actum eius qui togatus in re
publica cum potestate imperioque versatus sit quam lex?
30 Quaere acta Gracchi: leges Semproniae proferentur; quaere

1 non metu *D*: non modo metus *V* 3 et habeo et ago *D* L. Pisoni *D* 4 quisquam *post* quid *add* *Reid* 7 fecistis adhuc *D*: adhuc fecistis *V* (*peiore numero*) 9 enim çaṃ *V* 10 adesset M. *Halm*: adessem *V*: adesset *D* 12 licuit *V*[2]: *om.* *V*[1]: licebat *D* doceret *om.* *V*[1] 15 ac ne *D* 20 non facere *Muretus* 24 summo etiam studio praeclara illius *D* 25 ad Opis *lc*: ad opes *n*[1]*s*: ad opus *n*[2]*t*

Sullae: Corneliae. Quid? Pompei tertius consulatus in
quibus actis constitit? Nempe in legibus. De Caesare ipso
si quaereres quidnam egisset in urbe et in toga, leges multas
responderet se et praeclaras tulisse, chirographa vero aut
mutaret aut non daret aut, si dedisset, non istas res in actis 5
suis duceret. Sed haec ipsa concedo; quibusdam etiam in
rebus coniveo; in maximis vero rebus, id est in legibus, acta
8 19 Caesaris dissolvi ferendum non puto. Quae lex melior,
utilior, optima etiam re publica saepius flagitata quam ne
praetoriae provinciae plus quam annum neve plus quam 10
biennium consulares obtinerentur? Hac lege sublata viden-
turne vobis posse Caesaris acta servari? Quid? lege quae
promulgata est de tertia decuria nonne omnes iudiciariae
leges Caesaris dissolvuntur? Et vos acta Caesaris defenditis
qui leges eius evertitis? Nisi forte, si quid memoriae causa 15
rettulit in libellum, id numerabitur in actis et, quamvis iniquum et inutile sit, defendetur: quod ad populum centu-
20 riatis comitiis tulit, id in actis Caesaris non habebitur. At
quae est ista tertia decuria? 'Centurionum' inquit. Quid?
isti ordini iudicatus lege Iulia, etiam ante Pompeia, Aurelia 20
non patebat? 'Census praefiniebatur,' inquit. Non centurioni quidem solum sed equiti etiam Romano; itaque viri
fortissimi atque honestissimi qui ordines duxerunt res et
iudicant et iudicaverunt. 'Non quaero' inquit 'istos: quicumque ordinem duxit, iudicet.' At si ferretis quicumque 25
equo meruisset, quod est lautius, nemini probaretis; in
iudice enim spectari et fortuna debet et dignitas. 'Non
quaero' inquit 'ista: addo etiam iudices manipularis ex
legione Alaudarum. Aliter enim nostri negant posse se

1 Cornelii V^2 Cn. Pompei *D* 2 nempe V^2*D et Victorinus de defin. ed. Stangl p.* 31: *om.* V^1 a Caesare *D* 3 toga *cn*[2]: togam *Vn*[1]: tota *s*: totam *t* 6 ea ipsa *D* etiam in rebus *Vc*: in rebus etiam *nst* 7 in legibus *c et Victorinus p.* 32: *om.* in *celt.* 10 neve *Vc*: neu *nst* 12 posse *om. D* ea lege *D* 13 decuria iudicum *D* 15 evertistis *ct* 16 retulit V^1*D* 19 est *om. V* 20 etiamne Pompeia *D* 23 honestissimi atque fortissimi *D* 26 laudatius *D*

salvos esse.' O contumeliosum honorem eis quos ad iudicandum nec opinantis vocatis! Hic enim est legis index ut ei res in tertia decuria iudicent qui libere iudicare non audeant. In quo quantus error est, di immortales! eorum
5 qui istam legem excogitaverunt! Vt enim quisque sordidissimus videbitur, ita libentissime severitate iudicandi sordis suas eluet laborabitque ut honestis decuriis potius dignus videatur quam in turpem iure coniectus. Altera promulgata **9** 21 lex est ut et de vi et maiestatis damnati ad populum provo-
10 cent, si velint. Haec utrum tandem lex est an legum omnium dissolutio? Quis est enim hodie cuius intersit istam legem manere? Nemo reus est legibus illis, nemo quem futurum putemus. Armis enim gesta numquam profecto in iudicium vocabuntur. 'At res popularis.' Vtinam quidem
15 aliquid velletis esse populare! Omnes enim iam cives de rei publicae salute una et mente et voce consentiunt. Quae est igitur ista cupiditas legis eius ferendae quae turpitudinem summam habeat, gratiam nullam? Quid enim turpius quam qui maiestatem populi Romani minuerit per vim, eum damnatum
20 iudicio ad eam ipsam vim reverti propter quam sit iure damnatus? Sed quid plura de lege disputo? Quasi vero id agatur ut 22 quisquam provocet: id agitur, id fertur ne quis omnino umquam istis legibus reus fiat. Quis enim aut accusator tam amens reperietur qui reo condemnato obici se multitudini
25 conductae velit, aut iudex qui reum damnare audeat, ut ipse ad operas mercennarias statim protrahatur? Non igitur provocatio ista lege datur, sed duae maxime salutares leges quaestionesque tolluntur. Quid est aliud hortari adulescentis ut turbulenti, ut seditiosi, ut perniciosi cives velint esse? Quam

2 ut ii *t*: uti *V*: ut hi *cns* 3 res *om.* *D* 9 ut et *V*: ut *D* maiestatis *Halm*: maiestates *V*: de maiestate *D* 10 haec] haec cum *t*: haecum *cn*[1]*s*[1] 12 manere *V*: venire *D*: valere *Orelli* istis legibus *D* 14 ad res populares (-is *V*[2]) *codd.*: *corr.* *Naugerius* (1) 15 esse *del.* *Eberhard* 24 obici se *D*: obicere *V*[1]: obicere se *V*[2] 28 adhortari *D*

autem ad pestem furor tribunicius impelli non poterit his
23 duabus quaestionibus de vi et maiestate sublatis? Quid, quod
obrogatur legibus Caesaris, quae iubent ei qui de vi itemque
ei qui maiestatis damnatus sit aqua et igni interdici? quibus
cum provocatio datur, nonne acta Caesaris rescinduntur? 5
Quae quidem ego, patres conscripti, qui illa numquam probavi, tamen ita conservanda concordiae causa arbitratus sum
ut non modo, quas vivus leges Caesar tulisset, infirmandas hoc
tempore non putarem, sed ne illas quidem quas post mortem
10 Caesaris prolatas esse et fixas videtis. De exsilio reducti a 10
24 mortuo; civitas data non solum singulis sed nationibus et
provinciis universis a mortuo; immunitatibus infinitis sublata
vectigalia a mortuo. Ergo haec uno, verum optimo auctore
domo prolata defendimus: eas leges quas ipse nobis inspectantibus recitavit, pronuntiavit, tulit, quibus latis gloriabatur 15
eisque legibus rem publicam contineri putabat, de provinciis,
de iudiciis, eas, inquam, Caesaris leges nos qui defendimus
25 acta Caesaris evertendas putamus? Ac de his tamen legibus
quae promulgatae sunt saltem queri possumus: de eis quae
iam latae dicuntur ne illud quidem licuit. Illae enim sine 20
ulla promulgatione latae sunt ante quam scriptae. Quaero
autem quid sit cur aut ego aut quisquam vestrum, patres
conscripti, bonis tribunis plebi leges malas metuat. Paratos
habemus qui intercedant; paratos qui rem publicam religione defendant: vacui metu esse debemus. 'Quas tu mihi' 25
inquit 'intercessiones, quas religiones?' Eas scilicet quibus
rei publicae salus continetur. 'Neglegimus ista et nimis
antiqua ac stulta ducimus: forum saepietur; omnes claudentur aditus; armati in praesidiis multis locis conloca-

1 ad rei p. pestem *D* 2 de vi et maiestate *V*: de vi et de maiestate *D*, *del. Cobet* (*peiore numero*) 3 itemque ei qui *D et Arusian. K.* vii. *p.* 469: itemque *V* 7 tamen *om.* *D* 8 Caesar leges *D* 12 a mortuo *om. ns* 13 verum *V*: viro *D* 14 nobis] nouos *V*[1]: vobis *Naugerius* (1) 16 continere *D* 18 vertendas *D* putamus *Vc*: putabimus *nt*: putavimus *s* 20 illud *om.* *V*[1]: id *Halm* sine ulla *V*: nulla *D* 23 plebi *V*[1]: plebis (pl.) *V*[2]*D*

buntur.' Quid tum? quod ita erit gestum, id lex erit? et in 26
aes incidi iubebitis, credo, illa legitima: CONSULES POPULUM
IURE ROGAVERUNT — hocine a maioribus accepimus ius
rogandi? — POPULUSQUE IURE SCIVIT. Qui populus? isne
5 qui exclusus est? Quo iure? an eo quod vi et armis omne
sublatum est? Atque haec dico de futuris, quod est amicorum
ante dicere ea quae vitari possint: quae si facta non erunt,
refelletur oratio mea. Loquor de legibus promulgatis, de
quibus est integrum vobis, demonstro vitia: tollite! denuntio
10 vim: arma removete!

Irasci quidem vos mihi, Dolabella, pro re publica dicenti 11 27
non oportebit. Quamquam te quidem id facturum non arbitror — novi facilitatem tuam — conlegam tuum aiunt in
hac sua fortuna quae bona ipsi videtur—mihi, ne gravius
15 quippiam dicam, avorum et avunculi sui consulatum si
imitaretur, fortunatior videretur—sed eum iracundum audio
esse factum. Video autem quam sit odiosum habere eundem
iratum et armatum, cum tanta praesertim gladiorum sit
impunitas: sed proponam ius, ut opinor, aequum, quod
20 M. Antonium non arbitror repudiaturum. Ego, si quid in
vitam eius aut in mores cum contumelia dixero, quo minus
mihi inimicissimus sit non recusabo; sin consuetudinem
meam quam in re publica semper habui tenuero, id est si
libere quae sentiam de re publica dixero, primum deprecor
25 ne irascatur; deinde, si hoc non impetro, peto ut sic irascatur ut civi. Armis utatur, si ita necesse est, ut dicit, sui
defendendi causa: eis qui pro re publica quae ipsis visa
erunt dixerint ista arma ne noceant. Quid hac postulatione
dici potest aequius? Quod si, ut mihi a quibusdam eius 28
30 familiaribus dictum est, omnis eum quae habetur contra

3 hoc enim a V^2D 6 atque ego haec (haec ego *n*) *D* 10 vim: arma removete *ed. R* (*ita cns*): vim arma, removete *Poggius* 12 oportebat V^1 13 novi enim *D* 17 esse *om. D* iratum eundem *D* 22 sin *V*: si *D* 23 quam in re p. semper habui *om.* V^2

voluntatem eius oratio graviter offendit, etiam si nulla inest
contumelia, feremus amici naturam. Sed idem illi ita mecum
loquuntur: 'non idem tibi adversario Caesaris licebit quod
Pisoni socero,' et simul admonent quiddam quod cavebimus:
'nec erit iustior in senatum non veniendi morbi causa quam 5
12 mortis.' Sed per deos immortalis!—te enim intuens, Dola-
29 bella, qui es mihi carissimus, non possum de utriusque vestrum errore reticere. Credo enim vos nobilis homines magna
quaedam spectantis non pecuniam, ut quidam nimis creduli
suspicantur, quae semper ab amplissimo quoque clarissimo- 10
que contempta est, non opes violentas et populo Romano
minime ferendam potentiam, sed caritatem civium et gloriam
concupivisse. Est autem gloria laus recte factorum magno-
rumque in rem publicam fama meritorum, quae cum optimi
cuiusque, tum etiam multitudinis testimonio comprobatur. 15
30 Dicerem, Dolabella, qui recte factorum fructus esset, nisi te
praeter ceteros paulisper esse expertum viderem. Quem
potes recordari in vita inluxisse tibi diem laetiorem quam
cum expiato foro, dissipato concursu impiorum, principibus
sceleris poena adfectis, urbe incendio et caedis metu libe- 20
rata te domum recepisti? Cuius ordinis, cuius generis, cuius
denique fortunae studia tum laudi et gratulationi tuae se
non obtulerunt? Quin mihi etiam, quo auctore te in his
rebus uti arbitrabantur, et gratias boni viri agebant et tuo
nomine gratulabantur. Recordare, quaeso, Dolabella, con- 25
sensum illum theatri, cum omnes earum rerum obliti propter
quas fuerant tibi offensi significarent se beneficio novo
31 memoriam veteris doloris abiecisse. Hanc tu, P. Dolabella,—

2 mecum locuntur *V*: mecum *D* 7 qui es mihi carissimus *om.* V^1 de . . . errore *D*: errorem *V* 13 est autem V^1: ea est autem V^2*ct*: ea autem est *ns* et laus V^2D: *fort.* est autem gloria ea laus 14 fama *c et Isidorus Origg.* ii. 30. 2 (*cf. Marc.* 26; *de Invent.* ii. 166): *om. cett.* 17 praeter ceteros *om. D* 20 urbe incendio et caedis metu liberata V^2 (*cf. Fam.* ix. 14. 8): *om.* V^1D 23 obtulerunt *ct*: tulerunt *V*: optarent *ns* 27 significarent *Vt*: significa?t *c*: significaverunt *ns* se *om. V*

magno loquor cum dolore—hanc tu, inquam, potuisti aequo animo tantam dignitatem deponere? Tu autem, M. Antoni, 13 —absentem enim appello—unum illum diem quo in aede Telluris senatus fuit non omnibus his mensibus quibus te 5 quidam multum a me dissentientes beatum putant anteponis? Quae fuit oratio de concordia! quanto metu *senatus*, quanta sollicitudine civitas tum a te liberata est cum conlegam tuum, depositis inimicitiis, oblitus auspiciorum a te ipso augure populi Romani nuntiatorum, illo primum die conlegam 10 tibi esse voluisti; cum tuus parvus filius in Capitolium a te missus pacis obses fuit! quo senatus die laetior, quo popu- 32 lus Romanus? qui quidem nulla in contione umquam frequentior fuit. Tum denique liberati per viros fortissimos videbamur, quia, ut illi voluerant, libertatem pax conseque- 15 batur. Proximo, altero, tertio, denique reliquis consecutis diebus non intermittebas quasi donum aliquod cotidie adferre rei publicae; maximum autem illud quod dictaturae nomen sustulisti. Haec inusta est a te, a te, inquam, mortuo Caesari nota ad ignominiam sempiternam. Vt enim propter 20 unius M. Manli scelus decreto gentis Manliae neminem patricium Manlium *Marcum* vocari licet, sic tu propter unius dictatoris odium nomen dictatoris funditus sustulisti. Num te, cum haec pro salute rei publicae tanta gessisses, 33 fortunae tuae, num amplitudinis, num claritatis, num gloriae 25 paenitebat? Unde igitur subito tanta ista mutatio? Non possum adduci ut suspicer te pecunia captum. Licet quod cuique libet loquatur, credere non est necesse. Nihil enim

2 te *D* 3 enim *om. D* 6 oratio tua *Muretus* senatus *Ernesti*: veteranis *V*[1]: veteri *s*: veter *v*: cetera *n*: veterani *V*[2]*ct, del. Manutius* (*corruptelas e varia lectione ad* veteris § 30 *in mg. archetypi posita ortas esse arbitror, cf. Deiot.* 24) 7 cum collegam tuum *V*: tum collegam *t*: tu collegam *c*: tuum collegam *ns* 8 auspiciorum . . . nuntiatorum *Faernus*: auspiciorum a te ipso augure pronuntiate *V*[1] (-ante *V*[2]): auspicia te ipso augure nuntiante *D* 9 primo *D* 10 cum *Halm*: K. (R. *s*) *D*: *om. V* 11 populus Rom. *om. V*[1] 15 proximo *del. Eberhard* altero *del. Cobet* 21 Marcum *suppl. Gulielmius* 23 haec cum te *D* 24 num gloriae *V*[2]*D, Cus.*: *om. V*[1]

umquam in te sordidum, nihil humile cognovi. Quamquam
solent domestici depravare non numquam; sed novi firmi-
tatem tuam. Atque utinam ut culpam, sic etiam suspicionem
14 vitare potuisses! Illud magis vereor ne ignorans verum
iter gloriae gloriosum putes plus te unum posse quam omnis 5
et metui a civibus tuis quam diligi malis. Quod si ita putas,
totam ignoras viam gloriae. Carum esse civem, bene de re
publica mereri, laudari, coli, diligi gloriosum est; metui
vero et in odio esse invidiosum, detestabile, imbecillum,
34 caducum. Quod videmus etiam in fabula illi ipsi qui 10
'Oderint, dum metuant' dixerit perniciosum fuisse. Vtinam,
M. Antoni, avum tuum meminisses! de quo tamen audisti
multa ex me eaque saepissime. Putasne illum immortalitatem
mereri voluisse, ut propter armorum habendorum licentiam
metueretur? Illa erat vita, illa secunda fortuna, libertate esse 15
parem ceteris, principem dignitate. Itaque, ut omittam res
avi tui prosperas, acerbissimum eius supremum diem malim
quam L. Cinnae dominatum, a quo ille crudelissime est
35 interfectus. Sed quid oratione te flectam? Si enim exitus
C. Caesaris efficere non potest ut malis carus esse quam 20
metui, nihil cuiusquam proficiet nec valebit oratio. Quem
qui beatum fuisse putant, miseri ipsi sunt. Beatus est nemo
qui ea lege vivit ut non modo impune sed etiam cum summa
interfectoris gloria interfici possit. Qua re flecte te, quaeso,
et maiores tuos respice atque ita guberna rem publicam 25
ut natum esse te cives tui gaudeant: sine quo nec beatus
15 nec carus nec iucundus quisquam esse omnino potest. Po-
36 puli quidem Romani iudicia multa ambo habetis, quibus

1 in te . . . quamquam *om.* *D* 6 quam diligi malis *D* (*cf. Off.* ii. 29): *om.* *V* 10 in fabulis ipsi illi *D* 11 dixerint *D* 12 M. *Vc*: *om.* *nst* audisti multa ex me *V*: multa audisti ex me *cns*: multa ex me audisti *t* 13 eaque *Faernus*: aquae *V*: *om.* *D* 16 cum ceteris *D* 17 mallem *D* 22 fuisse *om.* *t* 26 te *om.* V^1 27 carus *scripsi*: clarus *codd.* (*cf.* v. 49, x 8, *Cael.* 72, *Deiot.* 15) nec iucundus *Weber* (*cf.* § 37): nec unctus *V*: *om.* *D*: nec tutus *Muretus*: nec diuturnus *Mittelmeyer*: nec munitus *P. R. Müller* esse quisquam *D* omnino potest *Muretus*: omni potestate *V*: potest *D*

vos non satis moveri permoleste fero. Quid enim gladiatoribus clamores innumerabilium civium? quid populi versus? quid Pompei statuae plausus infiniti? quid duobus tribunis plebis qui vobis adversantur? parumne haec significant incredibiliter 5 consentientem populi Romani universi voluntatem? Quid? Apollinarium ludorum plausus vel testimonia potius et iudicia populi Romani parum magna vobis videbantur? O beatos illos qui, cum adesse ipsis propter vim armorum non licebat, aderant tamen et in medullis populi Romani ac 10 visceribus haerebant! Nisi forte Accio tum plaudi et sexagesimo post anno palmam dari, non Bruto putabatis, qui ludis suis ita caruit ut in illo apparatissimo spectaculo studium populus Romanus tribueret absenti, desiderium liberatoris sui perpetuo plausu et clamore leniret. Equidem is sum 37 15 qui istos plausus, cum popularibus civibus tribuerentur, semper contempserim; idemque cum a summis, mediis, infimis, cum denique ab universis hoc idem fit, cumque ei qui ante sequi populi consensum solebant fugiunt, non plausum illum, sed iudicium puto. Sin haec leviora vobis 20 videntur quae sunt gravissima, num etiam hoc contemnitis quod sensistis tam caram populo Romano vitam A. Hirti fuisse? Satis erat enim probatum illum esse populo Romano, ut est; iucundum amicis, in quo vincit omnis; carum suis, quibus est ipse carissimus: tantam tamen sollicitudinem 25 bonorum, tantum timorem omnium in quo meminimus? Certe in nullo. Quid igitur? hoc vos, per deos immortalis! 38 quale sit non interpretamini? Quid? eos de vestra vita cogitare non censetis quibus eorum quos sperant rei publicae consulturos vita tam cara sit?

30 Cepi fructum, patres conscripti, reversionis meae, quoniam

1 vos non *Poggius*: vobis vo *V*: non *s*[2]: *om. cett.* gladiatoriis *D* 3 duobus *Faernus*: ii *V*: u *t*: hi *n*: his *cs* 7 parum magna *V*: parva *D* 11 non putabitis (-batis *t*) Bruto *D* 12 studium suum *V*[2] 13 tribueret *V*[2]: tribuerit *V*[1]*D* uț absenti *V*: absenti, ut *Faernus* 15 a popularibus *c* (*at vid. Madvig, Opusc.* i. 203): a populi parte *Campe* 21 A. *om. V*[1] 23 esset *D* 24 ipse *om. D* 25 omnium *om. V* 28 non *om D*

et ea dixi, ut quicumque casus consecutus esset, exstaret constantiae meae testimonium, et sum a vobis benigne ac diligenter auditus. Quae potestas si mihi saepius sine meo vestroque periculo fiet, utar: si minus, quantum potero, non tam mihi me quam rei publicae reservabo. Mihi fere satis 5 est quod vixi vel ad aetatem vel ad gloriam: huc si quid accesserit, non tam mihi quam vobis reique publicae accesserit.

1 et *om.* *D* 5 mihi fere *D*: qui mihi fere *V*: quia mihi fere *coni.* *Halm*

M. TVLLI CICERONIS

IN M. ANTONIVM

ORATIO PHILIPPICA SECVNDA

QUONAM meo fato, patres conscripti, fieri dicam ut nemo 1
his annis viginti rei publicae fuerit hostis qui non bellum
eodem tempore mihi quoque indixerit? Nec vero necesse
est quemquam a me nominari: vobiscum ipsi recordamini.
5 Mihi poenarum illi plus quam optarem dederunt: te miror,
Antoni, quorum facta imitere, eorum exitus non perhorrescere.
Atque hoc in aliis minus mirabar. Nemo enim
illorum inimicus mihi fuit voluntarius: omnes a me rei
publicae causa lacessiti. Tu ne verbo quidem violatus, ut au-
10 dacior quam Catilina, furiosior quam Clodius viderere, ultro
me maledictis lacessisti, tuamque a me alienationem commendationem
tibi ad impios civis fore putavisti. Quid putem? 2
contemptumne me? Non video nec in vita nec in gratia nec
in rebus gestis nec in hac mea mediocritate ingeni quid
15 despicere possit Antonius. An in senatu facillime de me
detrahi posse credidit? qui ordo clarissimis civibus bene
gestae rei publicae testimonium multis, mihi uni conservatae
dedit. An decertare mecum voluit contentione dicendi?
Hoc quidem est beneficium. Quid enim plenius, quid

4 a me quemquam *D* 5 optaram *Heumann* 6 pertimescere *t et Isidorus Origg.* ii. 9. 12 10 L. Catilina V^2D P. Clodius V^2D ultro me maledictis *Faernus*: ut romae maledictis V^1: ultro maledictis me V^2D 19 beneficium est *ns et Quintil.* xi. 1. 25

uberius quam mihi et pro me et contra Antonium dicere?
Illud profecto: non existimavit sui similibus probari posse
3 se esse hostem patriae, nisi mihi esset inimicus. Cui prius
quam de ceteris rebus respondeo, de amicitia quam a me
violatam esse criminatus est, quod ego gravissimum crimen 5
iudico, pauca dicam.

2 Contra rem suam me nescio quando venisse questus est.
An ego non venirem contra alienum pro familiari et
necessario, non venirem contra gratiam non virtutis spe,
sed aetatis flore conlectam, non venirem contra iniuriam 10
quam iste intercessoris iniquissimi beneficio obtinuit, non
iure praetorio? Sed hoc idcirco commemoratum a te puto
ut te infimo ordini commendares, cum omnes *te* recorda-
rentur libertini generum et liberos tuos nepotes Q. Fadi,
libertini hominis, fuisse. At enim te in disciplinam meam 15
tradideras—nam ita dixisti— domum meam ventitaras.
Ne tu, si id fecisses, melius famae, melius pudicitiae tuae
consuluisses. Sed neque fecisti nec, si cuperes, tibi id per
4 C. Curionem facere licuisset. Auguratus petitionem mihi
te concessisse dixisti. O incredibilem audaciam, o impu- 20
dentiam praedicandam! Quo enim tempore me augurem
a toto conlegio expetitum Cn. Pompeius et Q. Hortensius
nominaverunt—nec enim licebat a pluribus nominari—tu
nec solvendo eras nec te ullo modo nisi eversa re publica
incolumem fore putabas. Poteras autem eo tempore augu- 25
ratum petere cum in Italia Curio non esset, aut tum cum
es factus unam tribum sine Curione ferre potuisses? cuius
etiam familiares de vi condemnati sunt, quod tui nimis
3 studiosi fuissent. At beneficio sum tuo usus. Quo?
5

1 mihi quam *Campe* 2 profecto est *D* suis *D* (*cf.* I. 5) 3 se *om.* *V* 9 necessario meo *D* 12–15 sed hoc . . . fuisse *om.* *D* 13 ut] uit *V*: uti *Halm* cum omnes te *Halm*: cum omnes *V*²: *om.* *V*¹ 16 ventitabas *Cobet* 19 C. *om.* *V* 23 neque *D* 24 nec solvendo eras *Vc*: nec eras *t*: nec solus deeras *ns* 25 incolumem fore *c* ('quo numero ita iuvantur aures meae ut non dubitem quin ita scriptum sit a Cicerone' *Ferrarius*): fore incolumem *cett.* 26 Italiae *V*: Italia C. *Halm*

Quamquam illud ipsum quod commemoras semper prae me tuli: malui me tibi debere confiteri quam cuiquam minus prudenti non satis gratus videri. Sed quo beneficio? quod me Brundisi non occideris? Quem ipse victor qui 5 tibi, ut tute gloriari solebas, detulerat ex latronibus suis principatum, salvum esse voluisset, in Italiam ire iussisset, eum tu occideres? Fac potuisse. Quod est aliud, patres conscripti, beneficium latronum nisi ut commemorare possint eis se dedisse vitam quibus non ademerint? Quod 10 si esset beneficium, numquam qui illum interfecerunt a quo erant conservati, quos tu ipse clarissimos viros soles appellare, tantam essent gloriam consecuti. Quale autem beneficium est quod te abstinueris nefario scelere? Qua in re non tam iucundum mihi videri debuit non interfectum 15 *me* a te quam miserum te id impune facere potuisse. Sed 6 sit beneficium, quando quidem maius accipi a latrone nullum potuit: in quo potes me dicere ingratum? An de interitu rei publicae queri non debui, ne in te ingratus viderer? At in illa querela misera quidem et luctuosa, sed 20 mihi pro hoc gradu in quo me senatus populusque Romanus conlocavit necessaria, quid est dictum a me cum contumelia, quid non moderate, quid non amice? Quod quidem cuius temperantiae fuit, de M. Antonio querentem abstinere maledicto, praesertim cum tu reliquias rei publicae 25 dissipavisses, cum domi tuae turpissimo mercatu omnia essent venalia, cum leges eas quae numquam promulgatae essent et de te et a te latas confiterere, cum auspicia augur, intercessionem consul sustulisses, cum esses foedissime stipatus armatis, cum omnis impuritates impudica in domo 30 cotidie susciperes vino lustrisque confectus. At ego, tam- 7 quam mihi cum M. Crasso contentio esset, quocum multae

3 pudenti *Bake* 4 quod *Vc*: quo *nst* 7 tu] ut *V* (*cf.* § 76) 10 qui *V*: ii qui *D* 11 servati *D* ipse *om.* *V* appellare soles *D* 14 videri mihi *D* 15 me *suppl.* *Madvig* id te *D* 19 an in *D* 24 maledicti *V*: -tis *Faernus* 29 impudica V^1 *et Nonius, p.* 333: pudica V^2D 30 quamquam *t*: tam *V*

et magnae fuerunt, non cum uno gladiatore nequissimo, de re publica graviter querens de homine nihil dixi. Itaque hodie perficiam ut intellegat quantum a me beneficium tum 4 acceperit. At etiam litteras, quas me sibi misisse diceret, recitavit homo et humanitatis expers et vitae communis 5 ignarus. Quis enim umquam qui paulum modo bonorum consuetudinem nosset, litteras ad se ab amico missas offensione aliqua interposita in medium protulit palamque recitavit? Quid est aliud tollere ex vita vitae societatem, tollere amicorum conloquia absentium? Quam multa ioca 10 solent esse in epistulis quae, prolata si sint, inepta videantur, quam multa seria neque tamen ullo modo divol- 8 ganda! Sit hoc inhumanitatis: stultitiam incredibilem videte. Quid habes quod mihi opponas, homo diserte, ut Mustelae tamen Seio et Tironi Numisio videris? Qui cum 15 hoc ipso tempore stent cum gladiis in conspectu senatus, ego quoque te disertum putabo, si ostenderis quo modo sis eos inter sicarios defensurus. Sed quid opponas tandem, si negem me umquam ad te istas litteras misisse? Quo me teste convincas? An chirographo? in quo habes scientiam 20 quaestuosam. Qui possis? sunt enim librari manu. Iam invideo magistro tuo, qui te tanta mercede quantam iam 9 proferam nihil sapere doceat. Quid enim est minus non dico oratoris, sed hominis quam id obicere adversario quod ille si verbo negarit longius progredi non possit qui obie- 25 cerit? At ego non nego, teque in isto ipso convinco non inhumanitatis solum sed etiam amentiae. Quod enim verbum in istis litteris est non plenum humanitatis, offici,

1 et iam *V*: et tam *Halm* 6 paulum modo *D*: paulo *V* 9 ex *Halm*: et *V*: e *D* 10 ioca *n*: loca *cett.* 11 esse *om.* *V* 13 inhum. tuae *D* 15 ut Mustelae tamen Seio et Tironi Numisio *scripsi*, *ita fere D* (tamen scio *nst*: tam inscio *c*, *quod probat Landgraf*), *cf.* xii. 14: mus et laetam esse *V cett. omissis*: ut Tironi et Mustelae iam esse *Halm* 16 ipso] ipsūo *V*: isto *D* 17 te quoque *V* 20 convinces *D* 21 libera *D* 23 docuit *D* 27–28 solum . . . humanitatis *om.* *D*

benevolentiae? Omne autem crimen tuum est quod de te in his litteris non male existimem, quod scribam tamquam ad civem, tamquam ad bonum virum, non tamquam ad sceleratum et latronem. At ego tuas litteras, etsi iure poteram
5 a te lacessitus, tamen non proferam: quibus petis ut tibi per me liceat quendam de exsilio reducere, adiurasque id te invito me non esse facturum; idque a me impetras. Quid enim me interponerem audaciae tuae, quam neque auctoritas huius ordinis neque existimatio populi Romani
10 neque leges ullae possent coercere? Verum tamen quid 10 erat quod me rogares, si erat is de quo rogabas Caesaris lege reductus? Sed videlicet meam gratiam voluit esse, in quo ne ipsius quidem ulla esse poterat lege lata.

Sed cum mihi, patres conscripti, et pro me aliquid et in 5
15 M. Antonium multa dicenda sint, alterum peto a vobis ut me pro me dicentem benigne, alterum ipse efficiam ut, contra illum cum dicam, attente audiatis. Simul illud oro: si meam cum in omni vita tum in dicendo moderationem modestiamque cognostis, ne me hodie, cum isti, ut provo-
20 cavit, respondero, oblitum esse putetis mei. Non tractabo ut consulem: ne ille quidem me ut consularem. Etsi ille nullo modo consul, vel quod ita vivit vel quod ita rem publicam gerit vel quod ita factus est; ego sine ulla controversia consularis. Vt igitur intellegeretis qualem ipse se 11
25 consulem profiteretur, obiecit mihi consulatum meum. Qui consulatus verbo meus, patres conscripti, re vester fuit. Quid enim ego constitui, quid gessi, quid egi nisi ex huius ordinis consilio, auctoritate, sententia? Haec tu homo sapiens, non solum eloquens, apud eos quorum consilio
30 sapientiaque gesta sunt ausus es vituperare? Quis autem meum consulatum praeter te et P. Clodium qui vituperaret

1 tuum] meum n^2: *del. Manutius* 2 scribebam *V* 7 impetrasti *Bake* 8 quem *D* 20 respondero *V*: -deo *t*: -debo *cns* 22 est consul *D* 25 consulem *Vn*^{2}: consul *cett.* 31 te et P. Clod. *Muretus*: te P. aut Clod. *V*: P. Clod. *D*: te Publiumque Clod. *P. R. Müller*

inventus est? cuius quidem tibi fatum, sicuti C. Curioni, manet, quoniam id domi tuae est quod fuit illorum utrique fatale. 12 Non placet M. Antonio consulatus meus. At placuit P. Servilio, ut eum primum nominem ex illius temporis consularibus qui proxime est mortuus; placuit Q. Catulo, cuius semper in hac re publica vivet auctoritas; placuit duobus Lucullis, M. Crasso, Q. Hortensio, C. Curioni, C. Pisoni, M'. Glabrioni, M'. Lepido, L. Volcatio, C. Figulo, D. Silano, L. Murenae, qui tum erant consules designati; placuit idem quod consularibus M. Catoni, qui cum multa vita excedens providit, tum quod te consulem non vidit. Maxime vero consulatum meum Cn. Pompeius probavit qui, ut me primum decedens ex Syria vidit, complexus et gratulans meo beneficio patriam se visurum esse dixit. Sed quid singulos commemoro? Frequentissimo senatui sic placuit ut esset nemo qui mihi non ut parenti gratias ageret, qui mihi non vitam suam, fortunas, liberos, rem publicam referret acceptam. 6 13 Sed quoniam illis quos nominavi tot et talibus viris res publica orbata est, veniamus ad vivos qui duo de consularium numero reliqui sunt. L. Cotta, vir summo ingenio summaque prudentia, rebus eis gestis quas tu reprehendis supplicationem decrevit verbis amplissimis, eique illi ipsi quos modo nominavi consulares senatusque cunctus adsensus est; qui honos post conditam hanc urbem habitus est togato ante me nemini. 14 L. Caesar, avunculus tuus, qua oratione, qua constantia, qua gravitate sententiam dixit in sororis suae virum, vitricum tuum! Hunc tu cum auctorem et praeceptorem omnium consiliorum totiusque vitae debuisses habere, vitrici te similem

1 C. Curioni *V* (C. *om.* *V*[1]): C. Curionem *D* 2 domi *st et Arusian. K.* vii. *p.* 491: domui *c*: domu *n*: domus *V* 4 primo *D* 5 placuitque L. *D* 6 vivit *D* 8 M'. Lepido *ante* C. Pisoni *habent D* Volcatio *cns*: Vulcatio *Vt* 13 ut me primum *Vcn*[2]: ut te primum *n*[1]*s*: ut primum te *t* 14 congratulans *c* 17 non mihi *D* 20 ex (e *t*) consulari *D* 24 est] pĩ *add.* *V*[2] *sup. l.*

quam avunculi maluisti. Huius ego alienus consiliis consul
usus sum: tu, sororis filius, ecquid ad eum umquam de re
publica rettulisti? At ad quos refert? di immortales! Ad
eos scilicet quorum nobis etiam dies natales audiendi sunt.
5 Hodie non descendit Antonius. Cur? Dat nataliciam in 15
hortis. Cui? Neminem nominabo: putate tum Phormioni
alicui, tum Gnathoni, tum etiam Ballioni. O foeditatem
hominis flagitiosam, o impudentiam, nequitiam, libidinem
non ferendam! Tu cum principem senatorem, civem sin-
10 gularem tam propinquum habeas, ad eum de re publica
nihil referas, referas ad eos qui suam rem nullam habent,
tuam exhauriunt? Tuus videlicet salutaris consulatus,
perniciosus meus. Adeone pudorem cum pudicitia perdi- 7
disti ut hoc in eo templo dicere ausus sis in quo ego
15 senatum illum qui quondam florens orbi terrarum praeside-
bat consulebam, tu homines perditissimos cum gladiis
conlocavisti? At etiam ausus es—quid autem est quod tu 16
non audeas?—clivum Capitolinum dicere me consule plenum
servorum armatorum fuisse. Vt illa, credo, nefaria senatus
20 consulta fierent, vim adferebam senatui. O miser, sive illa
tibi nota non sunt—nihil enim boni nosti—sive sunt, qui
apud talis viros tam impudenter loquare! Quis enim eques
Romanus, quis praeter te adulescens nobilis, quis ullius
ordinis qui se civem esse meminisset, cum senatus in hoc
25 templo esset, in clivo Capitolino non fuit, quis nomen non
dedit? quamquam nec scribae sufficere nec tabulae nomina
illorum capere potuerunt. Etenim cum homines nefarii de 17
patriae parricidio confiterentur, consciorum indiciis, sua
manu, voce paene litterarum coacti se urbem inflammare,
30 civis trucidare, vastare Italiam, delere rem publicam consen-

1 esse maluisti *D* consultus ụṣsum *V*: consul tum usus sum *Halm* 3 publica *om.* V^1 at *Faernus*: ad *V*: *om. D* 5 natalicia *D* 6 putatote eum *D* 7 etiam *om. D* 11 refers, ad eos refers *D* suam rem *V*: domum suam *D* 20 consulta tum *D* miserum *D* 24 esse *om. D*

sisse, quis esset qui ad salutem communem defendendam non excitaretur, praesertim cum senatus populusque Romanus haberet ducem, qualis si qui nunc esset, tibi idem quod illis accidit contigisset? Ad sepulturam corpus vitrici sui negat a me datum. Hoc vero ne P. quidem Clodius dixit 5 umquam: quem, quia iure ei inimicus fui, doleo a te
18 omnibus vitiis iam esse superatum. Qui autem tibi venit in mentem redigere in memoriam nostram te domi P. Lentuli esse educatum? An verebare ne non putaremus natura te potuisse tam improbum evadere, nisi accessisset etiam 10
8 disciplina? Tam autem eras excors ut tota in oratione tua tecum ipse pugnares, non modo non cohaerentia inter se diceres, sed maxime diiuncta atque contraria, ut non tanta mecum quanta tibi tecum esset contentio. Vitricum tuum fuisse in tanto scelere fatebare, poena adfectum querebare. 15 Ita quod proprie meum est laudasti; quod totum est senatus reprehendisti. Nam comprehensio sontium mea, animadversio senatus fuit. Homo disertus non intellegit eum quem contra dicit laudari a se; eos apud quos dicit
19 vituperari. Iam illud cuius est, non dico audaciae—cupit 20 enim se audacem— sed, quod minime volt, stultitiae, qua vincit omnis, clivi Capitolini mentionem facere, cum inter subsellia nostra versentur armati, cum in hac cella Concordiae, di immortales! in qua me consule salutares sententiae dictae sunt, quibus ad hanc diem viximus, cum gladiis 25 homines conlocati stent? Accusa senatum; accusa equestrem ordinem qui tum cum senatu copulatus fuit; accusa omnis ordines, omnis civis, dum confiteare hunc ordinem hoc ipso tempore ab Ituraeis circumsederi. Haec tu non propter audaciam dicis tam impudenter, sed quia tantam 30 rerum repugnantiam non vides. Nihil profecto sapis. Quid

7 iam *D*: eum *V* (cui quia iure inimicus fui, doleo . . . eum esse *Stürenburg*) 11 tua *om. D* 12 ut non modo *D* 13 disiuncta *codd.*: *corr. Klotz* 16 est *post* totum *om. D* 21 audacem dici *D* 30 quia *Vc*: qui *nst* 31 vides *Ernesti*: videas *codd.*: quia, qui . . . videas . . . sapis *Halm*

est enim dementius quam, cum rei publicae perniciosa arma ipse ceperis, obicere alteri salutaria? At etiam quodam loco 20 facetus esse voluisti. Quam id te, di boni, non decebat! In quo est tua culpa non nulla. Aliquid enim salis a mima
5 uxore trahere potuisti. 'Cedant arma togae.' Quid? tum nonne cesserunt? At postea tuis armis cessit toga. Quaeramus igitur utrum melius fuerit libertati populi Romani sceleratorum arma an libertatem nostram armis tuis cedere. Nec vero tibi de versibus plura respondebo: tantum dicam
10 breviter, te neque illos neque ullas omnino litteras nosse; me nec rei publicae nec amicis umquam defuisse, et tamen omni genere monumentorum meorum perfecisse operis subsicivis ut meae vigiliae meaeque litterae et iuventuti utilitatis et nomini Romano laudis aliquid adferrent. Sed haec non
15 huius temporis: maiora videamus.

P. Clodium meo consilio interfectum esse dixisti. Quidnam 9 21 homines putarent, si tum occisus esset cum tu illum in foro inspectante populo Romano gladio insecutus es negotiumque transegisses, nisi se ille in scalas tabernae librariae
20 coniecisset eisque oppilatis impetum tuum compressisset? Quod quidem ego favisse me tibi fateor, suasisse ne tu quidem dicis. At Miloni ne favere quidem potui; prius enim rem transegit quam quisquam eum facturum id suspicaretur. At ego suasi. Scilicet is animus erat Milonis ut
25 prodesse rei publicae sine suasore non posset. At laetatus sum. Quid ergo? in tanta laetitia cunctae civitatis me unum tristem esse oportebat? Quamquam de morte Clodi 22 fuit quaestio non satis prudenter illa quidem constituta—quid enim attinebat nova lege quaeri de eo qui hominem

1 ipse *ante* rei publicae *hab. D* 3 te *V et Arusian. K.* vii. *p.* 465: *om. D* 4 culpa nulla *D* 9 plura *om. D* 10 te *om ct, ante* omnino *habent ns* 12 operis subsicivis (operis *om. t*) *D*: *om. V*: *cf. de Or.* ii. 364: *Legg.* I. 9 *et* 13 15 ad maiora veniamus *D* 18 inspectante *ct, Schol. Bob. ad Mil.* § 40: spectante *Vns* gladio *V et Schol.*: gladio stricto *D* 21 quod quidem *V*: sed quid *D* 23 eum *om. n*[2] fact. id suspicaretur *V*: suspicaretur (sciscitaretur *ct*) eum (rem *t*: *om. c*) fact. esse *D* 27 P. Clodii *D*

occidisset, cum esset legibus quaestio constituta?—quaesitum est tamen. Quod igitur, cum res agebatur, nemo in me dixit, id tot annis post tu es inventus qui diceres?

23 Quod vero dicere ausus es idque multis verbis, opera mea Pompeium a Caesaris amicitia esse diiunctum ob eamque causam culpa mea bellum civile esse natum, in eo non tu quidem tota re sed, quod maximum est, temporibus errasti. 10 Ego M. Bibulo, praestantissimo civi, consule nihil praetermisi, quantum facere enitique potui, quin Pompeium a Caesaris coniunctione avocarem. In quo Caesar felicior fuit. Ipse enim Pompeium a mea familiaritate diiunxit. Postea vero quam se totum Pompeius Caesari tradidit, quid ego illum ab eo distrahere conarer? Stulti erat sperare, suadere 24 impudentis. Duo tamen tempora inciderunt quibus aliquid contra Caesarem Pompeio suaserim. Ea velim reprehendas, si potes: unum ne quinquenni imperium Caesari prorogaret, alterum ne pateretur ferri ut absentis eius ratio haberetur. Quorum si utrumvis persuasissem, in has miserias numquam incidissemus. Atque idem ego, cum iam opes omnis et suas et populi Romani Pompeius ad Caesarem detulisset, seroque ea sentire coepisset quae multo ante provideram, inferrique patriae bellum viderem nefarium, pacis, concordiae, compositionis auctor esse non destiti, meaque illa vox est nota multis: 'Vtinam, Cn. Pompei, cum C. Caesare societatem aut numquam coisses aut numquam diremisses! Fuit alterum gravitatis, alterum prudentiae tuae.' Haec mea, M. Antoni, semper et de Pompeio et de re publica consilia fuerunt. Quae si valuissent, res publica staret, tu tuis flagitiis, egestate, infamia concidisses.

11 25 Sed haec vetera, illud vero recens, Caesarem meo consilio

3 id *Vcn*[2]: at *n*[1]*t*: et *s*   5 disiunctum *D*   8 civi (cui *t*) *D*: cive *V*   9 enitique *Vc*: innitique *nst*   11 disiunxit *D*   17 ñeri *D*   20 omnes opes *D*   22 nefarium viderem *D*   23 non *om.* *D*   24 Cn. Pompei *D et Priscian. K.* ii. *pp.* 395, 407: Pompei *V*   25 C. Caesare *D et Priscian.*: Caesare *V*   26 gravitatis alterum *om.* *V*[1]

interfectum. Iam vereor, patres conscripti, ne, quod turpissimum est, praevaricatorem mihi apposuisse videar, qui
me non solum meis laudibus ornaret sed etiam oneraret
alienis. Quis enim meum in ista societate gloriosissimi
5 facti nomen audivit? Cuius autem qui in eo numero fuisset
nomen est occultatum? Occultatum dico? cuius non statim
divolgatum? Citius dixerim iactasse se aliquos ut fuisse in
ea societate viderentur, cum conscii non fuissent, quam ut
quisquam celari vellet qui fuisset. Quam veri simile porro 26
10 est in tot hominibus partim obscuris, partim adulescentibus
neminem occultantibus meum nomen latere potuisse?
Etenim si auctores ad liberandam patriam desiderarentur illis
actoribus, Brutos ego impellerem, quorum uterque L. Bruti
imaginem cotidie videret, alter etiam Ahalae? Hi igitur his
15 maioribus ab alienis potius consilium peterent quam a suis
et foris potius quam domo? Quid? C. Cassius in ea familia
natus quae non modo dominatum, sed ne potentiam quidem
cuiusquam ferre potuit, me auctorem, credo, desideravit:
qui etiam sine his clarissimis viris hanc rem in Cilicia ad
20 ostium fluminis Cydni confecisset, si ille ad eam ripam
quam constituerat, non ad contrariam navis appulisset.
Cn. Domitium non patris interitus, clarissimi viri, non avun- 27
culi mors, non spoliatio dignitatis ad recuperandam libertatem, sed mea auctoritas excitavit? An C. Trebonio ego
25 persuasi? cui ne suadere quidem ausus essem. Quo etiam
maiorem ei res publica gratiam debet qui libertatem populi
Romani unius amicitiae praeposuit depulsorque dominatus
quam particeps esse maluit. An L. Tillius Cimber me est

3 oneraret *om. V* 4 istius conscientia glor. facti *ct*: istius f. conscientia glor. *ns* 8 ea *V*: ista *D* conscii *V*: socii *D*, *del. Ferrarius* 9 celare *D* fuisset *om. D* 13 actoribus *Madvig*: auctoribus *codd* 14 hi igitur his *V*: his igitur *D* 15 ab *V*: orti ab *D* 16 domo *Vcn*: domi *t*: modo *s* C. *V²c*: *om. V¹nst* 23 ad liberandam (patriam *add. n²*) ad recipiendam *D* 24-6 An C. . . . debet *ante* Cn. Domitium (*l.* 22) *hab. V* 24 ego *om D* 25 quo *D*: quae *V*: quare *coni. Halm* 28 Tillius *Barbadorius*: T. *V*: Tullius *D*

auctorem secutus? quem ego magis fecisse illam rem sum admiratus quam facturum putavi, admiratus autem ob eam causam quod immemor beneficiorum, memor patriae fuisset. Quid duos Servilios—Cascas dicam an Ahalas?—et hos auctoritate mea censes excitatos potius quam caritate rei 5 publicae? Longum est persequi ceteros, idque rei publicae
12 28 praeclarum fuisse tam multos, ipsis gloriosum. At quem ad modum me coarguerit homo acutus recordamini. 'Caesare interfecto' inquit 'statim cruentum alte extollens Brutus pugionem Ciceronem nominatim exclamavit atque ei recupe- 10 ratam libertatem est gratulatus.' Cur mihi potissimum? quia sciebam? Vide ne illa causa fuerit appellandi mei quod, cum rem gessisset consimilem rebus eis quas ipse gesseram, me potissimum testatus est se aemulum mearum
29 laudum exstitisse. Tu autem, omnium stultissime, non 15 intellegis, si, id quod me arguis, voluisse interfici Caesarem crimen sit, etiam laetatum esse morte Caesaris crimen esse? Quid enim interest inter suasorem facti et probatorem? aut quid refert utrum voluerim fieri an gaudeam factum? Ecquis est igitur exceptis eis qui illum regnare gaudebant qui illud 20 aut fieri noluerit aut factum improbarit? Omnes ergo in culpa. Etenim omnes boni, quantum in ipsis fuit, Caesarem occiderunt: aliis consilium, aliis animus, aliis occasio defuit;
30 voluntas nemini. Sed stuporem hominis vel dicam pecudis attendite. Sic enim dixit: 'Brutus, quem ego honoris 25 causa nomino, cruentum pugionem tenens Ciceronem exclamavit: ex quo intellegi debet eum conscium fuisse.' Ergo ego sceleratus appellor a te quem tu suspicatum aliquid suspicaris; ille qui stillantem prae se pugionem tulit, is a te

2 autem *V*: sum autem *cns*: autem sum *t* 4 Servilios *Vc*: Servilios nomina (-e *n*²) propria (-o *n*²) *nst* 7 tamen multo ipsis gloriosius est *D* 12 quia *Graevius*: qui *codd.*: quod *Ferrarius* mei *V*: me *D* 15 laudium *V* non] illud non *Cus.* 20 te excepto is qui *D*: te excepto et iis qui *Gruter* gaudebat *D* 21 improbavit *V* ergo *V*: enim *D* 25 M. Brutus *D* 28 a te *D*: ante *V*: abs te *coni. Halm* 29 ille (*vel* is) *del. Gruter*

honoris causa nominatur? Esto; sit in verbis tuis hic stupor:
quanto in rebus sententiisque maior? Constitue hoc, consul,
aliquando, Brutorum, C. Cassi, Cn. Domiti, C. Treboni,
reliquorum quam velis esse causam; edormi crapulam,
5 inquam, et exhala. An faces admovendae sunt quae excitent
tantae causae indormientem? Numquamne intelleges statuendum tibi esse utrum illi qui istam rem gesserunt homicidaene sint an vindices libertatis? Attende enim paulisper 13
cogitationemque sobrii hominis punctum temporis suscipe. 31
10 Ego qui sum illorum, ut ipse fateor, familiaris, ut a te
arguor, socius, nego quicquam esse medium: confiteor eos,
nisi liberatores populi Romani conservatoresque rei publicae
sint, plus quam sicarios, plus quam homicidas, plus etiam
quam parricidas esse, si quidem est atrocius patriae parentem
15 quam suum occidere. Tu homo sapiens et considerate,
quid dicis? si parricidas, cur honoris causa a te sunt et in
hoc ordine et apud populum Romanum semper appellati?
cur M. Brutus referente te legibus est solutus, si ab urbe
plus quam decem dies afuisset? cur ludi Apollinares in-
20 credibili M. Bruti honore celebrati? cur provinciae Bruto,
Cassio datae, cur quaestores additi, cur legatorum numerus
auctus? Atqui haec acta per te. Non igitur homicidas.
Sequitur ut liberatores tuo iudicio, quando quidem tertium
nihil potest esse. Quid est? num conturbo te? Non enim 32
25 fortasse satis quae diiunctius dicuntur intellegis. Sed
tamen haec summa est conclusionis meae: quoniam scelere
a te liberati sunt, ab eodem amplissimis praemiis dignissimos iudicatos. Itaque iam retexo orationem meam. Scribam
ad illos ut, si qui forte, quod a te mihi obiectum est, quaerent

5 quae te *V*[2]*D* 7 homicidaene *c*: -ne *om. Vt* (-ę rei *ns*) 8 enim *om. Cus.* 9 per punctum *Cus.* 10 ut a *Vns*: aut ut a *ct* 16 parricidae *D* 18 te referente *D* 20 Cassio et Bruto *D* 22 atqui *O. Jahn*: atque *codd.* homicidaę *D* 23 iudicio sint *D* 25 distinctius *nst*: *om. c* 26 est summa *D* 27 eodem te *D* dignissimos iudicatos *Vc*: -simi iudicantur *t*: -simi iudicati (-andi *n*[2]) *ns* 29 quaerent *Vc*: quaerenti *nst*

sitne verum, ne cui negent. Etenim vereor ne aut celatum me illis ipsis non honestum aut invitatum refugisse mihi sit turpissimum. Quae enim res umquam, pro sancte Iuppiter! non modo in hac urbe sed in omnibus terris est gesta maior; quae gloriosior, quae commendatior hominum memo- 5 riae sempiternae? In huius me tu consili societatem tam- 33 quam in equum Troianum cum principibus includis? Non recuso; ago etiam gratias, quoquo animo facis. Tanta enim res est ut invidiam istam quam tu in me vis concitare cum laude non comparem. Quid enim beatius illis quos tu 10 expulsos a te praedicas et relegatos? qui locus est aut tam desertus aut tam inhumanus qui illos, cum accesserint, non adfari atque appetere videatur? qui homines tam agrestes qui se, cum eos aspexerint, non maximum cepisse vitae fructum putent? quae vero tam immemor posteritas, quae 15 tam ingratae litterae reperientur quae eorum gloriam non immortalitatis memoria prosequantur? Tu vero ascribe me 14 talem in numerum. Sed unam rem vereor ne non probes: 34 si enim fuissem, non solum regem sed etiam regnum de re publica sustulissem; et, si meus stilus ille fuisset, ut dicitur, 20 mihi crede, non solum unum actum sed totam fabulam confecissem. Quamquam si interfici Caesarem voluisse crimen est, vide, quaeso, Antoni, quid tibi futurum sit, quem et Narbone hoc consilium cum C. Trebonio cepisse notissimum est et ob eius consili societatem, cum interfice- 25 retur Caesar, tum te a Trebonio vidimus sevocari. Ego autem—vide quam tecum agam non inimice—quod bene cogitasti aliquando, laudo; quod non indicasti, gratias ago; 35 quod non fecisti, ignosco. Virum res illa quaerebat. Quod si te in iudicium quis adducat usurpetque illud Cassianum, 30

2 ab ipsis illis *D* 5 erit hominum *D* 12 cum *ed. Crat.* (*in mg.*): quo *codd.*: quoquo *Angelius* 19 in eo fuissem *coni. Müller*: regnum etiam *D* 24 C. *om.* V^1 27 video *D* 28 non *om. V* 29 virum *Vcn*[2]: verum *n*[1]*st*

'cui bono fuerit,' vide, quaeso, ne haereas. Quamquam illud quidem fuit, ut tu dicebas, omnibus bono qui servire nolebant, tibi tamen praecipue qui non modo non servis sed etiam regnas; qui maximo te aere alieno ad aedem Opis liberavisti; 5 qui per easdem tabulas innumerabilem pecuniam dissipavisti; ad quem e domo Caesaris tam multa delata sunt; cuius domi quaestuosissima est falsorum commentariorum et chirographorum officina, agrorum, oppidorum, immunitatium, vectigalium flagitiosissimae nundinae. Etenim quae res 36 10 egestati et aeri alieno tuo praeter mortem Caesaris subvenire potuisset? Nescio quid conturbatus esse videris: num quid subtimes ne ad te hoc crimen pertinere videatur? Libero te metu: nemo credet umquam; non est tuum de re publica bene mereri; habet istius pulcherrimi facti clarissimos viros 15 res publica auctores; ego te tantum gaudere dico, fecisse non arguo. Respondi maximis criminibus: nunc etiam reliquis respondendum est.

15 37 Castra mihi Pompei atque illud omne tempus obiecisti. Quo quidem tempore si, ut dixi, meum consilium 20 auctoritasque valuisset, tu hodie egeres, nos liberi essemus; res publica non tot duces et exercitus amisisset. Fateor enim me, cum ea quae acciderunt providerem futura, tanta in maestitia fuisse quanta ceteri optimi cives, si idem providissent, fuissent. Dolebam, dolebam, patres con- 25 scripti, rem publicam vestris quondam meisque consiliis conservatam brevi tempore esse perituram. Nec vero eram tam indoctus ignarusque rerum ut frangerer animo propter vitae cupiditatem, quae me manens conficeret angoribus, dimissa molestiis omnibus liberaret. Illos ego praestan- 30 tissimos viros, lumina rei publicae, vivere volebam, tot

1 illud fuit tu ut dicebas quidem *V* 4 liberasti *n*: liberabis *V* 7 domus *D* 8 officina . . . oppidorum *om.* *V* immunitas *c*: -tatis *nst* 11 mihi esse *D* 16 nunc *ed. R*: num *Vcns*: tunc *t* 19 diximus consilium *V* 22 providem futuram *V* 29 illos] hos *Cus.*

consularis, tot praetorios, tot honestissimos senatores, omnem praeterea florem nobilitatis ac iuventutis, tum optimorum civium exercitus; qui si viverent, quamvis iniqua condicione pacis—mihi enim omnis pax cum civibus bello civili utilior videbatur—rem publicam hodie teneremus. 5
38 Quae sententia si valuisset ac non ei maxime mihi quorum ego vitae consulebam spe victoriae elati obstitissent, ut alia omittam, tu certe numquam in hoc ordine vel potius numquam in hac urbe mansisses. At vero Cn. Pompei voluntatem a me alienabat oratio mea. An ille quemquam plus 10 dilexit, cum ullo aut sermones aut consilia contulit saepius? Quod quidem erat magnum, de summa re publica dissentientis in eadem consuetudine amicitiae permanere. Ego quid ille et contra ille quid ego sentirem et spectarem videbat. Ego incolumitati civium primum, ut postea dignitati 15 possemus, ille praesenti dignitati potius consulebat. Quod autem habebat uterque quid sequeretur, idcirco tolerabilior
39 erat nostra dissensio. Quid vero ille singularis vir ac paene divinus de me senserit sciunt qui eum de Pharsalia fuga Paphum persecuti sunt. Numquam ab eo mentio de 20 me nisi honorifica, nisi plena amicissimi desideri, cum me vidisse plus fateretur, se speravisse meliora. Et eius viri nomine me insectari audes cuius me amicum, te sectorem
16 esse fateare? Sed omittatur bellum illud in quo tu nimium felix fuisti. Ne *de* iocis quidem respondebo 25 quibus me in castris usum esse dixisti: erant quidem illa castra plena curae; verum tamen homines, quamvis in turbidis rebus sint, tamen, si modo homines sunt, interdum
40 animis relaxantur. Quod autem idem maestitiam meam

10 abalienabat *D* 12 publica *om. D* dissidentes *n* 13 sed et (et *sup. l. in s*) ego *D*: *an* et ego? 15 ut *V*: et *cns*: ac *t* 16 possemus *om. D* dignitati *om. D* 17 quod sequeretur *Lambinus* 18 singularis *V*: consularis *D* 19 eum Pharsalica *D* 23 me *ante* amicum *om.* V^1: amicum me *coni. Halm* sectatorem s^2t 25 de iocis *Wesenberg*: iocis *D*: totis *V* 26 quidem illa *Vns*: illa quidem *ct*

reprehendit, idem iocum, magno argumento est me in utroque fuisse moderatum.

Hereditates mihi negasti venire. Vtinam hoc tuum verum crimen esset! plures amici mei et necessarii vive- 5 rent. Sed qui istuc tibi venit in mentem? Ego enim amplius sestertium ducentiens acceptum hereditatibus rettuli. Quamquam in hoc genere fateor feliciorem esse te. Me nemo nisi amicus fecit heredem, ut cum illo commodo, si quod erat, animi quidam dolor iungeretur; te 10 is quem tu vidisti numquam, L. Rubrius Casinas fecit heredem. Et quidem vide quam te amarit is qui albus aterne 41 fuerit ignoras. Fratris filium praeterit, Q. Fufi, honestissimi equitis Romani suique amicissimi, quem palam heredem semper factitarat, ne nominat quidem: te, quem numquam 15 viderat aut certe numquam salutaverat, fecit heredem. Velim mihi dicas, nisi molestum est, L. Turselius qua facie fuerit, qua statura, quo municipio, qua tribu. 'Nihil scio' inquies 'nisi quae praedia habuerit.' Igitur fratrem exheredans te faciebat heredem. In multas praeterea pecunias 20 alienissimorum hominum vi eiectis veris heredibus, tamquam heres esset, invasit. Quamquam hoc maxime admiratus 42 sum, mentionem te hereditatum ausum esse facere, cum ipse hereditatem patris non adisses.

17 Haec ut conligeres, homo amentissime, tot dies in aliena 25 villa declamasti? quamquam tu quidem, ut tui familiarissimi dictitant, vini exhalandi, non ingeni acuendi causa declamitas. At vero adhibes ioci causa magistrum suffragio tuo et compotorum tuorum rhetorem, cui concessisti ut in

3 hereditates *Naugerius* (1): -tate *V*: -tatem *D* 7 retuli *VD* 10 fecit heredem *del. Madvig* (*peiore numero*) 12 praeterit *Vns*: -riit *c*: -reo *t* 14 ne nomen quidem perscripsit *D* 15 aut certe numq. *Faernus*: ut (aut *V*[1]) cere numq. *V*: ac ne umq. *D* 16 Tursecius *D* 18 inques *V*: inquis *Klotz* is igitur *V*[2] 26 ingenii acuendi *D*: ingeniendi *V*: ingenii augendi *Stangl* 27 declamas *V* (*peiore numero*) at *Vt*: et *c*: tu *ns*

te quae vellet diceret, salsum omnino hominem, sed materia facilis in te et in tuos dicta dicere. Vide autem quid intersit inter te et avum tuum. Ille sensim dicebat quod
43 causae prodesset; tu cursim dicis aliena. At quanta merces rhetori data est! Audite, audite, patres con- 5 scripti, et cognoscite rei publicae volnera. Duo milia iugerum campi Leontini Sex. Clodio rhetori adsignasti et quidem immunia, ut populi Romani tanta mercede nihil sapere disceres. Num etiam hoc, homo audacissime, ex Caesaris commentariis? Sed dicam alio loco et de 10 Leontino agro et de Campano, quos iste agros ereptos rei publicae turpissimis possessoribus inquinavit. Iam enim, quoniam criminibus eius satis respondi, de ipso emendatore et correctore nostro quaedam dicenda sunt. Nec enim omnia effundam, ut, si saepius decertandum sit, 15 ut erit, semper novus veniam: quam facultatem mihi multitudo istius vitiorum peccatorumque largitur.

18 Visne igitur te inspiciamus a puero? Sic opinor; a
44 principio ordiamur. Tenesne memoria praetextatum te decoxisse? 'Patris' inquies 'ista culpa est.' Concedo. 20 Etenim est pietatis plena defensio. Illud tamen audaciae tuae quod sedisti in quattuordecim ordinibus, cum esset lege Roscia decoctoribus certus locus constitutus, quamvis quis fortunae vitio, non suo decoxisset. Sumpsisti virilem, quam statim muliebrem togam reddidisti. Primo volgare 25 scortum; certa flagiti merces nec ea parva; sed cito Curio intervenit qui te a meretricio quaestu abduxit et, tamquam stolam dedisset, in matrimonio stabili et certo
45 conlocavit. Nemo umquam puer emptus libidinis causa

2 facilis *D et Sueton. de Rhet.* 5: facilis est *V* vide autem quid intersit *V*: vide quid s^2: *om. cett.* 3 tuum] tum tuum *V* (*cf.* §§ 49, 88): tuum intersit *nst*: tuum quid intersit *c* sensim *om. V* 5 audite *semel habet Suetonius* 8 populi Romani *V*: pro *D*: *om. Suet.* 19 tenes V^1 23 constitutus *om.* V^1 24 virilem togam *D* 25 togam *V*: stolam *D* 28 et certo et V^1: et certo te *coni. Halm* 29 locavit *D*

tam fuit in domini potestate quam tu in Curionis. Quotiens te pater eius domu sua eiecit, quotiens custodes posuit ne limen intrares? cum tu tamen nocte socia, hortante libidine, cogente mercede, per tegulas demitterere. Quae
5 flagitia domus illa diutius ferre non potuit. Scisne me de rebus mihi notissimis dicere? Recordare tempus illud cum pater Curio maerens iacebat in lecto; filius se ad pedes meos prosternens, lacrimans, te mihi commendabat; orabat ut se contra suum patrem, si sestertium sexagiens
10 peteret, defenderem; tantum enim se pro te intercessisse dicebat. Ipse autem amore ardens confirmabat, quod desiderium tui discidi ferre non posset, se in exsilium iturum. Quo tempore ego quanta mala florentissimae 46 familiae sedavi vel potius sustuli! Patri persuasi ut aes
15 alienum fili dissolveret; redimeret adulescentem, summa spe et animi et ingeni praeditum, rei familiaris facultatibus eumque non modo tua familiaritate sed etiam congressione patrio iure et potestate prohiberet. Haec tu cum per me acta meminisses, nisi illis quos videmus gladiis confideres,
20 maledictis me provocare ausus esses? Sed iam stupra et 19 47 flagitia omittamus: sunt quaedam quae honeste non possum dicere; tu autem eo liberior quod ea in te admisisti quae a verecundo inimico audire non posses. Sed reliquum vitae cursum videte, quem quidem celeriter perstringam.
25 Ad haec enim quae in civili bello, in maximis rei publicae miseriis fecit, et ad ea quae cotidie facit, festinat animus. Quae peto ut, quamquam multo notiora vobis quam mihi sunt, tamen, ut facitis, attente audiatis. Debet enim talibus in rebus excitare animos non cognitio solum rerum sed
30 etiam recordatio; etsi incidamus, opinor, media ne nimis sero ad extrema veniamus.

2 domo *D* 4 demitt. *Ferrarius*: dimitt. *codd.* 9 se *Vn*[2]: te *cett.* 11 confirmauiat *V*: confirmavit *Halm* 13 esse iturum *D* tanta *D* 17 eumque a tua non modo *D* 30 etsi *V*: tametsi *ns*: iam etsi *ct* opinor *V*: oportet *D*

48 Intimus erat in tribunatu Clodio qui sua erga me beneficia commemorat; eius omnium incendiorum fax, cuius etiam domi iam tum quiddam molitus est. Quid dicam ipse optime intellegit. Inde iter Alexandream contra senatus auctoritatem, contra rem publicam et religiones; 5 sed habebat ducem Gabinium, quicum quidvis rectissime facere posset. Qui tum inde reditus aut qualis? Prius in ultimam Galliam ex Aegypto quam domum. Quae autem domus? Suam enim quisque domum tum obtinebat nec erat usquam tua. Domum dico? Quid erat in terris ubi 10 in tuo pedem poneres praeter unum Misenum quod cum
20 sociis tamquam Sisaponem tenebas? Venis e Gallia ad
49 quaesturam petendam. Aude dicere te prius ad parentem tuam venisse quam ad me. Acceperam iam ante Caesaris litteras ut mihi satis fieri paterer a te: itaque ne loqui 15 quidem sum te passus de gratia. Postea sum cultus a te, tu a me observatus in petitione quaesturae; quo quidem tempore P. Clodium approbante populo Romano in foro es conatus occidere, cumque eam rem tua sponte conarere, non impulsu meo, tamen ita praedicabas, te non existimare, nisi 20 illum interfecisses, umquam mihi pro tuis in me iniuriis satis esse facturum. In quo demiror cur Milonem impulsu meo rem illam egisse dicas, cum te ultro mihi idem illud deferentem numquam sim adhortatus. Quamquam, si in eo perseverares, ad tuam gloriam rem illam referri malebam 25
50 quam ad meam gratiam. Quaestor es factus: deinde continuo sine senatus consulto, sine sorte, sine lege ad Caesarem cucurristi. Id enim unum in terris egestatis, aeris alieni, nequitiae perditis vitae rationibus perfugium esse

3 quiddam iam tum *D* 4 Alexandiriem (*i.e.* -ream) *V*, *cf.* viii 23: Alexandriam *D* (*ubique*) 5 rem p. et *om.* *D* 9 domus *V*[1]: erat domus *cett.* nec *V*: neque *D* 12 venis e *Halm*: venisse *Vct*: venisti (in *add.* *n*) *ns* Galliam *D* 13 parentem *Vct*: patrem *ns* 14 tuam *Manutius*: tuum *codd.*: tum *Frotscher* 16 postea sum cultus *Muretus*: potense sum cultus *V*: postea cultus sum *c*: postea custoditus sum *nt* 17 observatus *D*: ovatus *V* 24 quamquam *codd.*: quoniam *Manutius* 25 rem . . . malebam *om.* *V*

ducebas. Ibi te cum et illius largitionibus et tuis rapinis explevisses, si hoc est explere, *expilare* quod statim effundas, advolasti egens ad tribunatum, ut in eo magistratu, si posses, viri tui similis esses.

5 Accipite nunc, quaeso, non ea quae ipse in se atque **21** in domesticum decus impure et intemperanter, sed quae in nos fortunasque nostras, id est in universam rem publicam, impie ac nefarie fecerit. Ab huius enim scelere omnium malorum principium natum reperietis. Nam cum 51
10 L. Lentulo C. Marcello consulibus Kalendis Ianuariis labentem et prope cadentem rem publicam fulcire cuperetis ipsique C. Caesari, si sana mente esset, consulere velletis, tum iste venditum atque emancipatum tribunatum consiliis vestris opposuit cervicesque suas ei subiecit securi qua
15 multi minoribus in peccatis occiderunt. In te, M. Antoni, id decrevit senatus et quidem incolumis, nondum tot luminibus exstinctis quod in hostem togatum decerni est solitum more maiorum. Et tu apud patres conscriptos contra me dicere ausus es, cum ab hoc ordine ego conservator essem,
20 tu hostis rei publicae iudicatus? Commemoratio illius tui sceleris intermissa est, non memoria deleta. Dum genus hominum, dum populi Romani nomen exstabit—quod quidem erit, si per te licebit, sempiternum—tua illa pestifera intercessio nominabitur. Quid cupide a senatu, quid 52
25 temere fiebat, cum tu unus adulescens universum ordinem decernere de salute rei publicae prohibuisti, neque semel, sed saepius, neque tu tecum de senatus auctoritate agi passus es? quid autem agebatur nisi ne deleri et everti rem publicam funditus velles, cum te neque principes civi-

2 expilare *supplevi* (*cf. Rull.* ii. 98, *Pis.* 52): devorare *aut* haurire *suppl. Faernus* quod] cum *Ernesti* 3 advolas *D* 6 decus *Madvig*: dedecus *codd.* 10 labentem *Vnt*: labantem *cs* 15 in te *Vc*: in mente *t*: in te autem *ns* 16 luminibus *Vc*: luminaribus *nst* 23 pro te *V* licuerit *D* 26 neque id semel *D* 28 deleri *cn¹s*: -ere *Vn²t* evertere *D*

tatis rogando neque maiores natu monendo neque frequens senatus agendo de vendita atque addicta sententia movere potuit? Tum illud multis rebus ante temptatis necessario tibi volnus inflictum est quod paucis ante te, quorum 53 incolumis fuit nemo: tum contra te dedit arma hic ordo 5 consulibus reliquisque imperiis et potestatibus: quae non **22** effugisses, nisi te ad arma Caesaris contulisses. Tu, tu, inquam, M. Antoni, princeps C. Caesari omnia perturbare cupienti causam belli contra patriam ferendi dedisti. Quid enim aliud ille dicebat, quam causam sui dementissimi 10 consili et facti adferebat, nisi quod intercessio neglecta, ius tribunicium sublatum, circumscriptus a senatu esset Antonius? Omitto quam haec falsa, quam levia, praesertim cum omnino nulla causa iusta cuiquam esse possit contra patriam arma capiendi. Sed nihil de Caesare: tibi certe 15 confitendum est causam perniciosissimi belli in persona tua 54 constitisse. O miserum te, si haec intellegis, miseriorem, si non intellegis hoc litteris mandari, hoc memoriae prodi, huius rei ne posteritatem quidem omnium saeculorum umquam immemorem fore, consules ex Italia expulsos, cumque 20 eis Cn. Pompeium quod imperi populi Romani decus ac lumen fuit, omnis consularis qui per valetudinem exsequi cladem illam fugamque potuissent, praetores, praetorios, tribunos plebis, magnam partem senatus, omnem subolem iuventutis, unoque verbo rem publicam expulsam atque 25 55 exterminatam suis sedibus! Vt igitur in seminibus est causa arborum et stirpium, sic huius luctuosissimi belli semen tu fuisti. Doletis tris exercitus populi Romani interfectos: interfecit Antonius. Desideratis clarissimos civis: eos quoque vobis eripuit Antonius. Auctoritas huius 30 ordinis adflicta est: adflixit Antonius. Omnia denique,

1 neque . . . monendo *om. V* 3 potuit] potuisset *Madvig. qui supra* velles? Cum (*ita ns*) *scribit* 4 est *om. D* 9 ferendi *Eberhard*: inferendi *codd.* 12 sublatum circ. *om.* V^1 15 de *om. D* 16 est *V*: si *ct*: sit *ns* causa *D* in *om.* V^1 17 haec *om. D* 20 cumque] que V^1 30 vobis *D*: bonis *V*: nobis *Halm*

quae postea vidimus—quid autem mali non vidimus?—si recte ratiocinabimur, uni accepta referemus Antonio. Vt Helena Troianis, sic iste huic rei publicae belli causa, causa pestis atque exiti fuit. Reliquae partes tribunatus
5 principi similes. Omnia perfecit quae senatus salva re publica ne fieri possent profecerat. Cuius tamen scelus in scelere cognoscite. Restituebat multos calamitosos: in **23** 56 eis patrui nulla mentio. Si severus, cur non in omnis? si misericors, cur non in suos? Sed omitto ceteros: Licinium
10 Lenticulam de alea condemnatum, conlusorem suum, restituit, quasi vero ludere cum condemnato non liceret, sed ut quod in alea perdiderat beneficio legis dissolveret. Quam attulisti rationem populo Romano cur eum restitui oporteret? Absentem, credo, in reos relatum; rem indicta
15 causa iudicatam; nullum fuisse de alea lege iudicium; vi oppressum et armis; postremo, quod de patruo tuo dicebatur, pecunia iudicium esse corruptum? Nihil horum. At vir bonus et re publica dignus. Nihil id quidem ad rem; ego tamen, quoniam condemnatum esse pro nihilo est, si
20 ita esset, ignoscerem. Hominem omnium nequissimum qui non dubitaret vel in foro alea ludere, lege quae est de alea condemnatum qui in integrum restituit, is non apertissime studium suum ipse profitetur? In eodem vero tribunatu, 57 cum Caesar in Hispaniam proficiscens huic conculcandam
25 Italiam tradidisset, quae fuit eius peragratio itinerum, lustratio municipiorum! Scio me in rebus celebratissimis omnium sermone versari, eaque quae dico dicturusque sum notiora esse omnibus qui in Italia tum fuerunt quam mihi qui non fui: notabo tamen singulas res, etsi nullo

3 belli causa, causa *Klotz*: belli causa *V*: causa belli, causa *D* 5 principii *h*: -iis *Vt*: -io *ns*: -ibus *c* 6 profecerat *scripsi*: perfecerat *codd.* (*cf.* x. 23): effecerat *Cobet*: *fort.* confecerat (*cf.* x. 4) 7 restituerat *V* 10 Lenticulam *ns* (Λεντίκουλον *nominat Dio Cassius* xlv. 47): Denticulam *Vct*: Denticulum *Bücheler* 11 sed *codd.*: scilicet *Koch* 19 et ego *D* est si ita esset *D*: si ita *V*: est ita *Halm*

modo poterit oratio mea satis facere vestrae scientiae. Etenim quod umquam in terris tantum flagitium exstitisse
24 58 auditum est, tantam turpitudinem, tantum dedecus? Vehebatur in essedo tribunus plebis; lictores laureati antecedebant, inter quos aperta lectica mima portabatur, quam ex 5 oppidis municipales homines honesti, obviam necessario prodeuntes, non noto illo et mimico nomine, sed Volumniam consalutabant. Sequebatur raeda cum lenonibus, comites nequissimi; reiecta mater amicam impuri fili tamquam nurum sequebatur. O miserae mulieris fecunditatem 10 calamitosam! Horum flagitiorum iste vestigiis omnia municipia, praefecturas, colonias, totam denique Italiam impressit.

59 Reliquorum factorum eius, patres conscripti, difficilis est sane reprehensio et lubrica. Versatus in bello est; saturavit 15 se sanguine dissimillimorum sui civium: felix fuit, si potest ulla in scelere esse felicitas. Sed quoniam veteranis cautum esse volumus, quamquam dissimilis est militum causa et tua—illi secuti sunt, tu quaesisti ducem—tamen, ne apud illos me in invidiam voces, nihil de genere belli dicam. 20 Victor e Thessalia Brundisium cum legionibus revertisti. Ibi me non occidisti. Magnum beneficium! potuisse enim fateor. Quamquam nemo erat eorum qui tum tecum
60 fuerunt qui mihi non censeret parci oportere. Tanta est enim caritas patriae ut vestris etiam legionibus sanctus 25 essem, quod eam a me servatam esse meminissent. Sed fac id te dedisse mihi quod non ademisti, meque a te habere vitam, quia non a te sit erepta: licuitne mihi per tuas contumelias hoc tuum beneficium sic tueri ut tuebar,

8 sequebantur rhedam *n* leonibus *h*, *ut voluit Victorius ex Plin. N. H.* viii. 16. 55 9 comites nequissimi *del. Koch* recta *V* 15 lubrice versatus *D* 16 fuit felix *D* 20 belli genere *D* 27 fac id (facit *n*) te *cns*[1]: faciut e (didisse) *V*: fac te *t*: fas sit te *s*[2]: fac illud te *coni. Halm* 28 quia *D*: qua *V*: quae *Graevius* non a te sit *Vc*: non sit a te *t*: a te non sit *ln* liceatne *D*

praesertim cum te haec auditurum videres? Venisti Brundisium, in sinum quidem et in complexum tuae mimulae. Quid est? num mentior? Quam miserum est id negare non posse quod sit turpissimum confiteri! Si te muni- 5 cipiorum non pudebat, ne veterani quidem exercitus? Quis enim miles fuit qui Brundisi illam non viderit? quis qui nescierit venisse eam tibi tot dierum viam gratulatum? quis qui non indoluerit tam sero se quam nequam hominem secutus esset cognoscere? Italiae rursus percursatio eadem 10 comite mima; in oppida militum crudelis et misera deductio; in urbe auri, argenti maximeque vini foeda direptio. Accessit ut Caesare ignaro, cum esset ille Alexandreae, beneficio amicorum eius magister equitum constitueretur. Tum existimavit se suo iure cum Hippia vivere et equos 15 vectigalis Sergio mimo tradere; tum sibi non hanc quam nunc male tuetur, sed M. Pisonis domum ubi habitaret legerat. Quid ego istius decreta, quid rapinas, quid hereditatum possessiones datas, quid ereptas proferam? Cogebat egestas; quo se verteret non habebat: nondum ei tanta 20 a L. Rubrio, non a L. Turselio hereditas venerat; nondum in Cn. Pompei locum multorumque aliorum qui aberant repentinus heres successerat. Erat vivendum latronum ritu, ut tantum haberet, quantum rapere potuisset.

25 61 62

Sed haec quae robustioris improbitatis sunt, omittamus: 25 loquamur potius de nequissimo genere levitatis. Tu istis faucibus, istis lateribus, ista gladiatoria totius corporis firmitate tantum vini in Hippiae nuptiis exhauseras ut tibi necesse esset in populi Romani conspectu vomere postridie. O rem non modo visu foedam sed etiam auditu! Si inter 30 cenam in ipsis tuis immanibus illis poculis hoc tibi acci-

63

1 ausurum viderem *Eberhard* 5 non *om.* *V* 7 viam *D*: via *V*: iter obviam *Müller* 8 quam nequam *V*: quem *D* 15 tum . . . legerat *om.* *D* 21 Cn. *om.* *V* 22 herus *Jeep* erat ei *ns* 30 et in illis imm. poc. tuis *Quintil.* viii. 4. 10: atque in ipsis tuis imm. poc. *Arusian.* *K.* vii. *p.* 482

disset, quis non turpe duceret? In coetu vero populi Romani negotium publicum gerens, magister equitum, cui ructare turpe esset, is vomens frustis esculentis vinum redolentibus gremium suum et totum tribunal implevit. Sed haec ipse fatetur esse in suis sordibus: veniamus ad splen- 5 dida.

26 64 Caesar Alexandrea se recepit, felix, ut sibi quidem videbatur, mea autem sententia, qui rei publicae sit infelix, felix esse nemo potest. Hasta posita pro aede Iovis Statoris bona Cn. Pompei—miserum me! consumptis enim lacri- 10 mis tamen infixus animo haeret dolor—bona, inquam, Cn. Pompei Magni voci acerbissimae subiecta praeconis. Una in illa re servitutis oblita civitas ingemuit servientibusque animis, cum omnia metu tenerentur, gemitus tamen populi Romani liber fuit. Exspectantibus omnibus quisnam esset 15 tam impius, tam demens, tam dis hominibusque hostis qui ad illud scelus sectionis auderet accedere, inventus est nemo praeter Antonium, praesertim cum tot essent circum hastam illam qui alia omnia auderent: unus inventus est qui id auderet quod omnium fugisset et reformidasset audacia. 20

65 Tantus igitur te stupor oppressit vel, ut verius dicam, tantus furor ut primum, cum sector sis isto loco natus, deinde cum Pompei sector, non te exsecratum populo Romano, non detestabilem, non omnis tibi deos, non omnis homines et esse inimicos et futuros scias? At quam insolenter statim 25 helluo invasit in eius viri fortunas cuius virtute terribilior

27 erat populus Romanus exteris gentibus, iustitia carior! In

1 duceret *Quintil.* viii. 4. 10, ix. 4. 107: diceret *codd.* 2 Romani *om. D* gerens *n*[2] *et Quintil.* viii. 4. 8, xi. 3. 39: gens *V*: regens *cett.* 5 splendidiora *V* (*malo numero*) 7 Alexandriam *D* 8 infelix *D*: hostis *V* 10 Cn. Pompei *Faernus*: subiecta Cn. Pompei *codd.* 11 animo haeret *D*: haberet animo *V*: haeret animo *Faernus*: pectori haeret *Quintil.* ix. 2. 26 12 Magni *om. Quintil.* acerbissimae voci *Quintil.* 14 cum . . . tenerentur *om. D* 23 exsecrandum *D* 24 non *post* deos *om. cns, ed. R* et esse *D*: esse *V*

eius igitur viri copias cum se subito ingurgitasset, exsultabat
gaudio persona de mimo, modo egens, repente dives. Sed,
ut est apud poetam nescio quem 'male parta male dilabun-
tur.' Incredibile ac simile portenti est quonam modo illa 66
5 tam multa quam paucis non dico mensibus sed diebus
effuderit. Maximus vini numerus fuit, permagnum optimi
pondus argenti, pretiosa vestis, multa et lauta supellex et
magnifica multis locis, non illa quidem luxuriosi hominis,
sed tamen abundantis. Horum paucis diebus nihil erat.
10 Quae Charybdis tam vorax? Charybdin dico? quae si 67
fuit, animal unum fuit: Oceanus, me dius fidius, vix videtur
tot res tam dissipatas, tam distantibus in locis positas tam
cito absorbere potuisse. Nihil erat clausum, nihil obsigna-
tum, nihil scriptum. Apothecae totae nequissimis homini-
15 bus condonabantur; alia mimi rapiebant, alia mimae;
domus erat aleatoribus referta, plena ebriorum; totos dies
potabatur atque id locis pluribus; suggerebantur etiam
saepe—non enim semper iste felix—damna aleatoria; con-
chyliatis Cn. Pompei peristromatis servorum in cellis lectos
20 stratos videres. Quam ob rem desinite mirari haec tam
celeriter esse consumpta. Non modo unius patrimonium
quamvis amplum, ut illud fuit, sed urbis et regna celeriter
tanta nequitia devorare potuisset. At idem aedis etiam et
hortos. O audaciam immanem! tu etiam ingredi illam 68
25 domum ausus es, tu illud sanctissimum limen intrare, tu
illarum aedium dis penatibus os impurissimum ostendere?
Quam domum aliquamdiu nemo aspicere poterat, nemo
sine lacrimis praeterire, hac te in domo tam diu deversari
non pudet? in qua, quamvis nihil sapias, tamen nihil tibi

1 viri *om* *D* 10 tam vorax, tam inexplebilis *Cus.* Charybdin *Quintil.* viii. 6. 70: Charybdim *V*: Caribdin *D* 11 animal unum fuit *V*, *Seneca Suasor.* vi. 5: anim. fuit unum *Servius ad Aen.* iii. 420: fuit anim. unum *cns*, *Quintil.*: fuit unum anim. *t* 18 ipse *D* 19 stratos lectos *Quintil.* viii. 4. 25 24 etiam *om.* *D* 26 importunissimum *D* 28 diversari *D*

28 potest esse iucundum. An tu illa in vestibulo rostra cum
aspexisti, domum tuam te introire putas? Fieri non potest.
Quamvis enim sine mente, sine sensu sis, ut es, tamen et te
et tua et tuos nosti. Nec vero te umquam neque vigilantem
neque in somnis credo posse mente consistere. Necesse 5
est, quamvis sis, ut es, violentus et furens, cum tibi obiecta
sit species singularis viri, perterritum te de somno excitari,
69 furere etiam saepe vigilantem. Me quidem miseret parie-
tum ipsorum atque tectorum. Quid enim umquam domus
illa viderat nisi pudicum, quid nisi ex optimo more et 10
sanctissima disciplina? Fuit enim ille vir, patres conscripti,
sicuti scitis, cum foris clarus tum domi admirandus, neque
rebus externis magis laudandus quam institutis domesticis.
Huius in sedibus pro cubiculis stabula, pro conclavibus
popinae sunt. Etsi iam negat. Nolite quaerere; frugi 15
factus est: illam suam suas res sibi habere iussit, ex duodecim tabulis clavis ademit, exegit. Quam porro spectatus
civis, quam probatus! Cuius ex omni vita nihil est honestius
70 quam quod cum mima fecit divortium. At quam crebro
usurpat: 'et consul et Antonius!' Hoc est dicere, et 20
consul et impudicissimus, et consul et homo nequissimus.
Quid est enim aliud Antonius? Nam si dignitas significa-
retur in nomine, dixisset, credo, aliquando avus tuus se et
consulem et Antonium. Numquam dixit. Dixisset etiam
conlega meus, patruus tuus, nisi si tu es solus Antonius. 25
Sed omitto ea peccata quae non sunt earum partium propria quibus tu rem publicam vexavisti: ad ipsas tuas partis
redeo, id est ad civile bellum, quod natum, conflatum, su-

1 in vestibulo *Muretus*: in vestibuloa *V*: vestibula *D* rostra *Orelli*: rostra (·an *V*) spolia *codd.*: rostra an (*vel* ac) spolia *Graevius* 2 *fort.* putas introire (*numeri gratia*) 3 et te et tua] te (*mg. add.*) ęț ei tua *V* 6 vinolentus *n*^{2}*t* 10 quid *om. D* 14 in aedibus *Vrsinus* conclavibus popinae *Halm*: conclavibus popinae triclinis *V*: tricliniis popinae *D* 16 illam suam *codd.* (minimam *sup. lin. in h add. m.* 1): illam mimam *Halm*: mimulam suam *Cornelissen* 17 clavis *Vc*: clausa *cett.* 19 cum *Vc*: *om. nst* 21 homi *V*: omnium *Nohl* 22 est enim *Vc*: est *t*: enim est *ns* 23 se et *V*: se *D* 24 numquam dixit *D*: numquid *V*: numquid dixit *Muretus*

29 71

sceptum opera tua est. Cui bello cum propter timiditatem tuam tum propter libidines defuisti. Gustaras civilem sanguinem vel potius exsorbueras; fueras in acie Pharsalica antesignanus; L. Domitium, clarissimum et nobilissimum
5 virum, occideras multosque praeterea qui e proelio effugerant, quos Caesar, ut non nullos, fortasse servasset, crudelissime persecutus trucidaras. Quibus rebus tantis talibus gestis quid fuit causae cur in Africam Caesarem non sequerere, cum praesertim belli pars tanta restaret? Itaque quem
10 locum apud ipsum Caesarem post eius ex Africa reditum obtinuisti? quo numero fuisti? Cuius tu imperatoris quaestor fueras, dictatoris magister equitum, belli princeps, crudelitatis auctor, praedae socius, testamento, ut dicebas ipse, filius, appellatus es de pecunia quam pro domo, pro
15 hortis, pro sectione debebas. Primo respondisti plane fero- 72 citer et, ne omnia videar contra te, prope modum aequa et iusta dicebas: 'A me C. Caesar pecuniam? cur potius quam ego ab illo? an sine me ille vicit? At ne potuit quidem. Ego ad illum belli civilis causam attuli; ego leges
20 perniciosas rogavi; ego arma contra consules imperatoresque populi Romani, contra senatum populumque Romanum, contra deos patrios arasque et focos, contra patriam tuli. Num sibi soli vicit? Quorum facinus est commune, cur non sit eorum praeda communis?' Ius postulabas, sed
25 quid ad rem? Plus ille poterat. Itaque excussis tuis voci- 73 bus et ad te et ad praedes tuos milites misit, cum repente a te praeclara illa tabula prolata est. Qui risus hominum, tantam esse tabulam, tam varias, tam multas possessiones, ex quibus praeter partem Miseni nihil erat quod is qui

1 cur ei bello tum *D* 5 praeterea *om.* *D* e *Vc*: eo *t*: de *ns* 6 servasset *Vns*: -aret *ct* 7 tantis ac *Schütz* 8 quid . . . Africam *om.* *V* 9 praestaret *V* 13 testamento *Vn*: -menti *cett.* dicebat *D* 17 C. *om.* *D* 18 at ne *V*: ac ne *t*: anne *cns* 19–20 ego . . . rogavi *om.* *V* (*contra Nonium p.* 383) 25 exclusis *Manutius* 27 prolata est *Halm*: prolatas *V*: prolata *D* hominum *V*: hominum de te erat *D*

auctionaretur posset suum dicere. Auctionis vero miserabilis aspectus: vestis Pompei non multa eaque maculosa; eiusdem quaedam argentea vasa conlisa, sordidata mancipia, ut doleremus quicquam esse ex illis reliquiis quod videre
74 possemus. Hanc tamen auctionem heredes L. Rubri de- 5
creto Caesaris prohibuerunt. Haerebat nebulo: quo se verteret non habebat. Quin his ipsis temporibus domi Caesaris percussor ab isto missus deprehensus dicebatur esse cum sica: de quo Caesar in senatu aperte in te invehens questus est. Proficiscitur in Hispaniam Caesar 10
paucis tibi ad solvendum propter inopiam tuam prorogatis diebus. Ne tum quidem sequeris. Tam bonus gladiator rudem tam cito? Hunc igitur quisquam qui in suis partibus, id est in suis fortunis, tam timidus fuerit pertimescat?
30 Profectus est aliquando tandem in Hispaniam; sed tuto, ut 15
75 ait, pervenire non potuit. Quonam modo igitur Dolabella pervenit? Aut non suscipienda fuit ista causa, Antoni, aut, cum suscepisses, defendenda usque ad extremum. Ter depugnavit Caesar cum civibus, in Thessalia, Africa, Hispania. Omnibus adfuit his pugnis Dolabella; in Hispaniensi etiam 20
volnus accepit. Si de meo iudicio quaeris, nollem; sed tamen consilium a primo reprehendendum, laudanda constantia. Tu vero quid es? Cn. Pompei liberi tum primum patriam repetebant. Esto, fuerit haec partium causa communis. Repetebant praeterea deos patrios, aras, focos, larem 25
suum familiarem, in quae tu invaseras. Haec cum peterent armis ei quorum erant legibus—etsi in rebus iniquissimis quid potest esse aequi?—tamen quem erat aequissimum contra Cn. Pompei liberos pugnare? quem? te sectorem.

4 reliquis *Vt*: reliqui *Pluygers* 7 quin *V*: quippe in *D* eis ipsis *coni. Halm* 13 cito accepisti *D* 14 fuerat *V* 15 tandem aliquando *D* 20 in *ns*: *om. Vct* 23 liberi tum *V*: liberam *c*: liberi *nst* 25 patrios *Faernus*: partios *V*: proprios *t*: penates patrios *cns* 26 in quencumque inv. *V* peterent *Vns*: repeterent *ct* 27 ei *t*: ii *V*: hi *ns*: eius *c* 28 tamen erat aequissimum contra Cn. P. liberos Cn. P. pugnare (te *add. c*) sectorem *D*

An ut tu Narbone mensas hospitum convomeres Dolabella 76
pro te in Hispania dimicaret?

Qui vero Narbone reditus! Etiam quaerebat cur ego
ex ipso cursu tam subito revertissem. Exposui nuper,
5 patres conscripti, causam reditus mei. Volui, si possem,
etiam ante Kalendas Ianuarias prodesse rei publicae.
Nam, quod quaerebas quo modo redissem, primum luce,
non tenebris; deinde cum calceis et toga, nullis nec Gallicis
nec lacerna. At etiam aspicis me et quidem, ut videris,
10 iratus. Ne tu iam mecum in gratiam redeas, si scias quam
me pudeat nequitiae tuae, cuius te ipsum non pudet. Ex
omnium omnibus flagitiis nullum turpius vidi, nullum audivi.
Qui magister equitum fuisse tibi viderere, in proximum
annum consulatum peteres vel potius rogares, per municipia
15 coloniasque Galliae, a qua nos tum cum consulatus pete-
batur, non rogabatur, petere consulatum solebamus, cum
Gallicis et lacerna cucurristi. At videte levitatem hominis. 31
Cum hora diei decima fere ad Saxa rubra venisset, delituit 77
in quadam cauponula atque ibi se occultans perpotavit ad
20 vesperum; inde cisio celeriter ad urbem advectus domum
venit capite involuto. Ianitor, 'Quis tu?' 'A Marco tabel-
larius.' Confestim ad eam deducitur cuius causa venerat,
eique epistulam tradidit. Quam cum illa legeret flens—erat
enim scripta amatorie; caput autem litterarum sibi cum
25 illa mima posthac nihil futurum; omnem se amorem abiecisse illim atque in hanc transfudisse—cum mulier fleret

1 ut tu *scripsi*: tutu *V*: ů *n*: tu *cst*: cum *Servius K*. iv. 416: cum tu *Klotz* convomeres *V*: cum vomeres *cns*: cum convom. *t* 3 etiam *V*: ẽ (ei' *c*) iam *ct*: et tamen *ns* 8 Gallicis *Gellius* xiii. 22. 6: caligis *codd.* (*ita mox*), *Rufinianus Rhet. p.* 40 12 turpius vidi nullum *om. V* 14 is (*add.* qui *ns*) per *D* 15 a *D*: *om. V*: e *Halm* nos tum *V*: nostrum *c*: nostrin *t*: noster *ns* 17 hominis *V et Gell.* vi. 11. 6: *om. D* 20 vesperum *D et Gell.*: vesperam *V* 21 capite *codd.*: ore *Gell.* involuto *D et Gell.*: obvol. *V* 22 deducitur *D et Gell.*: *om. V* 24 scripta amat. *V et Gell.*: amat. scripta *D* (am. causa script. *t*) litt. hoc erat *Gell.* 26 illim *Lambinus*: illinon *V*: illic *ct*: illinc *ns*

uberius, homo misericors ferre non potuit, caput aperuit, in collum invasit. O hominem nequam! Quid enim aliud dicam? magis proprie nihil possum dicere. Ergo, ut te catamitum, nec opinato cum te ostendisses, praeter spem mulier aspiceret, idcirco urbem terrore nocturno, Italiam 5
78 multorum dierum metu perturbasti? Et domi quidem causam amoris habuisti, foris etiam turpiorem ne L. Plancus praedes tuos venderet. Productus autem in contionem a tribuno plebis cum respondisses te rei tuae causa venisse, populum etiam dicacem in te reddidisti. Sed nimis multa 10 de nugis: ad maiora veniamus.

32 C. Caesari ex Hispania redeunti obviam longissime processisti. Celeriter isti, redisti, ut cognosceret te si minus fortem, at tamen strenuum. Factus es ei rursus nescio quo modo familiaris. Habebat hoc omnino Caesar: quem 15 plane perditum aere alieno egentemque, si eundem nequam hominem audacemque cognorat, hunc in familiaritatem
79 libentissime recipiebat. His igitur rebus praeclare commendatus iussus es renuntiari consul et quidem cum ipso. Nihil queror de Dolabella qui tum est impulsus, inductus, 20 elusus. Qua in re quanta fuerit uterque vestrum perfidia in Dolabellam quis ignorat? ille induxit ut peteret, promissum et receptum intervertit ad seque transtulit; tu eius perfidiae voluntatem tuam ascripsisti. Veniunt Kalendae Ianuariae; cogimur in senatum: invectus est copiosius multo in istum 25
80 et paratius Dolabella quam nunc ego. Hic autem iratus quae dixit, di boni! Primum cum Caesar ostendisset se, prius quam proficisceretur, Dolabellam consulem esse iussurum—quem negant regem, qui et faceret semper eius modi aliquid et diceret—sed cum Caesar ita dixisset, tum hic 30

3 nihili *Reid* 4 cum te *V*: cum *D*: cum os *Cobet* 7 habuit *codd.*: *corr. Ferrarius* 8 suos *h* 12 C. *om. D* 13 isti et *D* 17 cognoverat *D* 19 est *D* 20 qui tum . . . Dolabellam *om.* *V*[1] 21 utriusque *D* 22 induxit ut peteret *om. V* 26 iratus *Vc*: mihi iratus *nst* 29 negat *V*

bonus augur eo se sacerdotio praeditum esse dixit ut
comitia auspiciis vel impedire vel vitiare posset, idque se
facturum esse adseveravit. In quo primum incredibilem
stupiditatem hominis cognoscite. Quid enim? istud quod 81
5 te sacerdoti iure facere posse dixisti, si augur non esses et
consul esses, minus facere potuisses? Vide ne etiam facilius.
Nos enim nuntiationem solum habemus, consules et reliqui
magistratus etiam spectionem. Esto: hoc imperite; nec
enim est ab homine numquam sobrio postulanda prudentia,
10 sed videte impudentiam. Multis ante mensibus in senatu
dixit se Dolabellae comitia aut prohibiturum auspiciis aut
id facturum esse quod fecit. Quisquamne divinare potest
quid viti in auspiciis futurum sit, nisi qui de caelo servare
constituit? quod neque licet comitiis per leges et si qui
15 servavit non comitiis habitis, sed prius quam habeantur,
debet nuntiare. Verum implicata inscientia impudentia est:
nec scit quod augurem nec facit quod pudentem decet.
Atque ex illo die recordamini eius usque ad Idus Martias 82
consulatum, Quis umquam apparitor tam humilis, tam
20 abiectus? Nihil ipse poterat; omnia rogabat; caput in
aversam lecticam inserens, beneficia quae venderet a conlega
petebat. Ecce Dolabellae comitiorum dies. Sortitio prae- **33**
rogativae; quiescit. Renuntiatur: tacet. Prima classis
vocatur, deinde ita ut adsolet suffragia, tum secunda
25 classis, quae omnia sunt citius facta quam dixi. Confecto 83
negotio bonus augur—C. Laelium diceres—'Alio die' inquit.
O impudentiam singularem! Quid videras, quid senseras,
quid audieras? Neque enim te de caelo servasse dixisti nec
hodie dicis. Id igitur obvenit vitium quod tu iam Kalendis

4 enim est *V* 8 spectionem *ct*: spectationem *V*^{1}: inspectionem *cett.* 11 dixit se *Vn*^{2}: dixisse *cett.* 12 posset *V* 15 habitis comitiis *D*: comitiis *Cobet* 16 inscientia *Vn*: inscia *c*: inscitia *st* est (sed *c*) nec scit *Vc*: si nescit *cett.* 18 atque *D*: itaque *V* 21 adversam *D* inferens *D* venderet *D*: videret *V* 24 vocatur] renuntiatur *add. codd.*, *del. Madvig* ita *V*: *om.* *D* sex *ante* suffrag. *add. Niebuhr*: equitum *post* suffrag. *Mommsen* 25 classis vocatur *V* 26 C. *om* *D* 28 nec enim *D* neque hodie *D*

Ianuariis futurum esse provideras et tanto ante praedixeras. Ergo hercule magna, ut spero, tua potius quam rei publicae calamitate ementitus es auspicia; obstrinxisti religione populum Romanum; augur auguri, consul consuli obnuntiasti. Nolo plura, ne acta Dolabellae videar convellere, 5 quae necesse est aliquando ad nostrum conlegium deferantur.
84 Sed adrogantiam hominis insolentiamque cognoscite. Quam diu tu voles, vitiosus consul Dolabella; rursus, cum voles, salvis auspiciis creatus. Si nihil est, cum augur eis verbis nuntiat, quibus tu nuntiasti, confitere te, cum 'Alio die' 10 dixeris, sobrium non fuisse; sin est aliqua vis in istis verbis, ea quae sit augur a conlega requiro.

Sed ne forte ex multis rebus gestis M. Antoni rem unam pulcherrimam transiliat oratio, ad Lupercalia veniamus.
34 Non dissimulat, patres conscripti: apparet esse commotum; 15 sudat, pallet. Quidlibet, modo ne nauseet, faciat quod in porticu Minucia fecit. Quae potest esse turpitudinis tantae defensio? Cupio audire, ut videam ubi rhetoris sit tanta
85 merces, ubi campus Leontinus appareat. Sedebat in rostris conlega tuus amictus toga purpurea, in sella aurea, coronatus 20 Escendis, accedis ad sellam—ita eras Lupercus ut te consulem esse meminisse deberes—diadema ostendis. Gemitus toto foro. Vnde diadema? Non enim abiectum sustuleras, sed attuleras domo meditatum et cogitatum scelus. Tu diadema imponebas cum plangore populi; ille cum plausu reiciebat. 25 Tu ergo unus, scelerate, inventus es qui cum auctor regni esses, eumque quem conlegam habebas dominum habere velles, idem temptares quid populus Romanus ferre et pati posset.
86 At etiam misericordiam captabas: supplex te ad pedes

3 P. R. religione *D* 4 nuntiavisti *D* 9 si *Vc*: sed *nst* 12 augur *Vc*: auguris *nst* 16 nauseet] nausiet *codd*: *del. Cobet* 18 sit *om. D* 19 ubi . . . appareat *D*: id est ubi . . . appareat *V*: *del Campe* (*cf. Zielinski p.* 213) 21 ascendis *D* 25 reiciebat Vn^2s^1: recipiebat cn^1s^2: accipiebat *t* 27 eumque quem *c*: eum quem *cett.* collegam *Vc*: collegam regni *nst*

abiciebas. Quid petens? ut servires? Tibi uni peteres
qui ita a puero vixeras ut omnia paterere, ut facile servires;
a nobis populoque Romano mandatum id certe non habebas.
O praeclaram illam eloquentiam tuam, cum es nudus con-
5 tionatus! Quid hoc turpius, quid foedius, quid suppliciis
omnibus dignius? Num exspectas dum te stimulis fodiamus? Haec te, si ullam partem habes sensus, lacerat, haec
cruentat oratio. Vereor ne imminuam summorum virorum
gloriam; dicam tamen dolore commotus. Quid indignius
10 quam vivere eum qui imposuerit diadema, cum omnes
fateantur iure interfectum esse qui abiecerit? At etiam 87
ascribi iussit in fastis ad Lupercalia: C. Caesari, dictatori
perpetuo, M. Antonium consulem populi iussu regnum
detulisse; Caesarem uti noluisse. Iam iam minime miror
15 te otium perturbare; non modo urbem odisse sed etiam
lucem; cum perditissimis latronibus non solum de die sed
etiam in diem bibere. Vbi enim tu in pace consistes?
qui locus tibi in legibus et in iudiciis esse potest, quae tu,
quantum in te fuit, dominatu regio sustulisti? Ideone
20 L. Tarquinius exactus, Sp. Cassius, Sp. Maelius, M. Manlius
necati ut multis post saeculis a M. Antonio, quod fas non
est, rex Romae constitueretur?

35 88 Sed ad auspicia redeamus, de quibus Idibus Martiis fuit
in senatu Caesar acturus. Quaero: tum tu quid egisses?
25 Audiebam equidem te paratum venisse, quod me de emen-
titis auspiciis, quibus tamen parere necesse erat, putares
esse dicturum. Sustulit illum diem fortuna rei publicae.
Num etiam tuum de auspiciis iudicium interitus Caesaris
sustulit? Sed incidi in id tempus quod eis rebus in quas

1 abic. *cn*[2]*t*: obic. *n*[1]*s*: eic. *V* 2 ut facile servires *del. Cobet*
6 fodiamus *Vc*: fodiam *nst* 9 quid indignius quam vivere *V*: nonne
indignus tu tueri *D* 13 M. *om. V* 16 de *om. V* 17 bibere
Müller, alii (*cf.* § 104): vivere *codd.* 20 exactus est *Madvig* Sp.
(*ante* Maelius) *n*[2], *ed. R*: *om. cett.* 23 quibus rebus *D* Idibus
om. V 25 quidem *D* 27 rei p. *Vc*: populi R. *nst* (*peiore numero*)
28 tuum] tum *V*

ingressa erat oratio praevertendum est. Quae tua fuga, quae formido praeclaro illo die, quae propter conscientiam scelerum desperatio vitae, cum ex illa fuga beneficio eorum qui te, si sanus esses, salvum esse voluerunt, clam te domum 89 recepisti! O mea frustra semper verissima auguria rerum 5 futurarum! Dicebam illis in Capitolio liberatoribus nostris, cum me ad te ire vellent, ut ad defendendam rem publicam te adhortarer, quoad metueres, omnia te promissurum; simul ac timere desisses, similem te futurum tui. Itaque cum ceteri consulares irent, redirent, in sententia mansi: 10 neque te illo die neque postero vidi neque ullam societatem optimis civibus cum importunissimo hoste foedere ullo confirmari posse credidi. Post diem tertium veni in aedem Telluris et quidem invitus, cum omnis aditus armati ob- 90 siderent. Qui tibi dies ille, Antoni, fuit? Quamquam 15 mihi inimicus subito exstitisti, tamen me tui miseret quod 36 tibi invideris. Qui tu vir, di immortales, et quantus fuisses, si illius diei mentem servare potuisses! Pacem haberemus, quae erat facta per obsidem puerum nobilem, M. Bambalionis nepotem. Quamquam bonum te timor 20 faciebat, non diuturnus magister offici, improbum fecit ea quae, dum timor abest, a te non discedit, audacia. Etsi tum, cum optimum te putabant me quidem dissentiente, funeri tyranni, si illud funus fuit, sceleratissime praefuisti. 91 Tua illa pulchra laudatio, tua miseratio, tua cohortatio; tu, 25 tu, inquam, illas faces incendisti, et eas quibus semustilatus ille est et eas quibus incensa L. Bellieni domus deflagravit. Tu illos impetus perditorum hominum et ex maxima parte servorum quos nos vi manuque reppulimus in nostras domos immisisti. Idem tamen quasi fuligine abstersa 30 reliquis diebus in Capitolio praeclara senatus consulta

1 praetereundum *D* 2 praeclaro *om.* *D* 15 ille dies, M. Antoni *D* 17 et *D*: sed *V* 19 M. Antoni filium *post* nobilem *add.* *D* 20 te bonum *D* 24 tyranni illius sceleratissimi praef. *D* 26 inquam *om.* *D* 28 hominum *om.* *V*

fecisti, ne qua post Idus Martias immunitatis tabula neve cuius benefici figeretur. Meministi ipse de exsulibus, scis de immunitate quid dixeris. Optimum vero quod dictaturae nomen in perpetuum de re publica sustulisti: quo 5 quidem facto tantum te cepisse odium regni videbatur ut eius omnem propter proximum dictatorem metum tolleres. Constituta res publica videbatur aliis, mihi vero nullo modo, 92 qui omnia te gubernante naufragia metuebam. Num igitur me fefellit, aut num diutius sui potuit esse dissimilis? 10 Inspectantibus vobis toto Capitolio tabulae figebantur, neque solum singulis venibant immunitates sed etiam populis universis: civitas non iam singillatim, sed provinciis totis dabatur. Itaque si haec manent quae stante re publica manere non possunt, provincias universas, patres conscripti, 15 perdidistis, neque vectigalia solum sed etiam imperium populi Romani huius domesticis nundinis deminutum est. **37** Vbi est septiens miliens quod est in tabulis quae sunt ad 93 Opis? Funestae illius quidem pecuniae, sed tamen quae nos, si eis quorum erat non redderetur, a tributis posset 20 vindicare. Tu autem quadringentiens sestertium quod Idibus Martiis debuisti quonam modo ante Kalendas Aprilis debere desisti? Sunt ea quidem innumerabilia quae a tuis emebantur non insciente te, sed unum egregium de rege Deiotaro, populi Romani amicissimo, decretum in 25 Capitolio fixum: quo proposito nemo erat qui in ipso dolore risum posset continere. Quis enim cuiquam ini- 94 micior quam Deiotaro Caesar? aeque atque huic ordini, ut equestri, ut Massiliensibus, ut omnibus quibus rem publicam populi Romani caram esse sentiebat. Igitur a quo vivo nec

2 cuius (cui *c*) *Vc*: cuiusquam *cett.* 6 omnem *D*: omen nomen *V*: omne nomen *Muretus*: omen omne *Halm* proximum dictatorem *D*: proximum dictatoris *V*: proximi dictatoris *Muretus* metum tolleres *Vc*: tolleres metum *nst* 9 dissimilis esse *V* (*peiore numero*) 11 venibant *Heusinger*: veniebant *codd.* 17-22 ubi est . . . desisti *post* § 96 acta defendimus *transposuit Nägelsbach* 17 est in *V*: in *D* 18 Opis patebat *D* quae nos *post* redd. *hab. D* 22 sunt ea . . . defendimus (§ 96) *om. D*: *ante* sunt ea *hab. V* (*e* § 97) quid ego de commentaris Caesaris infinitos quiden numerabilibus cyrigraphis Caesaris loquar (*sic*) 23 a tuis *Faernus*: ad ius *V*: a diversis *Poggius* 29 is igitur *V*²

praesens nec absens rex Deiotarus quicquam aequi boni impetravit, apud mortuum factus est gratiosus. Compellarat hospitem praesens, computarat pecuniam, in eius tetrarchia unum ex Graecis comitibus suis conlocarat, Armeniam abstulerat a senatu datam. Haec vivus eripuit, 5
95 reddit mortuus. At quibus verbis? Modo aequum sibi videri, modo non iniquum. Mira verborum complexio! At ille numquam—semper enim absenti adfui Deiotaro—quicquam sibi quod nos pro illo postularemus aequum dixit videri. Syngrapha sesterti centiens per legatos, viros 10 bonos, sed timidos et imperitos, sine nostra, sine reliquorum hospitum regis sententia facta in gynaecio est, quo in loco plurimae res venierunt et veneunt. Qua ex syngrapha quid sis acturus meditere censeo: rex enim ipse sua sponte, nullis commentariis Caesaris, simul atque audivit eius 15
96 interitum, suo Marte res suas recuperavit. Sciebat homo sapiens ius semper hoc fuisse ut, quae tyranni eripuissent, ea tyrannis interfectis ei quibus erepta essent recuperarent. Nemo igitur iure consultus, ne iste quidem, qui tibi uni est iure consultus, per quem haec agis, ex ista syngrapha deberi 20 dicet pro eis rebus quae erant ante syngrapham recuperatae. Non enim a te emit, sed prius quam tu suum sibi venderes ipse possedit. Ille vir fuit; nos quidem contemnendi qui
38 auctorem odimus, acta defendimus. Quid ego de com-
97 mentariis infinitis, quid de innumerabilibus chirographis 25 loquar? quorum etiam institores sunt qui ea tamquam gladiatorum libellos palam venditent. Itaque tanti acervi nummorum apud istum construuntur ut iam expendantur, non numerentur pecuniae. At quam caeca avaritia est!

2 impetravit *Poggius*: imperavit *V* apud eum mortuum *Ernest* gratiosus *Vbaldinus*: gratus *V* 3 pecuniam] impetrarat *add. V, ego delevi, videtur varia lectio e l. 2 migrasse* (computarat, pecuniam imperarat *Poggius*) 4 tetrarchiam *Poggius* 6 reddidit *Poggius* 11 sine nostra *Muretus*: sinestra *V*: sine sua *Poggius*: sine Sexti *Ferrarius* (*cf. Att.* xvi. 3. 6) 12 est *Halm*: et *V*: *del. Poggius* 19 iure *Poggius*: iureis *V* 21 dicet *Halm*: dicit *V*. 24 actorem *Koch* 26 institores *Pantagathus*: imitatores *VD*

Nuper fixa tabula est qua civitates locupletissimae Cretensium vectigalibus liberantur, statuiturque ne post M. Brutum pro consule sit Creta provincia. Tu mentis compos, tu non constringendus? An Caesaris decreto Creta post 5 M. Bruti decessum potuit liberari, cum Creta nihil ad Brutum Caesare vivo pertineret? At huius venditione decreti—ne nihil actum putetis—provinciam Cretam perdidistis. Omnino nemo ullius rei fuit emptor cui defuerit hic venditor. Et de exsulibus legem quam fixisti Caesar 98 10 tulit? Nullius insector calamitatem: tantum queror, primum eorum reditus inquinatos quorum causam Caesar dissimilem iudicarit; deinde nescio cur non reliquis idem tribuas: neque enim plus quam tres aut quattuor reliqui sunt. Qui simili in calamitate sunt, cur tua misericordia 15 non simili fruuntur, cur eos habes in loco patrui? de quo ferre, cum de reliquis ferres, noluisti: quem etiam ad censuram petendam impulisti, eamque petitionem comparasti quae et risus hominum et querelas moveret. Cur autem ea comitia non habuisti? An quia tribunus plebis sini- 99 20 strum fulmen nuntiabat? Cum tua quid interest, nulla auspicia sunt; cum tuorum, tum fis religiosus. Quid? eundem in VII viratu nonne destituisti? intervenit enim cui metuisti, credo, ne salvo capite negare non posses. Omnibus eum contumeliis onerasti quem patris loco, si ulla in 25 te pietas esset, colere debebas. Filiam eius, sororem tuam, eiecisti, alia condicione quaesita et ante perspecta. Non est satis: probri insimulasti pudicissimam feminam. Quid est quod addi possit? Contentus eo non fuisti: frequentissimo senatu Kalendis Ianuariis sedente patruo hanc tibi

2 vectigalibus *om* *D* 3 pro consule *Halm*: pro cons. (cos. *V*) *codd.* mentis es *V*[2]*D* 4 an *Naugerius* (1): in *codd.*, *fort* num 8 defuit *V* 11 inquinatos] aequatos *Camerarius* dissimilem Caesar *D* 12 reliquis non *D* 14 calamitate sunt *Faernus*: calamitates at *V*: calamitate fuerint *D* 19 an quia *D*: aut qua *V* fulmen sin. *D* 20 cum *om.* *cns* 21 cum *om.* *D* sis *D* 22 septem viratu *codd.*, *ita fere semper, sed* v. 33, VII. virum *hab.* *V* cui *Madvig*: cũ *V*: quem *D*

esse cum Dolabella causam odi dicere ausus es quod ab eo sorori et uxori tuae stuprum esse oblatum comperisses. Quis interpretari potest, impudentiorne qui in senatu, an improbior qui in Dolabellam, an impurior qui patre audiente, an crudelior qui in illam miseram tam spurce, 5

39 tam impie dixeris? Sed ad chirographa redeamus. Quae 100 tua fuit cognitio? Acta enim Caesaris pacis causa confirmata sunt a senatu: quae quidem Caesar egisset, non ea quae egisse Caesarem dixisset Antonius. Vnde ista erumpunt, quo auctore proferuntur? Si sunt falsa, cur 10 probantur? si vera, cur veneunt? At sic placuerat ut ex Kalendis Iuniis de Caesaris actis cum consilio cognosceretis. Quod fuit consilium, quem umquam convocasti, quas Kalendas Iunias exspectasti? an eas ad quas te peragratis veteranorum coloniis stipatum armis rettulisti? 15

O praeclaram illam percursationem tuam mense Aprili atque Maio, tum cum etiam Capuam coloniam deducere conatus es! Quem ad modum illinc abieris vel potius paene 101 non abieris scimus. Cui tu urbi minitaris. Vtinam conere, ut aliquando illud 'paene' tollatur! At quam nobilis est 20 tua illa peregrinatio! Quid prandiorum apparatus, quid furiosam vinolentiam tuam proferam? Tua ista detrimenta sunt, illa nostra: agrum Campanum, qui cum de vectigalibus eximebatur ut militibus daretur, tamen infligi magnum rei publicae volnus putabamus, hunc tu compransoribus tuis et 25 conlusoribus dividebas. Mimos dico et mimas, patres conscripti, in agro Campano conlocatos. Quid iam querar de agro Leontino? quoniam quidem hae quondam arationes Campana et Leontina in populi Romani patrimonio grandiferae

1 ausus dicere es *D* 2 oblatum esse *ns*, *ed. R* 4 patre *D et Priscian. K.* ii. *p.* 93: patruo *V*, *Cus.* 7 tua *post* fuit *habent D* 9 quaeque *V* gessisse *V* 11 ut ex *D*: *om. V*: ut *Muretus* 13 advocasti *D* 17 coloniam *om. D* 18 illinc abieris *Faernus*: illī cauieris *V*: illam adieris *D* 19 abieris *Faernus*: habueris *V*: adieris *D* 20 nobilitata sit tua *D* 27 in agro P C. *D* queror *V* 28 Campani et Leontini *D*: *tria verba abesse malim* 29 grandifacere *D*

et fructuosae ferebantur. Medico tria milia iugerum: quid, si te sanasset? rhetori duo: quid, si te disertum facere potuisset? Sed ad iter Italiamque redeamus. Deduxisti 40 102 coloniam Casilinum, quo Caesar ante deduxerat. Consuluisti 5 me per litteras de Capua tu quidem, sed idem de Casilino respondissem: possesne ubi colonia esset, eo coloniam novam iure deducere. Negavi in eam coloniam quae esset auspicato deducta, dum esset incolumis, coloniam novam iure deduci: colonos novos ascribi posse rescripsi. Tu 10 autem insolentia elatus omni auspiciorum iure turbato Casilinum coloniam deduxisti, quo erat paucis annis ante deducta, ut vexillum tolleres, ut aratrum circumduceres; cuius quidem vomere portam Capuae paene perstrinxisti, ut florentis coloniae territorium minueretur. Ab hac perturba- 103 15 tione religionum advolas in M. Varronis, sanctissimi atque integerrimi viri, fundum Casinatem. Quo iure, quo ore? 'Eodem,' inquies 'quo in heredum L. Rubri, quo in heredum L. Turseli praedia, quo in reliquas innumerabilis possessiones.' Et si ab hasta, valeat hasta, valeant tabulae 20 modo Caesaris, non tuae, quibus debuisti, non quibus tu te liberavisti. Varronis quidem Casinatem fundum quis venisse dicit, quis hastam istius venditionis vidit, quis vocem praeconis audivit? Misisse te dicis Alexandream qui emeret a Caesare; ipsum enim exspectare magnum fuit. Quis vero 104 25 audivit umquam—nullius autem salus curae pluribus fuit—de fortunis Varronis rem ullam esse detractam? Quid? si etiam scripsit ad te Caesar ut redderes, quid satis potest dici de tanta impudentia? Remove gladios parumper illos quos videmus: iam intelleges aliam causam esse hastae 30 Caesaris, aliam confidentiae et temeritatis tuae. Non enim

2 quid si V^1: quasi V^2D sanum fecisset *D* quid si te] quidiste V^1: quid si *c*: quasiste V^2: quasi *nst* 6 respondisset *V* 7 quae est *D* 12 tolleres *V*, *Schol. Cruq. ad Hor. Od.* i. 16. 21: videres *D* ut aratr. *Vc*: et aratr. *nst*, *Schol. Cruq.* 19 valeat hasta *om. D* 20 tute te *D* 23 tè *om. V* 26 quid si *D*: quod *V*

te dominus modo illis sedibus sed quivis amicus, vicinus,
41 hospes, procurator arcebit. At quam multos dies in ea villa turpissime es perbacchatus! Ab hora tertia bibebatur, ludebatur, vomebatur. O tecta ipsa misera, 'quam dispari domino'—quamquam quo modo iste dominus—sed tamen 5 quam ab dispari tenebantur! Studiorum enim suorum M.
105 Varro voluit illud, non libidinum deversorium. Quae in illa villa antea dicebantur, quae cogitabantur, quae litteris mandabantur! iura populi Romani, monumenta maiorum, omnis sapientiae ratio omnisque doctrinae. At vero te inquilino 10 —non enim domino—personabant omnia vocibus ebriorum, natabant pavimenta vino, madebant parietes, ingenui pueri cum meritoriis, scorta inter matres familias versabantur. Casino salutatum veniebant, Aquino, Interamna: admissus est nemo. Iure id quidem; in homine enim turpissimo 15
106 obsolefiebant dignitatis insignia. Cum inde Romam proficiscens ad Aquinum accederet, obviam ei processit, ut est frequens municipium, magna sane multitudo. At iste operta lectica latus per oppidum est ut mortuus. Stulte Aquinates: sed tamen in via habitabant. Quid Anagnini? 20 Qui, cum essent devii, descenderunt ut istum, tamquam si esset consul, salutarent. Incredibile dictu, sed inter omnis constabat neminem esse resalutatum, praesertim cum duos secum Anagninos haberet, Mustelam et Laconem, quorum
107 alter gladiorum est princeps, alter poculorum. Quid ego 25 illas istius minas contumeliasque commemorem quibus invectus est in Sidicinos, vexavit Puteolanos, quod

1 aedibus *Pluygers* vicinus] *variam lectionem* vi^ci^nus *in mg. archetypi fuisse arbitror*: *cf. l.* 22 *et ad* xiv. 13 3 es *V*: est *ct*: *om. ns* 6 a *D* M *om.* V^1 7 illud *V*: esse *s*: esse illud *cnt*, *fort. recte* 8 ante *D* quae cogitabantur *om. D* 10 doctrina *D* 14 Casilino *D* 16 obsolefiebant *V*: obsolefaciebant *c*: obsolebant *nst* 19 est per oppidum *D* 21 devii *V*: devia ei *c*: devii (-via *t*) obviam ei *nst* 22 consul V^2D: colem V^1: consulem *Faernus* dictum *V*: dictu est *Ferrarius* sed] cū uinus *add. V*: et simul unū cinus *add c*, et sermulcinus *add. t*: simul *add. ns*: sum vicinus *Madvig* (*corruptelas ex* ui^ci^nus *ortas esse arbitror*, *cf. ad l.* 1 *et* xiv. 13) 25 gladiatorum *D*

C. Cassium et Brutos patronos adoptassent? Magno quidem studio, iudicio, benevolentia, caritate, non, ut te et Basilum, vi et armis, et alios vestri similis quos clientis nemo habere velit, non modo illorum cliens esse. Interea dum tu abes, 42
5 qui dies ille conlegae tui fuit, cum illud quod venerari solebas bustum in foro evertit? Qua re tibi nuntiata, ut constabat inter eos qui una fuerunt concidisti. Quid evenerit postea nescio—metum credo valuisse et arma—conlegam quidem de caelo detraxisti effecistique non tu quidem etiam
10 nunc ut similis tui, sed certe ut dissimilis esset sui. Qui 108 vero inde reditus Romam, quae perturbatio totius urbis! Memineramus Cinnam nimis potentem, Sullam postea dominantem, modo Caesarem regnantem videramus. Erant fortasse gladii, sed absconditi nec ita multi. Ista vero quae
15 et quanta barbaria est! Agmine quadrato cum gladiis sequuntur; scutorum lecticas portari videmus. Atque his quidem iam inveteratis, patres conscripti, consuetudine obduruimus. Kalendis Iuniis cum in senatum, ut erat constitutum, venire vellemus, metu perterriti repente diffu-
20 gimus. At iste, qui senatu non egeret, neque desideravit 109 quemquam et potius discessu nostro laetatus est statimque illa mirabilia facinora effecit. Qui chirographa Caesaris defendisset lucri sui causa, is leges Caesaris easque praeclaras, ut rem publicam concutere posset, evertit. Numerum
25 annorum provinciis prorogavit; idemque, cum actorum Caesaris defensor esse deberet, et in publicis et in privatis rebus acta Caesaris rescidit. In publicis nihil est lege gravius; in privatis firmissimum est testamentum. Leges alias sine promulgatione sustulit, alias ut tolleret promul-
30 gavit. Testamentum inritum fecit, quod etiam infimis

1 et *V*: quod *D* 4 esse illorum cliens *D* 5 fuit *om.* *D* quod tu *D* 9 et fecisti quae *D* 10 ut sit similis *D* 11 reditus inde *D* 12 L. Cinam *V* 14 sed *V*: sed ita *c*: sed tamen *nst* 16 scutati milites, lecticas *ns* 21 et (*del.* *n*[2]) *D*: est *V*: sed *Halm* 26 publicis *Vns*: publ. actis *ct*

civibus semper obtentum est. Signa, tabulas, quas populo Caesar una cum hortis legavit, eas hic partim in hortos Pompei deportavit, partim in villam Scipionis.

43 110 Et tu in Caesaris memoria diligens, tu illum amas mortuum? Quem is honorem maiorem consecutus erat quam 5 ut haberet pulvinar, simulacrum, fastigium, flaminem? Est ergo flamen, ut Iovi, ut Marti, ut Quirino, sic divo Iulio M. Antonius? Quid igitur cessas? Cur non inauguraris? Sume diem, vide qui te inauguret: conlegae sumus; nemo negabit. O detestabilem hominem, sive quod tyranni sacer- 10 dos es sive quod mortui! Quaero deinceps num hodiernus dies qui sit ignores? Nescis heri quartum in circo diem ludorum Romanorum fuisse? te autem ipsum ad populum tulisse ut quintus praeterea dies Caesari tribueretur? Cur non sumus praetextati? cur honorem Caesaris tua lege 15 datum deseri patimur? an supplicationes addendo diem contaminari passus es, pulvinaria noluisti? Aut undique 111 religionem tolle aut usque quaque conserva. Quaeris placeatne mihi pulvinar esse, fastigium, flaminem. Mihi vero nihil istorum placet: sed tu qui acta Caesaris defendis 20 quid potes dicere cur alia defendas, alia non cures? Nisi forte vis fateri te omnia quaestu tuo, non illius dignitate metiri. Quid ad haec tandem? exspecto enim eloquentiam. Disertissimum cognovi avum tuum, at te etiam apertiorem in dicendo. Ille numquam nudus est contionatus: tuum 25 hominis simplicis pectus vidimus. Respondebisne ad haec, aut omnino hiscere audebis? Ecquid reperies ex tam longa oratione mea cui te respondere posse confidas? Sed prae-

44 112 terita omittamus: hunc unum diem, unum, inquam, hodiernum diem, hoc punctum temporis, quo loquor, defende, si 30

8 inauguraris *Halm*: inauguraras *V*: inaugurare *D* 10 eo quod *V* tyranni *D*: Caesaris *V* 11 es] ē V^2 *in ras.*: est *D* 16 die *coni. Müller* 17 contaminari noluisti *V* 18 aut usque *nst*: aut ad usque *V*: actusque *c* quaeres *D* 23 eloquentiam ṭuạṃ *unus cod. Halmii* 29 hunc *post* diem *add. D*

potes. Cur armatorum corona senatus saeptus est, cur me
tui satellites cum gladiis audiunt, cur valvae Concordiae non
patent, cur homines omnium gentium maxime barbaros,
Ituraeos, cum sagittis deducis in forum? Praesidi sui causa
5 se facere dicit. Non igitur miliens perire est melius quam
in sua civitate sine armatorum praesidio non posse vivere?
Sed nullum est istuc, mihi crede, praesidium: caritate te et
benevolentia civium saeptum oportet esse, non armis.
Eripiet et extorquebit tibi ista populus Romanus, utinam 113
10 salvis nobis! Sed quoquo modo nobiscum egeris, dum istis
consiliis uteris, non potes, mihi crede, esse diuturnus.
Etenim ista tua minime avara coniunx quam ego sine contumelia describo nimium diu debet populo Romano tertiam
pensionem. Habet populus Romanus ad quos gubernacula
15 rei publicae deferat: qui ubicumque terrarum sunt, ibi
omne est rei publicae praesidium vel potius ipsa res publica,
quae se adhuc tantum modo ulta est, nondum recuperavit.
Habet quidem certe res publica adulescentis nobilissimos
paratos defensores. Quam volent illi cedant otio consulentes;
20 tamen a re publica revocabuntur. Et nomen pacis dulce
est et ipsa res salutaris; sed inter pacem et servitutem plurimum interest. Pax est tranquilla libertas, servitus postre-
mum malorum omnium, non modo bello sed morte etiam
repellendum. Quod si se ipsos illi nostri liberatores e con- 114
25 spectu nostro abstulerunt, at exemplum facti reliquerunt.
Illi quod nemo fecerat fecerunt. Tarquinium Brutus bello
est persecutus, qui tum rex fuit cum esse Romae licebat;
Sp. Cassius, Sp. Maelius, M. Manlius propter suspicionem
regni appetendi sunt necati: hi primum cum gladiis non in
30 regnum appetentem, sed in regnantem impetum fecerunt.
Quod cum ipsum factum per se praeclarum est atque

4 Ituraeos *del. O. Müller* 5 nonne *D* 7 te *om. D* 9 et *Vc*: *om. nst* 13 rei p. *D* 17 ulta *b*: vita *Vt*: victa *ns* 24 repellenda *Isid. Origg.* ii. 29. 13 27 Romae *Muretus*: Roma te *V* (-ae. te. *V*[2]): Romae regem *D* 29 primum *V*: primi *D* 31 est atque div. *V*: atque div. est *D*

divinum, tum expositum ad imitandum est, praesertim cum
illi eam gloriam consecuti sint quae vix caelo capi posse
videatur. Etsi enim satis in ipsa conscientia pulcherrimi
facti fructus erat, tamen mortali immortalitatem non arbitror
contemnendam. 5

45 115 Recordare igitur illum, M. Antoni, diem quo dictaturam
sustulisti; pone ante oculos laetitiam senatus populique
Romani; confer cum hac nundinatione tua tuorumque:
tum intelleges quantum inter laudem et lucrum intersit.
Sed nimirum, ut quidam morbo aliquo et sensus stupore 10
suavitatem cibi non sentiunt, sic libidinosi, avari, facinerosi
verae laudis gustatum non habent. Sed si te laus adlicere
ad recte faciendum non potest, ne metus quidem a foedissimis
factis potest avocare? Iudicia non metuis: si propter
innocentiam, laudo; sin propter vim, non intellegis, qui 15
116 isto modo iudicia non timeat, ei quid timendum sit? Quod
si non metuis viros fortis egregiosque civis, quod a corpore
tuo prohibentur armis, tui te, mihi crede, diutius non ferent.
Quae est autem vita dies et noctes timere a suis? Nisi vero
aut maioribus habes beneficiis obligatos quam ille quosdam 20
habuit ex eis a quibus est interfectus, aut tu es ulla re cum eo
comparandus. Fuit in illo ingenium, ratio, memoria, litterae,
cura, cogitatio, diligentia; res bello gesserat, quamvis rei
publicae calamitosas, at tamen magnas; multos annos
regnare meditatus, magno labore, magnis periculis quod 25
cogitarat effecerat; muneribus, monumentis, congiariis, epulis
multitudinem imperitam delenierat; suos praemiis, adversarios
clementiae specie devinxerat. Quid multa? Attulerat iam

1 est *V*: si n^1s^2: sit *c*: sic n^2: sed s^1: *om. t* 4 mortali] mortali immortali *V*: *om. D* arbitror esse *V* (*malo numero*) 6 igitur *om. D* 8 hac nundinatione *Lambinus* (hac immani nund. *A. Augustinus*): hac in manum latione *V*: nūmatione *D* 9 laudem et lucrum *D*: lucrum et laudem *V* (*peiore numero*) 12 gustatum *Vc*: gustum *nst* 15 intellegeris qui . . . et quid V^1: intellegis ei qui . . . quid V^2D: *corr. Muretus* 19 vita *Vc*: multas *nst* timere *ct*: timer V^1: timeri V^2ns 21 eo *V*: illo *D* 22 litterae, cura *Vc*: litteratura *nst* 25 magnis *D*: magmultis V^1: multis V^2 26 cogitabat *V* 27 delenierat *Garatoni*: deleniebat *V*: lenierat *D* 28 quid . . . attulerat *om.* V^1

liberae civitati partim metu partim patientia consuetudinem serviendi. Cum illo ego te dominandi cupiditate conferre possum, ceteris vero rebus nullo modo comparandus es. Sed ex plurimis malis quae ab illo rei publicae sunt inusta 5 hoc tamen boni est quod didicit iam populus Romanus quantum cuique crederet, quibus se committeret, a quibus caveret. Haec non cogitas, neque intellegis satis esse viris fortibus didicisse quam sit re pulchrum, beneficio gratum, fama gloriosum tyrannum occidere? An, cum illum homines 10 non tulerint, te ferent? Certatim posthac, mihi crede, ad hoc opus curretur neque occasionis tarditas exspectabitur. [46 117 118]

Respice, quaeso, aliquando rem publicam, M. Antoni, quibus ortus sis, non quibuscum vivas considera: mecum, ut voles: redi cum re publica in gratiam. Sed de te tu videris; 15 ego de me ipse profitebor. Defendi rem publicam adulescens, non deseram senex: contempsi Catilinae gladios, non pertimescam tuos. Quin etiam corpus libenter obtulerim, si repraesentari morte mea libertas civitatis potest, ut aliquando dolor populi Romani pariat quod iam diu parturit! 20 Etenim si abhinc annos prope viginti hoc ipso in templo negavi posse mortem immaturam esse consulari, quanto verius nunc negabo seni? Mihi vero, patres conscripti, iam etiam optanda mors est, perfuncto rebus eis quas adeptus sum quasque gessi. Duo modo haec opto, unum ut moriens 25 populum Romanum liberum relinquam—hoc mihi maius ab dis immortalibus dari nihil potest—alterum ut ita cuique eveniat ut de re publica quisque mereatur. [119]

3 es comparandus *D* 5 boni est V^2D: bonis et V^1: boni exstitit *Koch* 7 haec igitur non *D* neque *V*: nec *D* (*ita l.* 11) 8 re *om. D* 9 an *V*: et *D* 12 respice . . . quibus *D*: respice quaeso aliquibus *V med. omissis*: respice quaeso aliquando quibus *Halm*: resipisce q. a. q. *Seidler* 14 ut voles *D*: utiles *V* (v above i): uti voles *Halm* cum re p. redi *D* tu ipse *D* 15 ipse *V*: ipso *cns*: ipse ipso *t* 16 deseram sextimescam tu s V^1 (*e coll. mea*) *med. omissis, unde* extimescam *coni. Nohl* 19 parturii *D* 22 nunc *Vc*: non *nt*: *om. s* 23 adeptus . . . unum, ut *om.* V^1

COMMENTARY

FIRST PHILIPPIC

1. reversionis] Turning back before the completion of a journey, as distinct from *reditus*, 'return'.

aliquando] 'At last', after Caesar's murder. The senate had been a complete nonentity since the beginning of 49: perhaps Cicero is looking back to an even earlier period, say before Caesar's consulship in 59.

manendum . . . senatoria] This high-sounding protestation is at variance with the facts. From about 7th April to 31st August Cicero had been continuously absent from Rome. He spent most of his time at various places on the Gulf of Naples, writing querulous and ineffectual letters to his friends. Beyond this, he took no part whatever in public affairs: nor did he attend the important meetings of the senate in the first week of June.

eo die . . . Telluris] 17th March 44. See Introd., p. ix. The temple of Tellus was on the slopes of the Esquiline. It was built in 268, in fulfilment of a vow made two years before, by the consul P. Sempronius Sophus, in consequence of an earthquake which occurred during a battle against the Picentians.

Atheniensium vetus exemplum] The amnesty granted by the restored democrats under Thrasybulus to the oligarchs in 403. Dio (xliv. 23–33) purports to give the speech delivered by Cicero on this occasion. Plutarch (Brut. 19) says: Ἀντωνίου καὶ Πλάγκου καὶ Κικέρωνος εἰπόντων περὶ ἀμνηστίας καὶ ὁμονοίας, ἔδοξε μὴ μόνον ἄδειαν εἶναι τοῖς ἀνδράσιν . . . On what ground Halm[8] assumes the *Graecum verbum* to have been ἀμνηστία, I do not know. The word is not found in classical Greek, ἄδεια being the term used, or μὴ μνησικακεῖν. Either of these latter may have been employed by Cicero. But I think he probably said ὁμόνοια. Cf. Lysias, xxv. 27; 30; Demosthenes, Lept. 12. Dio puts the word into Cicero's mouth once or twice in this speech (xliv. 24, 2; 24, 3).

2. Praeclara . . . M. Antoni] The speech attributed to Antony by Appian (ii. 128) on this occasion is an unvarnished appeal to self-interest (Introd., p. ix). It was in this speech that Antony for the first time recognized Dolabella as his colleague in the consulship (§ 31).

liberos eius] According to Dio (xliv. 34, 6) and Appian (ii. 142) both Antony and Lepidus sent sons. Plutarch (Ant. 14, Brut. 19),

Velleius (ii. 58, 3), and Cicero himself elsewhere (§ 31, ii. 90) only mention Antony's son. De Mirmont cites Gellius' chapter (ii. 13) headed 'Liberos in multitudinis numero etiam unum filium filiamve veteres dixisse', and exx. from Cicero, Verr. II. i. 106; Rosc. Am. 96; Leg. Man. 33; Prov. Cons. 35.

domi de re publica] There is a touch of restrained and effective irony in the juxtaposition.

deferebat] *Deferre* is a word of general application, meaning to inform some one of something (in the present case of a decision taken). *Referre* means to refer a matter for decision, and is especially common in the technical phrase *referre ad senatum.* The two words are found side by side in Verr. II. iv. 85.

nihil tum, etc.] *Reliqua* two lines above and *tum* here refer to the period 17th March to 31st May, which is contrasted with the period beginning on 1st June (§ 6 'mutata omnia'). The statement is not borne out by Cicero's private correspondence. At first, it is true, he merely complained of the acceptance of the *Acta Caesaris* without questioning their authenticity. Cf. A. xiv. 9, 2, 18th April: 'Vivit tyrannis, tyrannus occidit! Eius interfecti morte laetamur, cuius facta defendimus'; A. xiv. 10, 1, 19th April: 'ut omnia facta, scripta, dicta, promissa, cogitata Caesaris plus valerent quam si ipse viveret.' But on 22nd April we already find the charge of forgery: 'Antonius accepta grandi pecunia fixit legem a dictatore comitiis latam, qua Siculi cives Romani; cuius rei vivo illo mentio nulla. Quid? Deiotari nostri causa non similis? Dignus ille quidem omni regno, sed non per Fulviam. Sescenta similia.' (A. xiv. 12, 1). For a further charge of forgery see below, note on § 3 *Unum, aiebat.*

commentariis] 'Notes.' Caesar called his histories *commentarii* because he regarded, or affected to regard, them as mere jottings for the use of subsequent historians (Brut. 262). Cicero, when asking one Lucceius to write a history of his consulship, promises him *commentarios rerum omnium* (F. v. 12, 10).

constantia] 'Steadiness,' 'directness.' He did not beat about the bush, as a man would who had something to conceal.

3. Num qui exsules restituti] Cicero had a horror of the restoration of exiles. In a letter written in 49 (A. x. 8, 2) he mentions this as one of the things to be dreaded if Caesar is victorious, together with massacre, abolition of debts, and an attack on private property. So too Servius Sulpicius declared (A. x. 14, 3) that if condemned persons were reinstated he would go into exile.

Unum aiebat, praeterea neminem] This was Sextus Clodius, a freedman of Publius Clodius, 'familiarissimus Clodi et operarum Clodianarum dux' (Ascon. in Pis. 7). He helped Publius to draft his laws (De Dom. 25; 47; 83; 129; Har. Resp. 11; Sest. 133). See Mil. 33 for a delightful picture of Sextus running about Rome on the night of his master's murder, guarding jealously, 'like the Palladium', 'a whole caseful of laws', and ready to present them to any suitable tribune. He was accused by Milo in 56, but acquitted (Q. F. ii. 4; Cael. 78). He played the leading part at Clodius's funeral, with its resultant incendiarism (Mil. 33; Ascon. in Mil. 29). He was brought to trial for his share in these proceedings and condemned by 46 votes to 5 (Ascon. in Mil. 49).

Before restoring him Antony wrote to Cicero: he had, he said, Caesar's authority, embodied in one of his posthumous papers, but would not use it without Cicero's permission. Cicero replied on 26th April (A. xiv. 13 b), consenting with fulsome politeness, and venturing incidentally on the remarkable assertion, 'accedit ut ne in ipsum quidem Clodium meum insigne odium fuerit umquam' (though two years after Publius' death he reckoned the time from that event, which he called *Leuctrica pugna* (A. vi. 1, 26)). Simultaneously he sent Atticus a copy of Antony's letter and his own reply, adding some abuse of Antony, who, he says, had forged a memorandum in support of a step which Caesar would never have taken or permitted: however, Antony would have done what he wanted in any case, so he had shown himself most compliant (A. xiv. 13, 6). Antony read out Cicero's letter to him in the senate on 19th September, an action which Cicero stigmatizes in the Second Philippic as a gross breach of political etiquette (ii. 7).

Num . . . respondebat] On this and the previous point contrast what Cicero says in a letter to Cassius on 3rd May (F. xii. 1, 1). 'Nec eius quidem rei finem video. Tabulae figuntur, immunitates dantur, pecuniae maximae discribuntur, exules reducuntur, senatus consulta falsa deferuntur . . .' See also ii. 92, 97.

Ser. Sulpicio] Servius Sulpicius Rufus: born in 65: studied oratory in Rhodes under Molon, with Cicero: returned to Rome, and devoted himself mainly to jurisprudence: stood for the consulship in 63, but was defeated by Murena, whom he prosecuted unsuccessfully for bribery, Cicero conducting the defence: as interrex in 52 nominated Pompey sole consul: consul in 51: during the civil war a lukewarm supporter of Caesar: governor of Achaia in 46: in January 43, with Piso and Philippus, went on embassy to Antony's camp outside Mutina: died there: in Ninth Philippic Cicero proposed that he should be given a public funeral and his statue placed on the Rostra. In one of the most famous letters of antiquity (F. iv. 5) Sulpicius offered Cicero consolation on the death of his daughter Tullia.

ne . . . figeretur] On this point and on the abolition of the dictatorship cf. ii. 91. For *figeretur* see note on *in aes incidit* (§ 16).

The measure is explained by historians as prohibiting any future use of Caesar's posthumous papers (Groebe-Drumann, i[2]. 77; Ferrero, iii. 31; Heitland, iii. 376, who however is doubtful, and thinks that 'this attempt to recall the general confirmation of Caesar's acts is perhaps not fairly reported'). Cicero refers to the measure in slightly different terms in ii. 91: 'ne qua post Idus Martias immunitatis tabula neve cuius benefici figeretur.' The only other authority for it is Dio, who says (xliv. 53, 4): τῆς βουλῆς τὸ μὲν πρῶτον ψηφισαμένης μηδεμίαν στήλην ὡς καὶ τοῦ Καίσαρος συγγεγραφότος τι ἀνατεθῆναι: xlv. 23, 7: ἐψηφίσασθε μηδεμίαν στήλην μετὰ τὸν τοῦ Καίσαρος θάνατον, ὡς καὶ παρ' ἐκείνου τῳ δεδομένον τι ἔχουσαν, στῆναι. Dio's words look like a puzzled attempt to translate the passages in Cicero, and can scarcely be regarded as independent evidence.

That Antony should have surrendered so powerful a weapon as the Acta, after once getting it into his hands, is remarkable. If he did surrender it, he regained it within a month, at any rate to a considerable extent. For as early as 18th April he was making free use of the Acta. (Note on *nihil tum*, etc., § 2.) If he regained it, that was a serious blow to the constitutionalists, of which our authorities tell us nothing. One might be tempted to take Cicero's words here as a rhetorical over-statement, of a kind not uncommon in his speeches (and so Heitland perhaps intends to suggest). But there is a sort of legal precision about the language, which tells against this view: and so does the repetition in ii. 91.

The traditional interpretation of the passage also involves a grammatical difficulty. The adverbial phrase *post Idus Martias* has to be taken, not with the verb *figeretur*, but with the substantival clause *ullius decreti Caesaris*, which scarcely seems possible Latin.

The very considerable difficulty of the passage has been ignored by all commentators and almost all historians.

de qua . . . diximus] The ordinary procedure for taking votes in the senate was as follows. The presiding magistrate asked each senator in turn for his opinion (*perrogatio sententiarum*) in the order, *consulares*, *praetorii*, and then, probably, *tribunicii*, *aedilicii*, *quaestorii*. The senator thus called upon could, if he chose, make a speech, ending with the declaration of his vote. The division (*discessio*) was then taken, the formula being 'qui haec sentitis in hanc partem, qui alia omnia in illam partem ite qua sentitis' (Plin. Ep. viii. 14, 19–20). But in cases where it was obvious that no serious difference of opinion existed, the division might be taken at once, without the preliminary *perrogatio sententiarum*. This is clearly explained by Varro (ap. Gell. xiv. 7, 9): 'senatus consultum fieri duobus modis: aut per discessionem, si consentiretur, aut, si res dubia esset, per singulorum sententias exquisitas.' (When Pompey, more at home in the camp than in the senate-house, was about to enter on his first consulship, he got his friend Varro to write him a little handbook on senatorial procedure, from which Gellius' extract is taken.)

Scriptum . . . attulit] Cicero wishes to emphasize that the abolition of the dictatorship was due to Antony's deliberate initiative. A magistrate might either simply ask the senate what it wished done (Cat. iii. 13: 'senatum consului de summa re publica quid fieri placeret'), or himself make proposals. In the latter case, he would naturally, when important matters were concerned, draft his proposals beforehand (iii. 20; x. 6; F. x. 13, 1).

4. dictatoris . . . fuisset] The last persons to be appointed dictator at a time of national crisis (*rei gerundae causa*, Fast. Capitol.: cf. Tac. Ann. i. 1, *ad tempus sumebatur*) were Q. Fabius Maximus Cunctator in 217, after Trasimene, and M. Iunius Pera in 216, after Cannae (Liv. xxii. 8, 6; 57, 9). Dictators continued after that date to be nominated as a constitutional convenience, *comitiorum habendorum causa* or for similar purposes, the last recorded case being in 202 (Fast. Capitol.). After a lapse of 120 years, Sulla was appointed dictator in 82 ἐπὶ θέσει νόμων καὶ καταστάσει τῆς πολιτείας (App. i. 99). Caesar was four times dictator and finally *dictator perpetuus* (ii. 87). Augustus refused the title (Suet. Aug. 52).

On the subject of the dictatorship see Greenidge, *R. P. L.* 191–5. 'The application of the name to Sulla and Caesar', he remarks, 'was the transference of the title of a constitutional office, in the first instance to a constituent authority, in the second to a monarchy.'

5. uncus impactus] The bodies of criminals were dragged after execution by a hook to the top of the Scalae Gemoniae, which led down from the Capitol in a direction which cannot be precisely determined. There they were exposed to public insult, and then thrown down and dragged by the hook into the Tiber. (Rab. Perd. 16; Dio lviii. 5, 6; 15, 3; Tac. Ann. v. 9; Suet. Tib. 61; Iuv. x. 86. Further references in Mayor's *Juvenal*, ad. loc., and in P.-W. s.v. *Gemoniae scalae* The details vary slightly.)

fugitivo] This was Herophilus, a 'vet' or oculist by profession (*medicus equarius* or *ocularius*: the reading in Val. Max. ix. 15 is uncertain), who changed his Greek name for the Roman one Amatius. He subsequently assumed the name Marius, and pretended to be the grandson of the great Caius. In April 45 he was prosecuted on some unknown charge and asked Cicero to defend him. Cicero (A. xii. 49) suggested that he should apply for protection to his 'kinsman' Caesar (whose aunt Julia was the wife of C. Marius). Instead of protecting him, Caesar banished him. But a year later, taking advantage of the confusion which followed the dictator's murder, he returned to Rome, and inflamed popular opinion against the conspirators. Antony, who was at this time on outwardly good terms with Brutus, arrested the pretender and executed him without trial, perhaps on 13th April. (So Becht. Ferrero gives 11th or 12th, Groebe 14th. The execution is first mentioned in A. xiv. 8, 15th April, from Sinuessa.) The date of the beginning of the riot was about 9th April. The first reference to it in Cicero's letters is in A. xiv. 5, 1, 11th April, from Astura: the previous day's letter mentions lack of news (A. xiv. 5, 1; 6, 1; 7, 1; 8, 1; Liv. Ep. 116; App. iii. 2–3; Dio xliv. 51, 1; Val. Max. ix. 15, 1).

nisi conlega afuisset] Antony left Rome for Campania on about 25th April See ii. 100, note on 'mense Aprili atque Maio'

The incident of Dolabella and the pillar must have occurred at the very end of April, as it is first mentioned in Cicero's letter written at Puteoli on 1st May (A. xiv. 15, 1). Cicero was greatly excited by the event, as his letters of the first week of May show. E.g. 'O mirificum Dolabellam meum! Iam enim dico meum, antea, crede mihi, subdubitabam' (A. xiv. 15, 1). 'O Dolabellae nostri magnam ἀριστείαν! Quanta est ἀναθεώρησις! Equidem laudare eum et hortari non desisto' (A. xiv. 16, 2). In a letter to Dolabella (A. xiv. 17 a) he writes that people are attributing the action to his own influence, and begs to be allowed to play Nestor to Dolabella's Agamemnon. After this Atticus intimated that he had had enough of the subject, and by 9th May Cicero's ardour had cooled, Dolabella having failed to pay a debt due on 1st January. 'Satis aculeatas ad Dolabellam litteras dedi' (A. xiv. 18, 1).

credo . . . communia] No doubt true. Dolabella's action was quite in line with Antony's execution of Amatius. 'Qua re . . . nuntiata . . . concidisti' in ii. 107 need not be taken seriously.

cum serperet . . . latius] Cicero used very similar language at the time. 'Manabat enim illud malum urbanum et ita corroborabatur cotidie, ut ego quidem et urbi et otio diffiderem urbano; sed ita seditio compressa est, ut mihi videamur omne iam ad tempus ab illo dumtaxat sordidissimo periculo tuti futuri' (F. xii. 1, 1).

bustum] Drumann (i^2. 94–5) understands this to include the βωμός erected by Amatius (App. iii. 2) and the *columna* mentioned below (which he identifies with the 20-foot column, inscribed 'parenti patriae', mentioned by Suetonius, Iul. 85). The *columna*, he thinks, was erected either by Amatius or by some one else after his death. But Cicero's words, 'cum serperet . . . infinitum malum . . . idemque bustum . . . facerent', if we may take them as a precise statement, seem to refer to something erected after Amatius's death, and I scarcely believe that Antony, when punishing the offender, would have suffered the objectionable monument to remain.

Appian (iii. 3, fin.; cf. A. xiv. 15, 1) appears to confound Antony's punishment of Amatius with Dolabella's overthrow of the pillar.

insepultam sepulturam] Oxymoron, common in Greek poetry, is rare in Latin, especially in prose. De Mirmont cites De Orat. iii. 219 (from a tragedy) 'innuptis nuptiis': A. vii. 13, 1 'Dux ἀστρατήγητος': the former obviously a translation of γάμος ἄγαμος (Soph. O.T. 1214), the latter containing a Greek word.

For descriptions of the funeral see Liv. Ep. 116; Plut. Caes. 68; Ant. 14; Brut. 20; Suet. Iul. 84–5; App. ii. 143–8; Dio, xliv. 35–51. The body was burned in the Forum, in violation of the Twelve Tables, which forbade funerals within the city precincts: and burned on an improvised pyre of benches and other random material. In general, the proceedings were not conducted 'decently and in order'.

animadversio] The slaves were crucified, the freemen hurled from the Tarpeian rock (A. xiv. 15, 1; 16, 2; App. iii. 3).

talisque eversio] 'Columnam tollere, locum illum sternendum locare!' (A. xiv. 15, 1).

6. Kalendis Iuniis] Introd., p. xiii; ii. 108–9.

mutata omnia] A cursory reading of the letters of April and May shows that the dramatic transformation of Antony from saint to devil on 1st June 44 is invented for the occasion.

Consules designati] Aulus Hirtius and Caius Vibius Pansa, nominated consuls by Caesar for the year 43. They were Caesarians, but moderate men, and by no means fond of Antony. Hirtius, clearly the more important man of the two, is warmly commended by Cicero in § 37. The winning over of the consuls elect by the constitutionalists would have been a success of the first magnitude, and it is not surprising to find Brutus and Cassius asking Cicero to bring all his influence to bear on them (A. xiv. 20, 4, 11th May). It even appeared that 1st January 43 might prove the beginning of a better era, and when Cicero left Italy he did so with the firm intention of returning before that date (cf. below, 'ea mente discessi', etc.). He saw the two constantly during May at various places on the Gulf of Naples, and his correspondence during this period illustrates both their attitude and his ever changing opinion of them. E.g. A. xiv. 19, 2: 'Pansa furere videtur de Clodio itemque de Deiotaro, et loquitur severe, si velis credere. Illud tamen non belle, ut mihi quidem videtur, quod factum Dolabellae vehementer improbat.' A. xiv. 20, 4: 'Quod Hirtium per me meliorem fieri volunt' (*sc.* Brutus et Cassius), 'do equidem operam et ille optime loquitur, sed vivit habitatque cum Balbo, qui item bene loquitur. Quid credas videris. . . . Cum Pansa vixi in Pompeiano. Is plane mihi probabat se bene sentire et cupere pacem.' A. xiv. 22, 1: 'Meus discipulus' (Hirtius), 'qui hodie apud me cenat, valde amat illum quem Brutus noster sauciavit.' A. xv. 1, 3: 'Ego perspexi, cum . . . proficisceretur Hirtius, omnem eius sensum. Seduxi enim et ad pacem sum cohortatus. Non poterat scilicet negare se velle pacem, sed non minus se nostrorum arma timere quam Antoni.' A. xv. 3, 2: 'Hirtius est tuus.' A. xv. 6, 1: 'Antonio est' (Hirtius) 'fortasse iratior, causae vero amicissimus.' (The letter encloses one from Hirtius to Cicero, begging him to restrain Brutus and Cassius from any rash action, and prophesying that Antony, if given his head, will ruin his own cause.) A. xv. 8, 1: (Hirtius) 'se scribit vehementer offensum esse veteranis.' A. xv. 22, 1: 'Pansam bene loqui credo. Semper enim coniunctum esse cum Hirtio scio. Amicissimum Bruto et Cassio puto, si expediet . . . inimicum Antonio: quando aut cur? quousque ludemur? . . . utrobi erit (Pansa) si bellum erit?' A. xvi. 1, 4: 'Ad Kal. Ian. in Pansa spes? Λῆρος πολὺς in vino et in somno istorum.'

negabant . . . venire] Cf. Hirtius's words in his letter in A. xv. 6: 'Noli autem me tam strenuum putare, ut ad Nonas recurram.'

patriae liberatores] M. Brutus and C. Cassius. The terms *liberatores* and *heroes* are frequently applied to them in the letters, as the two leading spirits in the conspiracy. The Amatius riots were particularly directed against them. App. iii. 2: φοβερὸς ἦν Ἀμάτιος τοῖς σφαγεῦσιν; iii. 3: τούτοις . . . ἐνεδρεύσειν ἐλέγετο. The day of their departure from Rome cannot be exactly determined. On 15th April Cicero writes from Formiae: 'Brutum . . . audio visum sub Lanuvio' (A. xiv. 7, 1), a rumour which he seems to doubt in A. xiv. 8, 1, written later on 15th, but definitely confirms in A. xiv. 10, 1, written on 19th, and which was probably therefore true from the first. They left Rome, then, not later than 13th, perhaps earlier. For safety, they moved secretly. Hence Cicero was in doubt as to their whereabouts for four days, though anxious to be informed. (A. xiv. 7, 1; 8, 2) Groebe gives the date of their departure as 'about 13th'; Ferrero as 13th; Merrill, as part of a wider chronological scheme, as 9th (*Class. Phil.* x. 255). The 9th is the *terminus a quo*, for 'parietibus contineri' in A. xiv. 5, 2, written at Astura on 11th, implies their presence in Rome two days before. Brutus, as Praetor Urbanus, needed leave to be absent from Rome for more than ten days: and this was granted him on Antony's motion (ii. 31), probably after his departure: had it been granted before, his going would not have been a secret.

Cicero was much affected by the news of their departure. He regarded their presence in Rome as vital to the constitutional cause: 'Quod errare me putas, qui rempublicam putem pendere a Bruto, sic se res habet: aut nulla erit aut ab isto istisve servabitur. . . . Atque utinam liceat isti (Bruto) contionari! Cui si esse in urbe tuto licebit, vicimus' (A. xiv. 20, 3).

From that time on we find the two living at Lanuvium, where Brutus owned a country estate, in which that admirer of ancient Lacedaemon had given Spartan names to the streams and porticos (A. xv. 9, 1). Like Cicero, he and Cassius were much exercised as to whether or not to attend the senate on 1st June. About 26th May they asked his advice on the point. Not knowing what to say, he left their letter unanswered (A. xv. 5, 1). At about the same time they wrote to Antony: 'scribitur nobis magnam veteranorum multitudinem Romam convenisse iam et ad Kalendas Iunias futuram multo maiorem: . . . cum ipsi . . . dimiserimus ex municipiis nostros necessarios, . . . digni sumus, quos habeas tui consili participes. . . . Qua re petimus a te, facias nos certiores tuae voluntatis in nos: putesne nos tutos fore in tanta frequentia militum veteranorum, quos etiam de reponenda ara cogitare audimus: quod velle et probare vix quisquam posse videtur, qui nos salvos et honestos velit. . . . Maximo timore de nobis adficiuntur amici nostri: quibus, etsi tua fides explorata est, tamen illud in mentem venit, multitudinem veteranorum facilius impelli ab aliis quolibet quam a te retineri posse. Rescribas nobis ad omnia rogamus: nam illud valde leve est ac nugatorium, ea re denuntiatum esse veteranis, quod de commodis eorum mense Iunio laturus esses'. (F. xi. 2.)

quos tamen . . . laudabant] For the relations between the 'liberators' and Antony cf. A. xiv. 6, 1: 'Antonio conloquium cum heroibus nostris pro re nata non incommodum'; A. xiv. 8, 1: 'Optime tam etiam Bruto nostro probari Antonium.' See also ii. 31.

Veterani qui appellabantur] 'The veterans whose assistance was being invoked.' Cf. F. xi. 2, quoted above; also A. xiv. 21, 2 (11th May): 'Antoni consilia narrabat (*sc.* Balbus): illum circumire veteranos, ut acta Caesaris sancirent idque se facturos esse iurarent, ut arma omnes haberent eaque duoviri omnibus mensibus inspicerent.' On 24th May Cicero writes to Atticus (A. xv. 4, 4): 'Cetera coram, et maxime quid nostris faciendum sit, quid etiam nobis, si Antonius militibus obsessurus est senatum.' He was even then contemplating attending on 1st. But after hesitating up to the last moment, he finally decided to absent himself.

(Graevius's interpretation of the words *veterani qui appellabantur*, given above, seems to me much the best. King prefers 'those who claimed the name of veterans': he thinks Cicero wished 'to intimate either that he thought those who had aided Caesar against the state to be unworthy of the name, or that many of them had not yet served the number of campaigns which entitled them to it'. I very much doubt, however, whether Cicero, when he delivered the First Philippic, would have ventured to speak in these terms of the veterans. Halm's explanation of the addition 'qui appellabantur' is that *veterani* was a new word only recently introduced into literature, after Caesar's example. But Cicero uses it elsewhere without explanation (e.g. ii. 59; 61; iii. 3; xi. 37; cf. F. xi. 2, quoted above): again, surely 'appellantur' would be required, as read by some inferior MSS.).

quibus . . . caverat] On 17th March, in addition to the general ratification of the *Acta Caesaris*, the senate confirmed in their tenure all persons to whom land allotments had been assigned or promised (App. ii. 135). Hence Antony's first agrarian law (ii. 100, note on *praeclaram percursationem*).

spem novarum praedarum] The agrarian measures of Caesar, carried out by Antony in May, had proved insufficient. 'Varro noster ad me epistolam misit sibi a nescio quo missam—nomen enim delerat—in qua scriptum erat veteranos eos, qui reiciantur—nam partem esse dimissam—, improbissime loqui, ut magno periculo Romae sint futuri qui ab eorum partibus dissentire videantur' (A. xv. 5, 3, 27th or 28th May). Hence the rumour that Antony was going to propose measures touching their interest (F. xi. 2, see note on *patriae liberatores* ad fin.), as he in fact did in his second agrarian law (ii. 100 n.).

quae . . . videre] The core of a feeble defence. Distance lent enchantment to the view.

ius legationis liberum] *Legatus* was a general term applied to persons dispatched by magistrates on special missions, and to persons in attendance on commanders in the field or provincial governors. During the closing years of the republic it became customary for senators, who wished to leave Italy on business or for other reasons, to obtain a special kind of *legatio* known as *legatio libera*, by which, while not attached to any official, they were enabled to travel at public expense and enjoy the advantages of ordinary *legati*. The privilege became so much abused that Cicero, during his consulship, attempted to abolish it, but only succeeded in limiting its duration to one year, a measure subsequently confirmed by a lex Iulia. Cicero appears to speak loosely in using the word *liberum* here. For, while his letters from as early as 17th March contain much discussion of the advantages and disadvantages of a *legatio libera*, he was finally appointed *legatus* by Dolabella on 2nd June. The advantage of this *legatio*, as opposed to a *libera*, was that it lasted five years, and enabled its holder to enter and quit Italy at pleasure, while it did not, any more than a *libera legatio*, entail the performance of any duties. 'A Dolabella mandata habebo quae mihi videbuntur, id est, nihil.' (A. xv. 19, 2; cf. A. iv. 2, 6). On the other hand a *libera legatio* 'looked better' (*honestior est*, A. xv. 8, 1). It would have given Cicero a more independent position, and he may not have wished to appear too intimate with, or indebted to, Dolabella. It is perhaps for this reason that in the present passage he speaks of his *legatio* as *libera*.

Groebe (Drumann, i². 431, followed by v. Premerstein in P.-W. xii. 1, 1136) lays stress on the form of the expression 'ius legationis liberum', which cannot, he says, equal 'ius legationis liberae'. But we do not know enough of the technical phraseology to dogmatize on this point. And it is natural, if Cicero wishes here to give the impression that his *legatio* was *libera*, when in reality it was not, that he should 'hedge' by using a not quite precise expression.

(De Leg. iii. 18; A. iv. 2, 6; xv. 8; xv. 11, 4; xv. 19; F. xi. 1, 2; xii. 21; Mommsen, *St. R.* ii. 690.)

ut . . . videbatur] Incoming consuls usually convened the senate on 1st January. Otherwise there were no fixed dates for meetings until the time of Augustus.

This passage can hardly mean that Antony was expected to suspend senatorial government altogether for the remainder of his term of office. For it is inconceivable that Cicero would refer thus casually to so revolutionary an intention. It can only mean that Antony meant to render senatorial government nugatory by methods of terrorism such as those which he employed on 1st June. It must be admitted, however, that it is extremely difficult to extract this sense from the words.

Atticus thought it most important that Cicero should be back by 1st January (A. xv. 25; xvi. 6, 2; 7, 2).

7. Cum Brundisium . . . vitavissem] The 'beaten track' was from Brundisium to Dyrrachium by sea, and thence by the Via Egnatia to Thessalonica. (For the road-system of Greece, cf. M. P. Charlesworth, *Trade-routes and Commerce of the Roman Empire*, ch. vii.) Cicero was uncertain up to the last moment what route to take. About 20th June he was consulting Atticus on the subject (A. xv. 20, 3). The advantage of Brundisium was the short sea voyage (only five hours, Atticus said), as against the much longer crossing from Puteoli, where Cicero then was. On the other hand, the legions which Antony meant to transport from Macedonia to Gaul were to disembark at Brundisium, making the place no safe one for a politician of Cicero's views (A. xv. 21, 3). Soon after, he heard that the seas were infested with pirates from Dyme, in Achaia, an additional argument for Brundisium; although, by taking the other route, he hoped to find some safety in having Brutus, with his ships, for a fellow-traveller, as it seemed he would (A. xvi. 1, 3). On 10th July (A. xvi. 4, 4) he had decided against Brundisium, owing to the reported imminent arrival of Antony's troops. By the next day (A. xvi. 2, 4), with characteristic vacillation, he had again changed his mind, thinking it would be 'easier to avoid the legions than the pirates'. However, he soon changed it yet again, and, definitely abandoning the Brundisium route, moved down the western coast to Pompeii (17th July), Velia (20th), and Vibo (25th) on his way to Rhegium. When he got to Rhegium there would be further alternatives to consider. He might cross to Corcyra; or to Patrae, either direct or via Syracuse (A. xvi. 6, 1). Meanwhile, every step south made Italy seem safer, his villas and Atticus' society more delightful. He became convinced that, whereas all was quiet now, he would be returning at the very moment when things were getting unpleasant again at the opening of the new year. In spite of these reflections he continued his journey, and from what he heard on the way decided on the Syracuse-Patrae route.

quae tamen . . . potuit] *Tamen*, in spite of the order, seems to go with *potuit*, *in apodosi* after 'urbs . . . coniunctissima', which is virtually a concessive clause.

Cicero had endeared himself to the Sicilians in 75, as quaestor at Lilybaeum (Planc. 64–5), and five years after had, at their request, conducted the prosecution of Verres, impeached for extortion as governor of the island.

suspicionis aliquid] Antony had recently conferred the franchise on the Sicilians, a step which Cicero, attached to them as he was, disapproved (A. xiv. 12, 1, 22nd April). They were presumably grateful, and Cicero's visit, if protracted, might have been construed as an attempt to wean them from their new benefactor. Moreover Sicily, near to Italy, yet separated from it by sea, manifestly offered a convenient jumping-off place for a *coup d'état*.

Cum autem me, etc.] The details are corroborated by a letter written to Atticus, on board ship, *en route* for Pompeii, on

19th August (A. xvi. 7). But Cicero there adds that the Rhegians told him that his absence was being criticized in Rome. And he received at the same time a letter from Atticus, which nettled him considerably, taunting him with deserting his country, after all his fine talk about a glorious death, and recommending him to turn out a short brochure in defence of his conduct.

conscendi] On 6th August.

nec ita multum] 300 stades (A. xvi. 7, 1).

8. Cumque . . . mansissemque] Rather an odd mixture of causal and temporal constructions. 'Since it was midnight, after I had (consequently) stopped the night with Valerius.'

P. Valeri] A friend of Cicero's mentioned in A. xiii. 15; xvi. 7, 1; F. xiv. 2, 2.

M. Antoni contionem] Nothing further is known of this speech. It is not mentioned in the letter (A. xvi. 7).

ea lecta . . . cogitare] Scarcely accurate. Cicero had been at any rate dallying with the idea since 17th July (A. xvi. 3, 4).

Nec ita multo post] In A. xvi. 7, 1 Cicero says that the edict and the optimistic prognostications were brought by the Rhegians. Brutus and Cassius were intensely dissatisfied with the duties assigned to them on 5th June of superintending the corn supply of Rome. Acceptance of the task meant virtual banishment, and Brutus' mother, the masterful Servilia, promised to get the measure amended (A. xv. 11, 2). Towards the end of July Brutus and Cassius issued a manifesto (*edictum*) in which they called upon Antony to allow them 'de suo iure decedere' (viz. I take it, to decline the corn-commission). This is the *edictum*, mentioned here, of which Cicero received a copy at Leucopetra on 7th August. Elated perhaps by the collapse of the senatorial party on 1st August, Antony replied with a counter-manifesto, and a violent and threatening letter, accusing Brutus and Cassius of raising money and men, tampering with the armies, and sending agents to the provinces. They replied on 4th August in a dignified letter, a copy of which is preserved in Cicero's correspondence (F. xi. 3). Brutus showed this letter, and the manifesto of Antony to which it was an answer, to Cicero at Velia on 17th August (A. xvi 7, 7). *Edictum*, which I render 'manifesto', seems to have been something not unlike a modern politician's 'letter communicated to the press'.

It has usually been assumed that the 'edictum Bruti et Cassi' is the document to which Velleius (ii. 62, 3) refers: 'testati edictis libenter se vel in perpetuo exilio victuros, dum rei publicae constaret concordia, nec ullam belli civilis praebituros materiam' (probably as a blind, to cover their intended move against Macedonia and Syria). See Halm[8] and King ad loc.; Ferrero, iii. 87. Groebe (Drumann, i[2]. 430–1) thinks that Brutus and Cassius demanded (1) that they should be relieved of the corn-commission, (2) that provinces should be allotted to them; in return, they would resign their praetorships and leave Italy.

But (1) the context of Velleius's statement suggests that the *edictum* to which he refers was published just before the departure of Brutus and Cassius from Italy (in the third week of August. See ii. 33, note on 'qui locus . . . videatur'). (2) 'Plenum aequitatis,' 'a very reasonable proposal,' would be a singular way of characterizing such a complete withdrawal from public life. (3) The Rhegians who brought Cicero a copy of the *edictum* expressed a hope that Brutus and Cassius would shortly be able to return to Rome (A. xvi. 7, 1.)

It therefore seems to me probable that what Brutus and Cassius proposed in this *edictum* was some arrangement by which they might resign the corn-commission (*de suo iure decedere*) and return to Rome, no doubt in return for certain concessions and promises on their side. Owing to the unfavourable course of the debates in the senate on 1st and 2nd August, these proposals for a compromise came to nothing, and we are consequently ignorant of their nature.

Kalendis] *Sextilibus* should be retained. The situation reported was the situation in Rome during the closing days of July.

malis suasoribus] With special reference, probably, to his wife Fulvia and his brother Lucius. Cf. § 33: 'Quamquam solent domestici depravare non numquam.'

remissis provinciis Galliis] See App. I.

ad auctoritatem . . . rediturum] Instead of carrying important measures through the comitia, a practice abhorrent to conservative Romans. Cf. i. 6: 'nihil per senatum.'

9. ut mihi . . . satis facerent . . . celeriter Veliam devectus] If Cicero started for Rome on 7th August, the day he received the Rhegians' news, he was ten days getting from Leucopetra to Velia, which he reached on 17th (A. xvi. 7, 5). This does not seem particularly quick going, as on the outward journey he got to Rhegium on the seventh day from Velia, and then the wind was giving him little help, and the ship was rowed a good part of the way; whereas on his return the wind seems to have been in the south. However, of course, he may have had to wait for a ship at Leucopetra. Clodius once reached Rome from Sicily in under seven days, and boasted of the speed of his journey (A. ii. 1, 5).

Brutum vidi] Brutus was with his grain-ships at the mouth of the river Hales, three miles north-west of Velia, when he heard of Cicero's arrival, and at once went on foot to meet him. He was overjoyed at Cicero's return, and apparently revealed for the first time his disapproval of the orator's journey. (Hitherto, perhaps, he had abstained from criticizing a much older man.) He said that people in Rome were accusing Cicero (1) of having deserted the state; (2) of having gone to see the Olympic games during a national crisis. He greatly regretted Cicero's absence from the senate on 1st August, and was loud in his praise of Piso. However, the interview left Cicero in a pessimistic mood. It brought, indeed, the overthrow of all the high hopes raised ten days before. 'Quid ista edicta valeant aut quo spectent, plane non video. Nec ego nunc, ut Brutus censebat, istuc ad rem publicam capessendam venio. Quid enim fieri potest? Num quis Pisoni est adsensus? Num rediit ipse postridie?' (A. xvi. 7, 7).

Turpe . . . videbatur] Is the point of *ipsi* that the incongruity between the positions of Cicero and Brutus might have been expected to have been the less apparent to Cicero, as one of the persons concerned?

10. L. Pisonis] L. Calpurnius Piso, father of Caesar's widow Calpurnia; consul in 58, governor of Macedonia in 57–6; on his return, attacked by Cicero for maladministration, in the speeches De Provinciis Consularibus and In Pisonem. But early in the Civil War we find Cicero speaking well of him: 'Amo etiam Pisonem, cuius iudicium de genero suspicor visum iri grave' (A. vii. 13, 1). He was one of the envoys sent to Antony in January 43 with the senate's ultimatum demanding the evacuation of Gaul. He proved most amenable to Antony's wishes, and Cicero complained of his conduct in public (viii. 28) as well as in private. 'Nihil autem foedius Philippo et Pisone legatis, nihil flagitiosius' (F. xii. 4, 1). His appearance as leader of the constitutionalists on 1st August cannot be accounted for; nor do we know the nature of the motion proposed by him. It may have referred to the Gallic provinces: Ferrero (iii. 86) thinks Piso supported the proposal to amalgamate Cisalpine Gaul with Italy (cf. App. iii. 30). But it may equally well have referred to the other burning question of the day, the position of Brutus and Cassius. (For an estimate of Piso see Butler and Cary's *De Provinciis Consularibus*, Appendix I.)

parum . . . adiutus] In particular, Cicero blames certain consulars for not supporting Piso (cf. §§ 14–15).

praeter . . . fatum] Aulus Gellius, in a rather unhelpful little essay (xiii. 1), discusses the meaning of these expressions, and whether they are synonymous or not. He compares Demosthenes, De Cor. 205, τὸν τῆς εἱμαρμένης καὶ τὸν αὐτόματον θάνατον. Cael. 79: 'nolite . . . hunc iam natura ipsa occidentem velle maturius exstingui volnere vestro quam suo fato,' which de Mirmont quotes, suggests that Cicero did not draw any definite distinction between *naturam* and *fatum* in such a context. The whole expression is reminiscent of the Homeric ὑπὲρ μόρον.

11. amicus] Cicero and Antony were by temperament fundamentally opposed, and there is no evidence that anything approaching real friendship ever existed between them, though Antony afterwards thought it worth his while to say so (ii. 3–4). But no open breach had so far occurred. In A. xiv. 13 b (cf. § 3, note) Cicero writes to Antony in almost fulsome terms; and even in writing to his confidential secretary Tiro, and as late as the end of June 44, he can say: 'Antoni inveteratam sine ulla offensione amicitiam retinere sane volo' (F. xvi. 23, 2); though perhaps, as Heitland (iii. 383, n. 4) suggests, this was meant to be repeated so as to reach Antony's ear. Cicero's private correspondence after Caesar's murder is full of virulent abuse of Antony; and we need not doubt the substantial truth of what he says in A. xi. 9, 1: 'Quid sperem ab eo (Antonio) qui mihi amicus numquam fuit?'

non nullo eius officio] In his speech on 19th September 44 Antony claimed to have done Cicero a favour by sparing his life at Brundisium. See ii. 5. (Cicero arrived at Brundisium in mid-October 48, two months after Pharsalus. For his previous movements see note on ii. 37, 'Castra mihi Pompei', etc.). What actually took place on that occasion is described in A. xi. 7, 2, 17th December 48: 'Nam ad me misit Antonius exemplum Caesaris ad se litterarum, in quibus erat se audisse Catonem et L. Metellum in Italiam venisse, Romae ut essent palam. Id sibi non placere, ne qui motus ex eo fierent; prohiberique omnis Italia, nisi quorum ipse causam cognovisset; deque eo vehementius erat scriptum. Itaque Antonius petebat a me per litteras, ut sibi ignoscerem; facere se non posse quin iis litteris pareret. Tum ad eum misi L. Lamiam qui demonstraret illum Dolabellae dixisse ut ad me scriberet ut in Italiam quam primum venirem; eius me litteris venisse. Tum ille edixit ita ut me exciperet et Laelium nominatim. Quod sane nollem; poterat enim sine nomine res ipsa excipi.'

Neither here, nor in any of Cicero's letters from Brundisium, is there the slightest hint that his life had been in danger. An over-zealous private might have been tempted to hit him over the head, but it is quite inconceivable that Antony, or any responsible person, would have ventured to execute in cold blood so valuable a waverer, who had taken so modest a part in the war. The real 'favour' that Antony conferred was to treat Cicero with marked courtesy and accept his statement without question. But Cicero is not displeased with the suggestion that his life had been in danger. He had always felt the ingloriousness of the role he had been playing in the war. If people thought that his life had once, at any rate, been in peril, so much the better: it might mitigate the unfavourable impression caused by the official labelling of himself and Laelius as harmless. This, not 'quamquam . . . videri' (ii. 5), was his reason for endorsing Antony's fiction. In the Second Philippic, on the other hand, blackening Antony is the paramount consideration. So he throws off the mask, and represents the matter in its true light (ii. 5: 'eum tu occideres'). See however ii. 59–60.

in senatum . . . cogerer] Cf. v. 19. Plutarch (Cic. 43) says that Cicero did not attend the senate because of an ambush laid for him by Antony. This is most improbable. Cicero had been out of Rome for five months, and no one knew whether on his return he would re-enter politics; he himself did not know a fortnight before (A. xvi. 7, 7), and while this remained uncertain Antony would scarcely risk assassinating him. Plutarch may be merely guessing, or he may be confusing 1st September with 19th September, when Cicero says Antony did plot his murder (v. 20). But between the two dates Cicero had shown his hand by delivering the First Philippic. The real motive for his absence was perhaps that he could not bring himself to support the motion before the house, yet dared not oppose it in the veterans' presence: attacking it on the following day, after it had been passed, was a different matter (if he really did attack it in the spoken First Philippic). Or he may have been waiting to sound opinion in Rome. Antony no doubt regarded his absence as tantamount to a protest, as indeed it was. Hence his fury.

Hannibal . . . portas] In 211, during the Second Punic War, Hannibal made a dash on Rome, hoping to cause a panic and induce the Romans to raise the siege of Capua. The ruse failed, and Capua capitulated shortly after (Polyb. ix. 4–7; Liv. xxvi. 7 ff.).

De Pyrrhi pace agebatur] In 280, after the Roman disaster at Heraclea, in Lucania, in the war against Pyrrhus of Epirus, the king's envoy Cineas came to Rome to treat for peace. Appius Claudius Caecus had himself carried down to the senate, and persuaded them to reject the terms (Liv. Ep. 13; Plut. Pyrrh. 18–19). A speech supposed to have been made by him on that occasion was extant in Cicero's day (Brut. 62).

de supplicationibus referebatur] 'No, the motion was about public thanksgivings.'

12. pignoribus] *Pignus capere* was the confiscation by a magistrate of a piece of an offender's property. The article was often destroyed (*pignus caedere, concidere*), apparently if the offender continued recalcitrant, or if he failed to offer a reasonable excuse for his delinquency. Liv. iii. 38 throws much light on the present passage: 'Postquam citati' (certain senators) 'non conveniebant, dimissi circa domos apparitores simul ad pignora capienda sciscitandumque num consulto detrectarent, referunt senatum in agris esse.' This disposes of the view that *pignora* were taken *before* the meeting of the senate: while the theory that *pignora* were securities for the payment of a fine is rendered untenable by our passage and others which clearly imply that *pignus* and *multa* were alternatives.

It is certainly not very clear what circumstances warranted the destruction of a *pignus*.

(De Orat. iii. 4; Liv. iii. 38; xxxvii. 51; xliii. 16; Tac. Ann. xiii. 28; Suet. Iul. 17; Gell. xiv. 7, 10; Mommsen, *St. R.* i. 160; Greenidge, *R. P. L.* 170.)

cum fabris . . . venturum] Cf. v. 19.

publice . . . domum] Cicero's house was on the Palatine Hill, over the Forum. It was destroyed at the time of his exile in 58, and was rebuilt at public expense on his return in the following year, in spite of the opposition of P. Clodius.

13. ut parentalia . . . . miscerentur] The Parentalia was a festival in commemoration of the dead, and lasted from 13th to 21st February. The most important day was the 21st, Feralia. The members of each family went to the necropolis outside the city, and there, at the family tomb, presented to their dead relatives offerings of water, wine, honey, milk, oil, and the blood of black victims: they decked the tomb with flowers, themselves partaking of the meal, and uttering the incantation 'Salve, sancte parens'.

The term *supplicatio* denoted both a thanksgiving to the gods and a service of humiliation for their appeasement.

The precise manner in which *parentalia* and *supplicationes* were combined by Antony's proposal is, in the absence of further evidence, difficult to determine. Reading this passage in conjunction with ii. 110, 'supplicationes addendo diem contaminari passus es', it would appear that what Antony proposed (or what Cicero says he proposed) was that at the end of every *supplicatio* a day should be added on which prayers were offered to the deified Caesar. Cicero objects that the proper occasion for honouring Caesar's memory was the *parentalia*, not the *supplicationes*. And so he stigmatizes the proposal as 'mixing up' the two ceremonies. (So Halm[3] and Heitland, iii. 387. Ferrero (iii. 94) maintains that the proposal affected the *parentalia*, not the *supplicationes*. He thinks that at the *parentalia*, in addition to the normal honours paid to the dead Caesar, *supplicationes* were to be held as well. But this is inconsistent with the language of ii. 110.)

For the *parentalia* see Varro, L.L. vi. 13; Ov. Fast. ii. 533 ff.; Warde Fowler, *Rom. Fest.* 306–10; Wissowa, 232 ff. For the whole question of the divine honours paid to Caesar see ii. 110 and notes.

Fuerit ille Brutus] For the supposed descent of M. Brutus from L. Iunius Brutus, the overthrower of the Tarquins, see note on ii. 26, *L. Bruti . . . Ahalae.*

ut, cuius sepulchrum . . . supplicetur] The emphatic *usquam* (anywhere at all) is difficult to understand. I take it that by 'he whose grave exists anywhere' Cicero means 'any one whose grave exists'; and that the gist of the whole sentence is: 'Any one whose body is laid in a grave must be a man, not a god, and so the proper tribute to pay him is the *parentalia*, not a *supplicatio*.

In connexion with the words 'adduci . . . religione', it is worth remembering that in March 45 Cicero was proposing to build a shrine in memory of his daughter Tullia (A. xii. 18, 1; 19, 1; 12, 1).

quae partim iam sunt] Pestilence they had not yet got, nor war, though they lived under the constant threat of war. The mission of Brutus and Cassius to organize the corn-supply suggests fear of a food shortage. Still, the statement seems exaggerated.

15. Quae, malum] A colloquial expression, but not uncommon in Cicero's speeches. Cf. x. 18; Scaur. 45; Verr. II. i. 54, and other instances quoted by de Mirmont. Our dignified parliamentary language hardly supplies a parallel.

hoc] The adoption of an independent attitude.

consulari loco] See note on i. 3, 'de qua . . . diximus'.

quid facere ipse deberet] 'What was his own personal duty.' He considered the situation from the subjective standpoint of morals, not from the objective standpoint of practical possibilities. Cicero takes exactly the same line himself in § 10 above, 'Hunc igitur . . . voluntatis'.

16. pacis atque oti] So he writes to Plancus in July: 'cum multa . . . non probentur quae Caesar statuerit, tamen oti pacisque causa acerrime illa soleo defendere' (A. xvi. 16 B, 9).

advocatis] In Cicero's time the term *advocati* was applied to persons who attended in court and assisted one of the parties with legal advice or moral support (as the emperor Augustus did on one occasion: Suet. Aug. 56). They were distinct from the *patroni* or *oratores*, who actually pleaded the case. Cf. Pseudo-Asconius, In Verr., p. 104: 'qui defendit alterum in iudicio, aut patronus dicitur, si orator est; aut advocatus, si aut ius suggerit aut praesentiam suam commodat amico.' The distinction is well brought out by Clu. 110: 'quis eum umquam non modo in patroni, sed in lautioris advocati loco viderat?' Cf. also De Orat. ii. 301: 'orat reus, urgent advocati, ut invehamur, ut male dicamus.'

Under the empire the meaning of the term changed, and it is used by Quintilian as a synonym for *patronus*, *orator*, or *causidicus*. (P.-W., s.v. *advocatus*.)

Cicero uses the word sarcastically here of the soldiers with whom Antony had packed the Senate House on 1st September and on previous occasions.

in aes incidit] §§ 16–26 contain many references to Roman legislative procedure, and it will be convenient to consider all these together.

Notice of a bill had to be given twenty-four days (*tria nundina*) ahead: simultaneously the text of the bill was published (*promulgatio*), and a copy deposited in the *aerarium* to prevent any alterations from being made in it. On the proposal coming before the Comitia, the text was read aloud by the herald (*praeco*) prompted by the clerk (*scriba*), the reading being termed *pronuntiatio* or *recitatio* (Ascon. in Cornel. 51). Strictly speaking, the proposer of a law was said to *ferre* or *rogare*. But in § 24 he is said to *pronuntiare* or *recitare* because the herald does so for him. (Cases are known, it is true, when a tribune, on the herald being obstructed, read out his bill himself: cf. Ascon. loc. cit. And Mommsen, *St. R.* iii. 391, n. 4, thinks that Cicero means in § 24 that Caesar did so. It seems to me unnecessary to press Cicero's words so literally.)

When passed, or rather, from 62 B.C., when promulgated, laws were deposited in the *aerarium*. No regular provision appears to have been made for their publication. But very frequently whole laws, or important clauses of laws, were posted up (*fixa*) in conspicuous places, in early times painted on wood, later, to ensure permanence, engraved on bronze.

(Mommsen, *St. R.* iii. 370-419; Greenidge, *R. P. L.* 256-60.)

17. Pecunia . . . maneret] 'Ops mater', the goddess of the harvest, later of plenty and riches in general, had her temple on the Capitoline Hill (Wissowa, 203). The treasure amounted to 700,000 sesterces. It is sometimes stated (e.g. by Groebe-Drumann, i². 61, 410) that Antony appropriated the whole sum at one sweep on the night after Caesar's murder. But the passages in the ancient authorities (see below) show that what he really did was to perpetrate a series of embezzlements lasting over several weeks (so Halm⁸, Intr. n. 164; Ferrero, iii. 315; Becht, 89-90). These embezzlements began not later than the first week of April (A. xiv. 14, 5: 'Rapinas scribis ad Opis fieri; quas nos quoque tum (viz. before leaving Rome about 7th April) videbamus'): possibly before the end of March, if 'ante Kalendas Apriles' in ii. 93 is an allusion to this particular source of income; and they had not stopped when A. xiv. 14 and 18 were written (in May).

(ii. 35; 93; v. 11; vi. 3; vii. 15; viii. 26; xii. 12; xiii. 12; A. xiv. 14, 5; xiv. 18, 1; App. iii. 52, 54; Vell. ii. 60, 4; Dio, xlv. 24, 1.)

18. qui . . . versatus sit] *Imperium* includes *potestas*. All magistrates had *potestas* (though the term is predominantly used in reference to the lower magistrates); only the higher magistrates (dictator, consul, and praetor), had *imperium*. This *imperium* they possessed both as magistrates proper in Rome, and as pro-magistrates in command of provinces. But, while for the magistrate *imperium* was limited by the right of *provocatio*, for the pro-magistrate it was unlimited. Consequently we sometimes find *imperium* contrasted with *magistratus*. In the present passage *togatus* limits the application to the *imperium* of the magistrate in Rome (*domi*). The pro-magistrate abroad (*militiae*) is *paludatus*, and his *acta* are not laws, but the enactments of a practically absolute ruler (Greenidge, *R.P.L.*, 152-3).

acta Gracchi] Gaius Sempronius Gracchus, as the more famous of the two brothers, is mentioned without *praenomen*. The most important measures of his tribunate in 123 were: a law that only the assembly might pass a sentence affecting a Roman citizen's *caput* (life or civil rights); a law providing for the selling of corn by the state to citizens in Rome at an uneconomic price; a law for the distribution of land-allotments, on the lines of Tiberius' measure; a law for the farming out of the Asiatic taxes to private contractors; a law transferring the right of sitting on juries from the senate to the equites; a law for the foundation of citizen colonies in Italy; and a law providing that the senate should select provinces for the incoming consuls before those consuls were elected.

Corneliae] The chief measures passed by P. Cornelius Sulla, as dictator in 81, were: laws limiting the powers of the tribunate;

reconstitution of the regulations for the holding of successive magistracies (*cursus honorum*); restoration of the law courts to an enlarged senate; distribution of land to discharged soldiers; systematization of the provincial commands; organization and increase of the standing courts (*quaestiones perpetuae*).

Pompei tertius consulatus] As sole consul in 52 (he had already been consul in 70 and 55) Pompey passed laws 'de vi', 'de ambitu' (in connexion with the disturbances following upon the murder of Clodius: see ii. 22), and 'de iure magistratuum' (see ii. 24, note on 'ne . . . haberetur').

aut . . . duceret] A curiously unnecessary addition, made perhaps on stylistic grounds, which somewhat obscures the logic.

19. ne praetoriae provinciae] After the reorganization of provincial commands by Sulla, a province was normally held, whether by a proconsul or by a propraetor, for one year only. But in practice the limit was frequently overstepped. Thus Verres governed Sicily, Fonteius Gaul, and Q. Cicero Asia for three years each. In 46 Caesar, who owed his own supremacy to his ten years' command in Gaul, and was doubtless determined, as Dio suggests (xliii. 25, 3), that others should not follow his example, fixed the tenure of consular provinces at two years, of praetorian at one. See v. 7; viii. 28; Appendix I.

'Optima re publica flagitata' is likely enough, but we cannot fix the reference to any particular occasion.

lege . . . de tertia decuria] For this law, and for previous judiciary legislation, see Appendix II.

decuria] Under the Sullan constitution, when the juries were drawn exclusively from the senate, the term *decuriae* was applied to the sections into which the roll of jurymen (*Album iudicum*) was divided (Verr. II. ii. 79; Schol. Gronov., p. 392, Orelli; Greenidge, *Leg. Proc.* 437–8). After the passing of the Aurelian law of 70 B.C., the term was used in a new sense, to denote the classes of jurymen.

The strength of the decuries is uncertain. F. viii. 8, 5 (51 B.C.) gives the senatorial decury as 300 strong; A. viii. 16, 2 (49 B.C.) gives it as 360 strong. It may be assumed that the other decuries were of the same strength. Greenidge accepts 360, Mommsen and Kübler 300, citing also Plin. N. H. 33, 1, 31 (*nongenti* for the total of three decuries). Strachan-Davidson (*Problems of the Roman Criminal Law*, ii. 75–6) would read 400 in F. viii. 8, 5, thinking 300 too small. May not the number have varied in different years?

20. lege Iulia] The Lex Iulia Iudiciaria of 46 abolished the decury of Tribuni Aerarii. 'Iudicia ad duo genera iudicum redegit, equestris ordinis ac senatorii; tribunos aerarios, quod erat tertium, sustulit (Suet. Iul. 41). *τά τε δικαστήρια τοῖς τε βουλευταῖς καὶ τοῖς ἱππεῦσι μόνοις ἐπέτρεψεν, ὅπως τὸ καθαρώτατον ὅτι μάλιστα ἀεὶ δικάζοι· πρότερον γὰρ καὶ ἐκ τοῦ ὁμίλου τινὲς συνδιεγίγνωσκον αὐτοῖς* (Dio, xliii. 25, 1).

According to Suetonius (Aug. 32), Augustus added a fourth decury to three which he found in existence: 'Ad tres iudicum decurias quartam addidit ex inferiore censu, quae ducenariorum vocaretur iudicaretque de levioribus summis.' Mommsen infers from this (*St. R.* iii. 535) that Caesar left the third decury in existence, but constituted it, like the second, of 'equites Romani equo publico'. But this theory is inconsistent with *tertia decuria* above.

Pompeia] For the Lex Pompeia Iudiciaria see Appendix II p. 176. Greenidge's interpretation of the words 'amplissimo ex censu', which I there give, seems to me the correct one. Mommsen (*St. R.* iii. 192, n. 4) maintains that the effect of the law was to raise the property qualification for the Tribuni Aerarii to the Census Equester, and he thus explains (p. 193, n. 2) the inclusion of the Tribuni among the Equites by Cicero in certain passages. But some of the passages occur in speeches delivered before the passing of the Lex Pompeia. Moreover, it is quite impossible to make Asconius mean what Mommsen wants. He says plainly, not that the qualification of the third order was made equal to that of the second, but that in all three orders the richest men were given the preference. Hence *amplissimo*, not *ampliore*.

quicumque equo meruisset] The reference is, I think, to the ex-officers who had served under Caesar. Many were under the legal age required for a juryman (*dignitas*), and many lacked the required equestrian census of 400,000 sesterces (*fortuna*). For other explanations, and for a full discussion of difficulties, see Appendix II.

dignitas] The Lex Acilia Repetundarum fixed thirty as the minimum age for a juryman. Subsequently the age seems to have been raised to thirty-five (Mommsen, *Strafrecht*, 212, n. 4, thinks, by the Lex Aurelia of 70 B.C.); for Suetonius) Aug. 32) says: 'iudices a tricesimo (*M*: vicesimo *cett.*) anno aetatis adlegit, id est quinquennio maturius quam solebant.' Naturally, many of the ex-officers would be under thirty-five.

addo . . . Alaudarum] The legion *Alauda*, so called from the plume on their helmets shaped like a lark's crest, had been recruited by Caesar in Transalpine Gaul and had received the franchise at his hands (Suet. Iul. 24; Plin. N.H. xi. 121). They were therefore likely to be loyal to his memory, and to Antony, his old Master of Horse.

Whether these men were actually included in Antony's proposal is difficult to say. The way in which Cicero here argues the case against the centurions in detail, while passing lightly over the much more sensational inclusions of these privates, who a few years before had not even been Roman citizens, suggests that the statement about the *Alaudae* is rhetorical exaggeration. On the other hand v. 12-15 implies that Cicero's words here are to be taken literally. 'Antesignanos et manipularis et Alaudas iudices se constituisse dicebat: at ille legit aleatores, legit exsules, legit Graecos' (v. 12). It is difficult to say where truth ends and exaggeration begins.

Vt enim . . . coniectus] An adroit argument. While objecting to the appointment of these military jurymen, Cicero manages to compliment them on their integrity.

21. et de vi et maiestatis] The first *et* cannot mean 'also', 'even', as that would imply that *provocatio* was allowed in the case of other offences, which was not so. (See note on 'ad populum provocent' below.) 'Et . . . et' must mean 'both . . . and . . .'. But perhaps, with *D*, we should omit the first *et*.

maiestatis] Defined by Cicero as 'De dignitate aut amplitudine aut potestate populi aut eorum quibus populus potestatem dedit aliquid derogare' (De Inv. ii. 53). The *quaestio maiestatis* was one of the Sullan courts. The *quaestio de vi* was established by a Lex Plautia at about the same period.

ad populum provocent] During the early Republic, appeal to the people against the sentence of a magistrate played a prominent part, and was perhaps the origin of the *iudicia populi*, trial before the people assembled in the *Comitia Centuriata*. Since, however, the magistrate, rather than pronounce a sentence against which he thought appeal would be made, tended to refer the matter to the people in the first instance, *provocatio* became rarer. And when, in 149 and the following years, standing courts (*quaestiones perpetuae*) began to be constituted, it was held that the judicial functions of the people were delegated to these courts, and appeal against their verdicts is unheard of. (The appeal of C. Rabirius Postumus, whom Cicero defended in a speech still extant, was against the verdict, not of a *quaestio perpetua*, but of two specially appointed commissioners.)

In spite of the theory of delegation, however, Antony might possibly urge that, as *vis* and *maiestas* were in a special sense offences against the community, an appeal to the direct decision of the people should in such cases be allowed. His real object, however, clearly was to secure immunity for his own violent and lawless acts. The law was passed, but was repealed with Antony's other measures at the end of 44, and does not seem to have been revived. (Greenidge, *Leg. Proc.* 307–12, 516–19: Strachan-Davidson, *Problems of the Roman Criminal Law*, I. capp. viii–ix. The latter holds (p. 134) that all trials before the people resulted from appeal, and that where *provocatio* is not mentioned it is to be assumed.)

Vtinam . . . populare] Cicero insists that Antony's professedly democratic policy is really an anti-democratic military tyranny. Cf. § 6: 'multa et magna per populum et absente populo et invito.'

ad eam . . . damnatus . . . reo condemnato . . . conductae] The *provocatio ad populum* could easily be used as a means of inflaming popular opinion, and of organizing mob violence against the prosecutor and the jurymen who had condemned the accused.

22. operas mercennarias] *Operae* is almost a technical term for the gangs of rowdies organized by unscrupulous demagogues like Clodius. Cf. A. i. 13, 3 and A. i. 14, 5 (*operae Clodianae*).

duae . . . tolluntur] Each *quaestio perpetua* was introduced by a separate law, which bore the name of its proposer; e.g. 'Lex Calpurnia repetundarum', 'Lex Pompeia de vi'. Consequently *lex* and *quaestio* stood or fell together.

Quid est aliud] For 'quid est aliud quam'. Cf. ii. 7; v. 5; x. 5. So, in Greek, ἄλλο τι for ἄλλο τι ἤ.

23. obrogatur] 'Obrogare est legis prioris infirmandae causa legem aliam ferre' (Festus, p. 203, Lindsay). 'Huic legi neque obrogari fas est neque derogari ex hac aliquid licet neque tota abrogari potest' (De Rep. iii. 33).

quibus . . . rescinduntur] Because an outlaw, being outside the pale of the people, had no right to appeal to the people.

Before the passing of Caesar's law, the penalty for *vis* seems to have been exile (Sull. 31–2; Sest. 69, 146).

24. De exsilio . . . a mortuo] Contrast § 3.

civitas . . . universis] E.g. Sicily. See § 2, note on 'nihil . . . omnibus'.

immunitatibus] E.g. Crete. See ii. 97.

domo] Cf. § 2 *domi*.

25. intercedant] *Intercessio* was the right possessed by a magistrate to veto the actions of another magistrate of equal or inferior authority. Tribunes possessed this right against all magistrates except a dictator. It was employed against the decree of a magistrate (*edictum* or *decretum*), against a *rogatio*, and against a *senatus consultum*. *Intercessio* against a *rogatio* early became confined to the tribunes (Mommsen, *St. R.* i. 266–88; Greenidge, *R. P. L.* 176–80).

The Lex Clodia of 58 (see App. II) is said by Cicero to have abolished *intercessio*, at any rate against a *rogatio* (Sest. 33; Prov. Cons. 46; Post Red. in Sen. 11; De Har. Resp. 58). But no such clause was in operation a few years later (Prov. Cons. 17; A. iv. 17, 3 (16, 6)). We must suppose, either that the Lex Clodia was ignored (a possibility supported by other evidence: see App. II), or, with Mommsen (*St. R.* ii. 1, 308, with n. 3), that the law only forbade the use of *intercessio* to support *obnuntiatio* (a sense, however, not easy to extract from the texts).

For the use of tribunician *intercessio* against a praetor trying a civil case see ii. 3 and Greenidge (*R. P. L.* 178, n. 4), who cites the Pro Quinctio and Pro Tullio as parallels.

religione] For Antony's neglect of the auspices cf. the description in v. 8 of the way in which he carried his provincial law during a violent thunderstorm.

27. avorum] (1) M. Antonius, the Orator: in 102, as praetor with proconsular powers, conducted a successful campaign against the Cilician pirates; consul in 99; censor in 97; put to death by the soldiers of Marius and Cinna in 87. He and L. Licinius Crassus, the principal characters in Cicero's *De Oratore*, were the foremost orators of their generation. (2) L. Iulius Caesar: consul in 90, when he commanded in southern Italy in the Social War; proposer of the Lex Iulia in that year, bestowing the franchise on all allies not in arms against Rome; a victim of the Marian reign of terror in 87.

avunculus] 'Maternal uncle.' Paternal uncle is *patruus*. L. Iulius Caesar: son of the last-named; consul in 64; advocated the execution of the Catilinarians in 63 (cf. ii. 14). His attitude during the Civil War is uncertain, but he held the post of *praefectus urbi* for a time in 47. In A. xiv. 17, 2; 17 A, 3 Cicero mentions him as expressing dissatisfaction with Antony. On the outbreak of the Mutinensian War, his attitude to his nephew, though moderated by kinship, was hostile enough to earn him subsequently the second place on the proscription lists, from which his sister's prayers with difficulty saved him. His degree of relationship with the Dictator is uncertain. Lactantius, Div. Inst. i. 15, 30, speaks of the two as *propinqui* (P.-W. x. 1, 469).

sin consuetudinem] The implication, that Cicero normally avoided personalities in his political speeches, comes oddly from the author of the In Pisonem, the De Provinciis Consularibus, and the In Vatinium.

sui defendendi causa] According to Appian (iii. 5), Antony persuaded the senate to allow him a bodyguard after his execution of Herophilus, to protect him against the anger of the mob. The story is rejected by Groebe (Drumann i². 421-2): and it is hardly possible that Cicero would have passed over such an incident in his letters. The veterans collected by Antony are probably the origin of the myth.

Antony was, or pretended to be, in considerable fear of Brutus and Cassius, whom he accused of raising troops (F. xi. 3, 2). 'Umbras timet', Cicero writes in June (A. xv. 20, 4), and 'de consulum ficto timore cognoveram' (A. xv. 17, 1). It is difficult to say how far this fear was genuine, how far it was a mere pretext for collecting soldiers. Hirtius said 'non minus se nostrorum arma timere quam Antoni' (A. xv. 1, 3).

28. Pisoni socero] See note on § 10, *L. Pisonis*.

nec erit...mortis] Grim irony. '(Antony will kill you, and then) being dead will be as good an excuse for non-attendance as being ill.' So Halm⁸. This seems to me much better than King's explanation: 'if sickness is, as all allow, a valid excuse for absence from the senate, surely the danger of death is at least as valid, and Cicero would be fully justified, if these threats continue, in refusing to expose himself to obvious peril of his life.' It is not easy to get 'danger of death' out of *mortis*, though De Mirmont renders *causa* *mortis* by 'une excuse venant de la crainte de la mort'. For *causa mortis*, 'death as an excuse', cf. ii. 78, *causam amoris*.

29. non pecuniam . . . concupivisse] Cf. § 33: 'non possum adduci ut suspicer te pecunia captum.' Cicero is betrayed into an error in tactics by his love of irony. Doubtless every one knew that Antony had pillaged the temple of Ops, and many knew that Dolabella had got part of the spoils (A. xiv. 14, 5; 18, 1). But why indulge in such covert sneers in a speech of which the whole tone was meant to be conciliatory? It is possible, however, that these touches were added to the spoken oration when it was revised for publication.

In A. xvi. 15, 1 (Nov. 44) Cicero speaks of Dolabella as abandoning, *emptus pecunia*, and doing his best to ruin, the cause of a client.

30. Quem potes . . . gratulabantur] See § 5 and notes.

incendio] Arson was a common feature of the riots of the time. Cf. ii. 91: 'quibus incensa L. Bellieni domus deflagravit.'

consensum illum theatri] Nothing is known of the incident. The demeanour of Roman audiences was carefully watched by statesmen, and was regarded as a barometer of popular opinion. Any sign of a political allusion was quickly taken up by the spectators. Thus, at the Apollinarian games of 59, the words 'nostra miseria tu es magnus', thought to refer to Pompey, were repeatedly encored (A. ii. 19, 3). It was easy, Cicero remarks (Sest. 115), to distinguish spontaneous expressions of popular feeling from the demonstrations of hired claqueurs. Cf. § 36 'Apollinarium ludorum plausus'; A. xiv. 2, 1: 'Ex priore (epistula) theatrum Publiliumque cognovi, bona signa consentientis multitudinis.'

earum rerum obliti] In 48 Dolabella, overwhelmed by debt, and unable to obtain assistance from Caesar, got himself adopted into a plebeian family, in order to become eligible for the tribuneship. Having obtained this office, he proposed, early in 47, a general abolition of debts (*novae tabulae*) and of rent. Riots ensued, which were suppressed by Antony with much bloodshed (Liv. Ep. 113; Dio, xlii. 32). Cicero refers to the occurrence in A. xi. 12, 4 (8th March 47), 'praeclaras generi actiones', and in A. xi. 23, 3, where he regrets not having divorced Tullia from Dolabella 'tabularum novarum nomine'.

31. in aede Telluris . . . Quae fuit oratio] See § 2.

depositis . . . auspiciorum] See ii. 79-83.

tuus parvus filius] See § 2.

32. M. Manli] After the battle of the Allia, twelve miles from Rome, in 390, the Gauls captured all the city, except the Capitol, to which they laid siege. According to a famous story recounted by Livy (v. 47) on one occasion a night assault was betrayed by the sacred geese, whose clamour woke Manlius. His subsequent career and downfall is described by Livy (vi. 11-20). In 384 or 385, seeing a centurion being led off to prison, for inability to pay his debts, he publicly discharged the debt: moreover, he sold his farm, in order to have money available for similar contingencies, and he openly accused the senate of embezzling money captured from the Gauls, which might have been used to relieve poverty. Cornelius Cossus, the dictator, gave him the choice between substantiating the charge and going to prison. He could not, or would not, do the first, and was compelled to undergo the second. But popular discontent increased, and it was decided to take him out of prison and try him. The *Comitia Centuriata*, sitting in full view of the Capitol, to which he pointed in his peroration, were in the act of acquitting him; but the trial was postponed and transferred to a locality whence the Capitol could not be seen. There he was condemned, and, according to Varro and Livy, hurled from the Tarpeian rock, according to Nepos, beaten to death (Gell. xvii. 21, 24).

Mommsen (*Röm. Forsch.* ii. 179–99) maintains that the story as told by Livy has been considerably watered down. He points to Diodorus's brief notice, Μάρκος Μάνλιος ἐπιβαλόμενος τυραννίδι καὶ κρατηθεὶς ἀνῃρέθη (xv. 35, 3), and to certain features in Livy's narrative, notably *Manliana seditio* (vi. 18, 1), which imply actual armed insurrection. He believes that the story of the saving of the Capitol originated in family history, and that the incident was associated with M. Manlius Capitolinus on the strength of his cognomen, which cannot, however, have been derived from the exploit (as Livy and other authorities say) since it is several times found at an earlier period. Mommsen will accept as historical only Diodorus's notice and the 'decretum gentis Manliae'. He thinks that the debt-paying motif was added in the Sullan epoch, when *novae tabulae* were in the air.

neminem . . . licet] Festus, pp. 112, 135, Lindsay; Liv. vi. 20, 14; Dio, Fr. 26, 1. So the senate, in 30, passed a decree that in future no Antonius should be called Marcus (Plut. Cic. 49; Dio, li. 19, 3). *Patricium* because there were also plebeian families of Manlii.

33. domestici] There is certainly a reference to his wife Fulvia, perhaps also to his brother Lucius. Another sneer which impairs the conciliatory tone of the speech.

34. illi ipsi] Atreus, in Accius's tragedy of that name. He was killed by his nephew, Aegisthus. Cf. Sest. 102; De Off. i. 97; Sen. de Ira i. 20 ff.

avum] See § 27, note on *avorum*. Both Antony's grandfathers were put to death during the Marian reign of terror, but, in the absence of any indication to the contrary, the paternal grandfather, M. Antonius, is no doubt meant. 'Audisti multa ex me' makes this the more certain, as M. Antonius plays an important part in Cicero's oratorical works, the Brutus and the De Oratore.

res . . . prosperas] With special reference to the triumph which M. Antonius celebrated in honour of his victory over the Cilician pirates.

36. gladiatoribus] 'At the gladiatorial shows.' Nothing is known of the incident.

populi versus] Lampoons and political verses, circulated by word of mouth or in writing. English history supplies plenty of examples. But in our own day the normal channel of expression is the newspaper. Catullus's fierce lampoons on Caesar are examples of *populi versus* in the hands of a master.

Pompei statuae] Nothing is known of the incident; but Pompey's statue, in the Curia Pompei, at the foot of which Caesar fell, was a natural place for manifestations in favour of the assassins.

duobus . . . adversantur] In iii. 23 three tribunes are mentioned as opposing Antony: L. Cassius, D. Carfulenus, and Ti. Cannutius. Velleius (ii. 64, 3) says that Cannutius 'canina rabie lacerabat Antonium'. F. xii. 3, 2 (October 44) describes a passage at arms between Cannutius and Antony.

Cicero mentions an ovation to L. Cassius in a letter of 8th April 44: 'Plausus vero L. Cassio datus etiam facetus mihi quidem visus est' (A. xiv. 2, 1).

Apollinarium ludorum] These games were first celebrated in 212, with the object of enlisting Apollo's help in the Second Punic War. On the occasion of a pestilence in 208 they were made annual (the first games held annually in honour of a Greek deity), and were celebrated at first on 13th July, and finally, after gradual extension, on the eight days 6th to 13th July. Unlike other games, they were organized, not by the Aediles, but by the Praetor Urbanus. Dramatic representations played from the first a particularly prominent part in these games (Wissowa, p. 295).

On the present occasion, in the absence of the urban praetor, M. Brutus, the games were undertaken by Antony's brother Gaius, Atticus helping to finance them (A. xv. 18, 2). That Cicero considered the games a great success, as far as they went, is shown by his letters. Brutus had asked him to go to Rome for the occasion, but he had refused. However, he got Atticus to write to Brutus and tell him all about the games, an act of courtesy which Brutus greatly appreciated: (he was much annoyed, however, by the official use of the expression *Nonis Iuliis*, as he considered that the new name for the month Quinctilis should have been allowed to lapse after Caesar's death). (x. 7; A. xv. 26, 1; 28; 29, 1; xvi. 2, 3; 4, 1.)

But Cicero did not, at the time, think quite so much of the demonstration as he now pretends: 'Mihi . . . molestiae est populum Romanum manus suas non in defendenda re publica, sed in plaudendo consumere' (A. xvi. 2, 3, 11th July).

Accio] Accius, the last of the great Roman tragedians, lived from 170 to 90, or later. The play in question was the *Tereus* (A. xvi. 5, 1).

37. A. Hirti] Details as to this illness of Hirtius are lacking. He was slowly recovering in the latter part of September (F. xii. 22, 2), but was still 'weak and emaciated' (vii. 12; cf. viii. 5) when he marched against Antony in January 43 to relieve Mutina, the campaign in which he met his death.

38. satis est quod vixi] Cicero was born in 106.

SECOND PHILIPPIC

1. nemo] As King remarks, it is unfortunate for the completeness of Cicero's list that he is unable to mention Caesar, 'from whom he had received too many favours to enumerate him among his personal enemies'.

his annis viginti] Ever since the Catilinarian conspiracy of 63.

bellum . . . indixerit] Thus early the key-note of the speech is struck. Contrast i. 11 'cui sum amicus', 28 'feremus amici naturam'.

poenarum . . . plus quam optarem] Catiline fell in battle in 62. Clodius was killed by Milo in 52. See § 21.

hoc] The coincidence of enmity towards Cicero with enmity towards the state. The pronoun refers back to the first sentence of the speech, 'Nec vero . . . perhorrescere' being virtually parenthetical.

lacessiti] In particular, Clodius, who prosecuted Catiline for extortion in 65, was at first on good terms with Cicero (Plut. Cic. 29). Cicero provoked the breach in 61 by supporting a bill for the appointment of a special court for the trial of Clodius for sacrilege, and by giving evidence which disproved Clodius's alibi.

2. mihi uni conservatae] After the suppression of the Catilinarian conspiracy. See § 12 and notes.

Illud] Referring to what follows, 'non existimavit . . . inimicus'. So Peskett. This is much better than, with Mayor, making it refer back to 'tuamque . . . putavisti' in § 1. So distant a reference would not be clear; and the review of alternative explanations does not formally begin till § 2.

3. Contra rem suam . . . fuisse] The facts of the case are lost beyond possibility of recall. In A. xvi. 11, when Cicero is acknowledging certain suggestions made by Atticus for alterations in the Second Philippic, he writes (§ 1): 'De Sicca ita est, ut scribis. † Asta ea aegre me tenui. Itaque perstringam sine ulla contumelia Siccae aut Septimiae, tantum ut sciant παῖδες παίδων, sine † vallo Luciliano, eum ex Galli Fadi filia liberos habuisse. Atque utinam eum diem videam, cum ista oratio ita libere vagetur ut etiam in Siccae domum introeat! Sed illo tempore opus est quod fuit illis IIIviris. Moriar nisi facete!'

This clearly refers to our passage; but, beyond telling us that the *familiaris* is Sicca, it does not help us. Sicca was a friend of Cicero's, often mentioned in the letters, with whom he stayed at Vibo.

For *intercessio* see i. 25, n.

It seems clear that Antony had prevented Sicca from obtaining a verdict, by persuading a tribune, won over by companionship in profligacy, to interpose his veto; and that Cicero had done his best to frustrate the manœuvre.

How Q. Fadius and his daughter Fadia, Antony's first wife, come into the business, remains obscure. Cicero is fond of taunting Antony with the mésalliance: iii. 17 'ipse ex libertini filia susceperit liberos'; xiii. 23 'Is autem humilitatem despicere audet cuiusquam, qui ex Fadia sustulerit liberos?' Drumann (i². 380) says that the children were now dead, relying apparently on the tense of *fuisse*. But the perfect is used, as Halm rightly points out, because, according to Roman ideas, the relationship ceased with the death of Fadius.

iure praetorio] *Ius praetorium* was the body of judge-made law, which supplemented *ius civile*, and which grew out of the *edicta* published by the successive urban praetors at the commencement of their terms of office, setting forth the general lines on which each intended to administer justice. Such *edicta* were based on previous *edicta*, and were meant to have an effect on future *edicta*. Hence they were called *perpetua* and *tralaticia*. (See Greenidge, *Leg. Proc.*, pp. 85–7.)

te in disciplinam meam tradideras] So Hirtius and Dolabella, for example, took lessons in declamation from Cicero at Tusculum in 46 (F. ix. 16, 7), as did Hirtius and Pansa at Puteoli in 44 (A. xiv. 12, 2).

C. Curionem] C. Scribonius Curio the younger, son of C. Scribonius Curio the elder (see § 12, note): married Clodius's widow Fulvia; quaestor in Asia; tribune in 50; at first a Pompeian, but won over by Caesar, who paid his debts; supported proposal that both Pompey and Caesar should be required to lay down their *imperium*; towards the end of 50 left Rome and went to Caesar at Ravenna; on outbreak of Civil War raised troops for Caesar in Umbria and Etruria; propraetor of Sicily in 49; in the same year crossed to Africa and fell at Utica.

Cicero tries here to convey the impression that the younger Curio was bitterly hostile to him, perhaps on account of the events recorded in §§ 44–6 below. In point of fact, though *filiola Curionis* had been a prominent Clodian in 61 (A. i. 14, 5), Cicero was on good terms with him as early as 59 (cf. A. ii. 7; ii. 8; ii. 12, *Curio meus*), and wrote him several letters in 53 (F. ii. 1–7).

4. **Auguratus petitionem**] The numbers of the augural college were raised by Caesar to sixteen. The procedure for election was as follows. Two members of the college nominated probably three candidates. Out of these, by the Lex Domitia of 104, one was elected by seventeen tribes out of the thirty-five, the seventeen electing tribes being determined by lot.

Cicero became augur in 53, on the death of P. Crassus, the

Triumvir's son; Antony in 50 (20th to 24th September, according to O. E. Schmidt, *Briefwechsel Ciceros*, ii. 88, 19). The circumstances of Antony's election are described by M. Caelius Rufus in one of his racy letters to Cicero, then governor of Cilicia (F. viii. 14): 'You've missed a sight here worth all your military exploits, Domitius's face when Antony beat him in the election for the augurship. He's perfectly furious: thinks I am at the bottom of it all, and has prosecuted young Cn. Saturninus.' This agrees well with our passage. Caelius was intimate with Curio, and *familiares* presumably refers to Saturninus. L. Domitius Ahenobarbus had some cause for annoyance. He had been consul in 54: Antony had only reached the quaestorship, and was hardly qualified by his past life for the position of augur.

cum . . . esset] He was quaestor in Asia at the time (F. ii. 6, 1).

unam . . . potuisses] Cicero omits to mention a far more important factor in the situation. Caesar (as Hirtius tells us in B. G. viii. 50) hastened to Italy, 'quam maximis itineribus', to support Antony's candidature, both on personal and on political grounds. Before reaching Italy he heard the news of Antony's election.

5. **At beneficio sum tuo usus**] See i. 11, 'non nullo eius officio', and note.

ex latronibus suis principatum] The Italian command and the post of Magister Equitum (§§ 57, 62, 71).

6. **querela**] The whole tone of the First Philippic is one of remonstrance. Cf. i. 11 'querar', 27 'proponam ius aequum'.

leges . . . armatis] The reference is to the agrarian and provincial laws of 2nd June. See Introd. and v. 7–10.

et de te et a te latas] The Licinian and Aebutian laws debarred the proposer of any extraordinary office, and also his relations, connexions, and colleagues, from holding that office (Leg. Agr. ii. 21). The date of these laws is uncertain, but they are plausibly referred to the period of Tiberius Gracchus' small holdings law of 133, when he proposed the appointment of a commission consisting of himself, his brother Gaius, and his father-in-law Appius Claudius. Antony violated these measures by establishing a land commission consisting of himself, his brother Lucius, Dolabella, a writer of mimes named Nucula, a tragic actor named Lento, and two others unknown (xi. 13). His uncle Gaius seems to have been promised a place and then thrown over (§ 99; A. xv. 19, 2. Groebe (Drumann, i[2]. 83, n. 4), followed by Sternkopf, *Hermes*, xlvii. 146–51, concludes from these passages, I think wrongly, that Antony's *brother* Gaius was on the commission).

The transactions of the commission were repealed in 43, on the motion of L. Iulius Caesar (vi. 14). (On the general question of Antony's agrarian legislation see § 100, note on 'praeclaram . . . percursationem'.)

auspicia . . . intercessionem] See i. 25 and notes.

7. **M. Crasso**] In a letter written to Crassus in 54, after his departure for Syria (F. v. 8, 1), Cicero speaks of 'interruptions' in their friendship. We can guess the nature of these 'interruptions', the *contentiones* to which Cicero here refers. At the time of the Catilinarian conspiracy, Crassus communicated to Cicero an anonymous letter of warning which he had received. Three years after, in his *De Consulatu*, Cicero recounted the incident, and Crassus bore him a grudge for doing so, as the reception of warning might be held to imply complicity in the plot (Plut. Cic. 15; Crass. 13; Dio, xxxvii. 31). Crassus did in fact, at the time of the conspiracy, believe that Cicero suspected him of complicity. On 4th December 63 (the day before the execution of Lentulus and his associates), when a certain L. Tarquinius stated in the senate that he had been dispatched by Crassus with a secret message to Catiline, it was rumoured that Tarquinius had been suborned by Cicero, and Crassus himself actually told Sallust that he believed this to be so (Sall. Cat. 48).

Subsequently Cicero suspected Crassus, perhaps of intriguing for his banishment (A. ii. 22, 5), certainly of obstructing his recall (F. xiv. 2, 2; A. iii. 23, 5). On Cicero's return from exile, in 57, the relations between the two men were outwardly friendly, but in 56 they quarrelled again, when Crassus took up the cause of Gabinius, accused of maladministration in Syria, and seized the opportunity to deliver a violent attack on Cicero. This quarrel was patched up by the intervention of Caesar and Pompey, and Crassus left for Syria, 'almost from Cicero's door', after dining with him the night before (F. i. 9, 20). Cicero's letters show mistrust and dislike of the man: e.g. 'o hominem nequam' (A. iv. 13, 2); 'Crassum tamen metuo' (F. xiv. 2, 2).

See further § 12, note on *Maxime . . . probavit*.

uno . . . nequissimo] Probably *uno* goes closely with the superlative, and strengthens it, as we say 'the one most . . .'. Cf. Planc. 97 'urbem unam mihi amicissimam'. This is better, I think, than to take *uno* as = 'a certain', as King does. (In § 84 below *unam* is differently used.)

gladiatore] Cicero so often applies this term to Antony, both in the speeches and in the letters, that I suspect it to have been something like a regular nickname, perhaps coined by Cicero himself. Cf. § 63; iii. 18; v. 32; vii. 17; xiii. 25; F. xii. 2, 1. In vii. 17 he explains that Marcus was figuratively a gladiator, Lucius literally one, having fought in the gladiatorial ring at Mylasa in Caria (v. 20). When Cicero uses the phrase 'gladiatore omnium nequissimo' of Antony in F. xii. 22, 1, he is perhaps quoting consciously from the present passage. Cf. also Rosc. Am. 17; Mur. 50, 83 (Catiline).

litteras recitavit] i. 3, note on *unum aiebat*.

8. **Mustelae . . . Numisio**] These two are mentioned elsewhere as hangers-on of Antony (ii. 106; viii. 26; xii. 14; xiii. 3). **Mustela**

came from Anagnia, and is styled by Cicero *gladiorum princeps*. Otherwise nothing is known of them.

tamen] 'In spite of the fact that you are nothing of the kind.'

inter sicarios] The 'quaestio inter sicarios' perhaps dates back to the middle of the second century (Greenidge, *Leg. Proc.* 420).

scientiam quaestuosam] This, taken literally, would suggest that Antony did his forging (of *acta Caesaris*) for himself; and the accounts of Velleius (ii. 60, 4) and Dio (xliv. 53, 2; xlv. 23, 5) give rather the same impression, or, at least, do not mention an amanuensis. Appian, however (iii. 5), says that Antony used Caesar's clerk Faberius for the purpose (perhaps identical with the Faberius often mentioned in Cicero's letters in 45). And Cicero (A. xiv. 18, 1) says of Dolabella: 'cum se maximo aere alieno Faberi manu liberarit et opem ab Ope petierit.' See Münzer in P.-W. vi. 2, 1736–7.

magistro] For Sextus Clodius, the Sicilian rhetorician, and his 'enormous fee', see § 42 and note.

9. hominis] 'A reasonable being.' See L. and S. s.v. *homo*, I. B. 1 a.

10. quid . . . rogares] A poor argument. It is possible to possess a right, yet not insist on it against a friend's wishes.

lege] Certainly an exaggeration. In the letter in question (A. xiv. 13 a, 2) Antony only suggests an informal consent given in private. 'A Caesare petii ut Sex. Clodium restitueret; impetravi.'

pro me aliquid . . . in M. Antonium multa] Respectively, §§ 11–42, 44–114.

vel . . . factus est] Because he had been nominated by Caesar, not elected by the free vote of the people. See § 79 'iussus es renuntiari consul'; Plut. Ant. 11; App. ii. 107; Dio, xliii. 49, 1.

11. ex huius . . . sententia] With special reference to Cicero's suppression of the Catilinarian conspiracy. For the senate's share in this see § 18. For the argument that the senate was the worst possible place in which to attack Cicero, see § 2.

id] His third wife, Fulvia. Her two previous husbands had both died violent deaths, P. Clodius at the hands of Milo in 52, C. Scribonius Curio at the battle of Utica in 49, during the war against Juba.

Cf. *tertiam pensionem*, § 113.

12. P. Servilio] P. Servilius Vatia Isauricus: consul in 79, and in the following year sent out as commander against the Cilician pirates; conducted the war, which lasted till 75, with conspicuous success, and won the name Isauricus by a brilliant victory over the Isaurians, whose capital he destroyed: died in 44.

Q. Catulo] Q. Lutatius Catulus: consul in 78; died in 60: son of the victor of Vercellae, where the Cimbri were defeated in 101: he and Cato saluted Cicero as *pater patriae* after the execution of the Catilinarians.

duobus Lucullis] (1) L. Licinius Lucullus: consul in 74; conducted the war against Mithradates (74-66) with great ability, until superseded by Pompey; died in 56, or earlier. (2) M. Licinius Lucullus, his less distinguished brother, was consul in 73: in 72-1, as governor of Macedonia, advanced eastward across the Struma, and subdued Thrace.

M. Crasso] M. Licinius Crassus: see note on § 7.

Q. Hortensio] 114-50: the foremost pleader of his time up to 70, when Cicero by his successful prosecution of Verres deprived him of first place; politically a supporter of the optimates; his oratory was of the florid Asiatic type.

C. Curioni] C. Scribonius Curio the elder: consul in 76: proconsul in Macedonia, 75-3, where, confining his attention to the northern frontier, he subdued the Dardani (in Serbia) and reached the Danube; an opponent of Caesar; a friend of Cicero, whose consulship he called *ἀποθέωσις*, though his championship of Clodius in 61 caused a temporary estrangement; died in 53; father of Fulvia's second husband (for whom see note on § 3).

C. Pisoni] C. Calpurnius Piso: consul in 67; opposed the Lex Gabinia; governor of Gallia Narbonensis in 66-5; on his return defended by Cicero in 63, on a charge of maladministration.

M'. Glabrioni] M'. Acilius Glabrio: praetor in 70, in which capacity he presided at the trial of Verres; governor of Cilicia, and succeeded L. Lucullus as commander in the Mithradatic War, in which capacity he proved himself most inefficient.

M'. Lepido . . . . L. Murenae] M'. Aemilius Lepidus and L. Volcatius Tullus: consuls in 66. C. Marcius Figulus: consul in 64. D. Iunius Silanus and L. Licinius Murena: consuls in 62.

Silanus, as consul elect, was the first senator called upon for his opinion in the debate on the punishment of the Catilinarian conspirators. He declared himself in favour of the death penalty, but after Caesar's speech changed his mind.

Murena served under Lucullus in the Third Mithradatic War. In 63, after his election to the consulship, he was prosecuted for bribery by Serv. Sulpicius, one of the unsuccessful candidates, and defended by Hortensius and Cicero, whose speech is extant.

M. Catoni] M. Porcius Cato, the type, for all ages, of political and personal severity and uprightness: as tribune in 63, spoke strongly in favour of the execution of the Catilinarians; subsequently opposed Pompey and Caesar with obstinacy and courage, but without success; in 58, when Cicero was banished, Cato was entrusted with the task of carrying out the annexation of Cyprus, as a pretext for removing him from Rome; praetor in 54; in 52 stood unsuccessfully for the consulship; in the Civil War served for a time as governor of Sicily, subsequently, during the campaign of Pharsalus, as governor of Dyrrachium, and finally under Scipio in Africa; committed suicide at Utica in 46, after the battle of Thapsus.

Maxime . . . probavit] The assertion needs qualification. While Pompey was completing his conquest of the East, Cicero had written him a letter (since lost) describing the events of his consulship. Pompey apparently answered without much enthusiasm. He was essentially cautious by disposition, and was probably reluctant to commit himself to a definite expression of opinion before his return to Italy, and so run the risk of offending Caesar in particular, who was looking after his interests in Rome, and the democratic party in general, with which his past history connected him. (Cicero at any rate hints in F. v. 7, 3 at reluctance of such a kind.) Besides we may conjecture that he was galled by the orator's bombastic self-assertiveness, particularly if any mischief-maker had communicated to him the passages in the Catilinarians (iii. 26 : iv. 21) in which Cicero places his own achievements on a level with Pompey's. Finally, he had himself desired the task of crushing the conspiracy, and could hardly be expected to feel warmly towards the man who had forestalled him.

In a further letter (F. v. 7) Cicero expresses his mortification with characteristic *naïveté*. Pompey reached Rome in January 61, and treated him with outward cordiality. But Cicero doubted his sincerity. 'Tuus autem ille amicus (scin, quem dicam?) de quo tu ad me scripsisti, postea quam non auderet reprehendere, laudare coepisse, nos, ut ostendit, admodum diligit, amplectitur, amat, aperte laudat, occulte, sed ita ut perspicuum sit, invidet. Nihil come, nihil simplex, nihil ἐν τοῖς πολιτικοῖς illustre, nihil honestum, nihil forte, nihil liberum' (A. i. 13, 4). In Pompey's first speech in the senate he praised the proceedings of that body in general terms, and remarked to Cicero, on sitting down, 'se putare satis ab se etiam "de istis rebus" esse responsum'. Crassus thereupon stepped into the breach, and eulogized Cicero's consulship in the warmest terms, saying, 'se, quod esset senator, quod civis, quod liber, quod viveret, mihi acceptum referre ; quotiens coniugem, quotiens domum, quotiens patriam videret, totiens se beneficium meum videre'. Pompey, sitting next Cicero, was visibly perturbed at seeing Crassus seize the chance he had missed himself (A. i. 14, 3).

However, circumstances quickly drew the two men together. Pompey's main objects were the ratification of his Eastern settlement and the allotment of land to his veterans, and many senators were opposed to these measures, in spite of the conservative tone of his public utterances. Cato had rejected his offers for a marriage connexion. It was clearly worth his while to cultivate Cicero's friendship. Cicero, on his side, was nettled by the jealousy of some of the optimates, and disgusted by their selfishness and luxuriousness. He lived in peril of prosecution, and the recent acquittal of Clodius showed what Roman justice was worth. He must needs look for allies, and Pompey's help was not to be despised. By the end of May 61 the two were fast friends, and people were calling Pompey 'Gnaeus Cicero'. 'Eum qui nimium diu de rebus nostris tacuerat, Pompeium adduxi in eam voluntatem ut in senatu non semel, sed saepe multisque verbis huius mihi salutem imperi atque orbis terrarum adiudicarit' (A. i. 19, 7). 'Quem de meis rebus, in quas eum multi incitarant, multo scito gloriosius quam de suis praedicare; sibi enim bene gestae, mihi conservatae rei publicae dat testimonium' (A. ii. 1, 6). Atticus warned Cicero repeatedly against going too far in his friendship with Pompey (A. i. 20, 2; ii. 1, 6), and he promised to be careful. Actually, the prospect of aid in time of trouble, and the pleasing illusion that he might convert Pompey, perhaps even Caesar, to constitutionalism, proved irresistible attractions.

Frequentissimo senatui] The adjective shows that a particular meeting is referred to: clearly, I think, the meeting of 3rd December (described in the Third Catilinarian, delivered in the assembly later on the same day), when the senate authorized the conspirators' arrest and decreed a *supplicatio* in Cicero's honour (§ 13 below). The language, 'qui mihi . . . acceptam', resembles that used by Crassus on a later occasion (see previous note).

13. L. Cotta] L. Aurelius Cotta, proposer of the Lex Aurelia of 70 (i. 20), in which year he was praetor: consul in 65. The terms of the motion are given in Cat. iii. 15: 'quod urbem incendiis, caede civis, Italiam bello liberassem.' In 57, when the motion for Cicero's recall from exile was brought forward, Cotta, as *Princeps Senatus*, expressed the opinion that, as Cicero had not been legally banished, no law was necessary for his restoration. (De Dom. 68; Sest. 73; De Leg. iii. 45.)

rebus . . . reprehendis] This is quite untrue. The *supplicatio* was voted on 3rd December, after the conspirators' arrest. What Antony 'censured' was their execution, which was voted and carried out on 5th. On 3rd Cicero had a united senate behind him, on 5th he met with considerable opposition. He intentionally confuses the chronology here, in order to give the impression that the whole senate was in favour of the death penalty. For the Catilinarian conspiracy see further §§ 16–19 and notes.

14. L. Caesar] i. 27, n. It appears that Cicero is still speaking of the meeting of 3rd December, and that the speech is the one to which he refers in Cat. iv. 13, in which L. Caesar said that Lentulus ought to be put to death. But it does not seem likely, from Cat. iii. 14–15 and Sall. Cat. 47, that the punishment of the conspirators was formally debated on that occasion. The senate confined itself to compelling Lentulus to abdicate from the praetorship, and handing over him and the other conspirators to the safe keeping of prominent senators.

sororis] Lentulus' wife Julia. Cicero speaks of her in Cat. iv. 13 as *femina lectissima*. ii. 58.

15. in hortis] Presumably the gardens which had once been Pompey's. §§ 67, 109.

Phormioni . . . Gnathoni . . . Ballioni] Figures from comedy, typical of the company which Antony kept. Phormio is a parasite in Terence's play of that name, Gnatho a parasite in his *Eunuchus*, Ballio a pander in Plautus's *Pseudolus*.

eo templo] The temple of Concord.

16. olivum Capitolinum] On 5th December 63 the ascent to the Capitol was guarded by Equites, prominent among whom was Atticus. 'Equitatus ille quem ego in clivo Capitolino te signifero ac principe collocaram' (A. ii. 1, 7). The Forum and adjoining temples, and the approaches to the temple of Concord, were also occupied by volunteers of every class and description (Cat. iv. 14). The assistance which the Equites gave the senate on this occasion was bitterly remembered by the popular party, as all union between antagonistic sections of the 'Haves' is naturally resented by the 'Have-nots'. In 58, just before Cicero's banishment, Gabinius threatened that the 'knights should pay for the day when they stood on the slope of the Capitoline with swords in their hands' (Sest. 28; cf. Post Red. in Sen. 32). The knights did not make themselves more popular by threatening Caesar as he left the senate (Sall. Cat. 49, 4; Plut. Caes. 8).

servorum armatorum] That a certain number of reliable slaves were armed by their masters for the occasion is *a priori* not improbable (for, though Roman sentiment was opposed to the arming of slaves, necessity knows no law), and is suggested, I think, by Cat. iv. 16: 'Servus est nemo, qui modo tolerabili condicione sit servitutis . . . qui non quantum audet et quantum potest conferat ad communem salutem voluntatis.' At any rate, Antony meant that slaves were armed: it seems to me most unlikely that he meant by *servorum* the knights, 'mere slaves to Cicero', as some editors explain.

adulescens] The date of Antony's birth cannot be determined with certainty. The evidence is:

(1) App. v. 8 ἔτη τεσσαράκοντα γεγονώς (when he met Cleopatra in 41).

(2) Plut. Ant. 86 Ἀντώνιον δὲ οἱ μὲν ἕξ, οἱ δὲ τρισὶ τὰ πεντήκοντα ὑπερβαλεῖν φασιν (at his death in August, 30).

(3) The date of his election to the quaestorship, which is itself debatable (§ 50). It appears probable that a man could not be elected quaestor till the completion of his thirtieth year, though it is possible that he could be elected during his thirtieth year (Mommsen, *St. R.* i. 570–1). We cannot, however, assume that Antony was elected quaestor directly he became eligible.

I do not think the evidence warrants a decision. (1) Points to 82–1, (2) to 87–6 or 84–3. Arguments based on (3) are card-houses of uncertainties. Groebe, arguing from (1) and (3), decides for 82 (Drumann, i². 401; P.-W. i. 2, 2595). I accept this, under reserve, as a basis for estimating Antony's age on various occasions.

nomen non dedit] Ὁ Κικέρων τό τε Καπιτώλιον καὶ τὴν ἀγορὰν τῆς νυκτὸς φρουρᾷ προκατέσχε, καὶ . . . τὸν μὲν δῆμον τοῖς στρατηγοῖς ὁρκῶσαι *εἰς τὸν κατάλογον, εἰ δή τις χρεία στρατιωτῶν γένοιτο, ἐκέλευσεν, αὐτὸς δὲ ἐν τούτῳ τὴν βουλὴν ἤθροισε* (Dio, xxxvii. 35, 4).

quamquam] The concessive is rather curious. Halm's explanation is no doubt right: 'quamquam omnes, qui voluerunt, ne dederunt quidem, quia nec scribae, etc.'

17. **voce . . . coacti]** Envoys from the Gallic tribe of Allobroges, who happened to be in Rome, were won over to the conspiracy by Lentulus, but subsequently turned informers. Cicero instructed them to continue negotiations with their confederates. On the night of 2nd/3rd December 63 they left Rome for Gaul, escorted by a certain Volturcius, with a dispatch for their own government and a letter and verbal messages for Catiline, whom they were to meet in Etruria. At the Mulvian bridge, two miles outside Rome, they found a picket waiting for them, under the command of two of the praetors, to which they surrendered. They were brought to Cicero's house at daybreak. He immediately sent for Lentulus and the other leaders of the conspiracy in Rome, who walked unsuspectingly into the trap. He then at once summoned the senate. Volturcius gave his evidence: Cicero produced the incriminating letters, which he had intentionally refrained from opening. The leaders of the conspiracy, Lentulus, Cethegus, and Statilius, were shown their respective seals, which they could not but acknowledge. The letters were opened and read. The culprits made no serious attempt to deny their guilt, which was indeed manifest. The senate then passed a resolution, thanking Cicero 'quod virtute, consilio, providentia mea res publica maximis periculis sit liberata' (Cat. iii. 14): the conspirators were handed over to prominent senators for safe keeping: and finally a *supplicatio* was voted in Cicero's honour. Later in the day he delivered the Third Catilinarian before the people in the Forum. On the following day, 4th December, the senate met again. A certain L. Tarquinius endeavoured, without success, to implicate Crassus. Volturcius and the Gallic envoys were rewarded, and Lentulus and his associates were declared public enemies. On 5th December Cicero summoned the senate to the temple of Concord, to consult them as to the punishment to be inflicted on the conspirators. As a result of the debate (for the details of which see below, note on 'animadversio senatus fuit') the senate voted by a large majority for the death penalty. Without delay, as night was approaching, Lentulus, Cethegus, Statilius, Gabinius, and Caeparius were strangled in the Tullianum. Cicero announced their fate to the expectant populace by the single word *vixerunt*.

urbem . . . Italiam] Minute arrangements were made for all this, and each conspirator knew exactly what he had to do. Rome was to be fired simultaneously in twelve places by Statilius and Gabinius: the resulting confusion would facilitate the tasks of Cethegus, who was to kill Cicero, and of his fellow assassins. Various districts of Italy, and even Gaul, were assigned to different conspirators (Cat. ii. 6; Sull. 53; Sall. Cat. 43, 1–3).

quis esset] Probably potential subjunctive. 'Who could there be?' Cf. De Fin. ii. 55 'quis enim redargueret?' (Roby, ii. § 1538).

praesertim cum] Usually concessive (§ 64, n.); but here clearly causal in sense, 'especially in view of the fact that'.

Ad sepulturam] Plutarch (Ant. 2) says that Antony accused Cicero of refusing to give up Lentulus's body for burial, until finally Lentulus' mother begged Cicero's wife for it. But he adds that this is admittedly false, as Cicero gave up all the bodies.

ne P. quidem Clodius] And Clodius, who got Cicero banished for his execution of the Catilinarians, presumably left nothing unsaid which tended to Cicero's discredit in the matter.

18. domi P. Lentuli] Lentulus was consul in 71, but was expelled from the senate by the censors in the following year for immoral conduct (Plut. Cic. 17). He was praetor in 63.

diiuncta] In the Topics (§ 56) Cicero gives as types of argument *ex diiunctione*: 'Aut hoc aut illud; hoc autem; non igitur illud. Itemque: Aut hoc aut illud; non autem hoc; illud igitur.' (*Aut* differs from *or* in having a disjunctive force, excluding one term: otherwise the former syllogism would of course be fallacious.) In the present passage we have the former type of *diiunctio* (two things which cannot both be true): in § 32, the latter (two things of which one must be true).

Cicero's argument is a singularly poor one. That a man is guilty does not make it legal to execute him without trial.

fatebare] Antony may have merely admitted his stepfather's guilt implicitly by not denying it, or he may have made a show of fairness by admitting it explicitly. Nothing could have been gained by denial, as Lentulus himself had confessed (Cat. iii. 11).

Ita] Not 'so', but 'by so doing'. Cicero has finished the charge of inconsistency: he proceeds to the charge of tactlessness.

animadversio senatus fuit] The debate took place on 5th December. Cicero first asked the opinion of Silanus, consul elect, who declared for the death penalty, followed by the other senators in turn, until Caesar proposed, as an alternative, confiscation of property and imprisonment for life, with the proviso that it should be illegal to propose the prisoners' release. His opinion carried great weight, but the scale was turned by the speeches of Cicero and Cato in favour of the death penalty. Cato's motion was put to the house by Cicero and carried by a large majority. Eighteen years later Brutus, in his *Cato*, aroused Cicero's indignation by exaggerating the importance of the part played by Cato in the debate. Cicero retorted that, with the exception of Caesar, all the senators who spoke before Cato advocated the death penalty, and that the division was only taken on Cato's motion because it was 'more fully and lucidly expressed' (A. xii. 21, 1).

The legality of the penalty has been hotly contested. Mommsen once styled the execution a 'brutal judicial murder', but later modified his view. On the one hand a Lex Porcia of 197 confirmed the right of appeal against the death sentence, and a Lex Sempronia of 123 forbade a magistrate to put a citizen to death without the command of the people. On the other it might be maintained that men who, after the passing of the 'senatus consultum ultimum' (see § 51, note on 'in te . . . senatus'), continued in rebellion, *ipso facto* ceased to be citizens. This was the argument which Cicero used (Cat. i. 28), and it might be held to apply not only to Catiline, under arms in Etruria, but to his confederates in the capital. It is, however, clear that the senate, while possessing the power to authorize a consul, by the 'senatus consultum ultimum', to inflict the death penalty, had no power to inflict that penalty itself. And though Cicero gained great moral support from the senate's opinion, he was not thereby relieved from personal responsibility for the act, as his language here and Pis. 14 seems to suggest. His chief justification lay in two precedents to which he alludes in Cat. i. 4, the killing of C. Gracchus by Opimius in 121, and the killing of Saturninus by Marius in 100. The former was the classical test case, Opimius being tried for his action and acquitted: Cicero puts the issue in De Orat. ii. 134: 'num poena videatur esse adficiendus, qui civem ex senatus consulto patriae conservandae causa interemerit, cum id per leges non liceret.' It must be admitted, however, that neither precedent provides an exact parallel for the judicial execution of an untried person. (Strachan-Davidson, *Cicero*, 151–8; Watson, *Select Letters of Cicero*, App. iv. 132–3; Meyer, 35–6; Rice Holmes, i. 278–82; E. G. Hardy, *The Catilinarian Conspiracy*, 85–97.)

19. qui tum . . . fuit] § 16, note on *clivum Capitolinum*. The common fear of mob violence united the two orders, as it had united them against Glaucia and Saturninus in 100. Cicero was most anxious to preserve this *concordia ordinum*. In A. i. 14, 4 (13th Feb. 61) he describes a speech which he had made on the subject. But in the course of that year serious differences arose between the orders. It was proposed in the senate to hold an inquiry on judicial corruption, and the knights were attempting without success to obtain alteration in the terms under which they had contracted for the collection of the Asiatic taxes (A. i. 17, 8–9, 5th December 61). Cicero deplored the consequent alienation of the knights from the senate, although he admitted that they were in the wrong, and gave it as one of the excuses for his rapprochement with Pompey (A. i. 18, 3; ii. 1, 6–8).

Ituraeis] This tribe, situated north-east of the Sea of Galilee, was subjugated by Pompey in 63. It is conceivable that he may have recruited archers from it (see § 112), and, as Antony served in the campaign, his connexion with the Ituraeans may have originated then. Or he may have met them when serving under Gabinius in 57. Caesar used Ituraean archers in his African campaign in 47 (Bell. Afr. 20).

20. uxore] A sarcastic designation for Antony's mistress. Cf.

§ 69, 'illam . . . divortium.' She was the freedwoman and mistress of one Volumnius Eutrapelus, and after manumission went on the stage. (For a similar case cf. Antiphon in A. iv. 15, 6.) Following a prevalent custom, she now called herself Volumnia, after her former owner, but her stage-name was Cytheris, chosen no doubt for its suggestion of Aphrodite. (In Rosc. Com. 23 we hear of a similar stage-name, Dionysia.) The poet Gallus wrote love-poems to her under the name Lycoris. Hence:

tua cura Lycoris
Perque nives alium perque horrida castra secutast.
(Verg. Ecl. x. 22-3 and Servius ad loc.)

In A. xv. 22 (June 44) Cicero refers to Antony as 'our friend Cytherius', and already in May 49 he complains that Antony is going about accompanied by Cytheris in an open litter (A. x. 16, 5; cf. § 58). F. ix. 26 is written from Volumnius's dinner-table in 46. 'Cytheris is sitting below Eutrapelus. Strange company, you say, for the grave and reverend Cicero. But, on my honour, I never knew she was to be here.'

Cedant arma togae] No doubt from Cicero's poem De Consulatu meo, written in 60. The complete line is quoted in De Off. i. 77, and runs:

Cedant arma togae, concedat laurea laudi.

(*Laudi* seems to mean 'true desert'. Perhaps the next line made the sense clearer, or perhaps the alternative reading *linguae* is right: 'let the sword yield to the pen'.)

Cicero tells us there that the line was selected for attack by the malicious. It is not a good line, with its crude, archaic assonances; but it is better than 'O fortunatam natam me consule Romam' from the same poem. The line was also attacked by Piso, on political rather than literary grounds it would seem. Piso maintained that *arma* could only refer to Pompey, then at the zenith of his military success, and that the disparaging reference had earned Cicero Pompey's enmity, and thus led to his exile; to which Cicero answers that the meaning of the line was universal, not particular, 'that war and disorder were to yield to peace and quiet' (Pis. 72–5).

A long passage from the De Consulatu is quoted in De Div. i. 17. Another political poem by Cicero, De meis Temporibus, was composed in 55 or 54.

neque . . . nosse] Antony's only purely literary work seems to have been his De Ebrietate sua, written shortly before Actium (Plin. N. H. xiv. 148). His epistolary style may be gauged by two letters to Cicero (A. x. 8 a and A. xiv. 13 a). The former is particularly characteristic; it is clumsily and laboriously written, with an occasional colloquialism and an occasional Greek word. The latter contains a common solecism, *non contempseris* for *ne contempseris* (cf. Quint. I. v. 50). There is another solecism, the superlative *piissimus*, in the letter quoted in the Thirteenth Philippic (§ 43). Cf. iii. 21-2, *facere contumeliam*.

monumentorum] The term includes anything which records the past, either in stone or, as here, in writing. Cf. De Orat. i. 201: 'monumenta rerum gestarum'; Rab. Post. 43, 'monumenta annalium'.

subsicivis] The word is originally applied to odd bits of land left over after a distribution. 'Subsiciva, quae divisis per veteranos agris carptim superfuerunt' (Suet. Dom. 9). Hence it is also used, as here, of odd bits of time. 'Subsiciva quaedam tempora incurrunt, quae ego perire non patior' (De Leg. i. 9).

The whole description would fit Caesar, who had an amazing faculty for writing in the midst of distractions, far better than Cicero, whose periods of literary activity were his periods of political impotence.

21. For further details of Antony's attempt on Clodius see § 49 and Mil. 40. The two had been intimate friends five years before (§ 48). We cannot say what motive induced a democratic candidate for the quaestorship to attack the idol of the populace in a public place, but a love intrigue may well have been at the bottom of the business (cf. § 48: 'cuius etiam domi iam tum quiddam molitus est (Fulvia)). Cicero's language in § 49, 'ultro mihi idem illud deferentem', suggests a deliberate, premeditated attempt. Why, in that case, Antony chose the Forum for the place and broad daylight ('inspectante populo Romano') for the time, remains obscure.

In the elections for 52 the candidates for the consulship were T. Annius Milo, P. Plautius Hypsaeus, and Q. Caecilius Metellus Scipio. Clodius was standing for the praetorship. The elections dragged on, with much disorder and bribery. The year 52 began with no consuls or praetors, and the proposal to appoint an interrex was vetoed by a tribune. On 18th January, in a fray on the Appian Way, Milo killed Clodius. The murder was followed by wild tumult. The dead body was exposed to view in the Forum, and then burned in the Curia, which caught fire and was burned to the ground. M. Aemilius Lepidus, the newly appointed interrex, was besieged in his house by the mob for five days, because he refused to hold the elections at once. The senate, by a 'senatus consultum ultimum', gave Pompey, the tribunes, and the interrex powers of martial law for the maintenance of order. But these proved unavailing, and finally Pompey was made sole consul. His first action, early in March, was to establish courts *de vi* and *de ambitu* to deal with Milo's case. Altogether, Milo was summoned to appear before four courts, the new *quaestiones extraordinariae de vi* and *de ambitu*, and the old *quaestiones perpetuae de vi* and *de sodaliciis*.

in scalas] 'Under the stairs.' This was a favourite place for slaves to hide when they were afraid of a beating. Cf. Hor. Ep. ii. 2. 15. It seems to have been used as a sort of lumber-room, entered by a door (Frag. A. vii. 11, Müller: 'aperuit fores scalarum'; cf. ib. 12 'correpsit in scalas'; 13 'latet in scalis tenebrosis

Cominius), like a boot-hole in a modern house. The description of the incident in Mil. 40: 'cum se ille fugiens in scalarum tenebras abdidisset,' proves that Clodius attempted to escape by hiding under the stairs, not by running up them.

22. The argument is: an inquiry, whether or not wisely constituted, was held about the death of Clodius: an opportunity was thereby given to any one who wished to accuse Cicero of complicity; no one did so; therefore the accusation is groundless.

The answer is simple: the charge *was* made. 'Scitis, iudices, fuisse qui in hac rogatione suadenda diceret (v. l. dicerent) Milonis manu caedem esse factam, consilio vero maioris alicuius. Me videlicet latronem ac sicarium abiecti homines et perditi describebant' (Mil. 47).

quid . . . quaeri] The object (a quite justifiable one: see *Pro Milone*, Clark, p. xxv) was to provide speedier procedure and severer penalties. Ascon. in Mil. 31: 'Duas (*sc.* leges) promulgavit (*sc.* Pompeius), alteram de vi . . . alteram de ambitu: poena graviore et forma iudiciorum breviore. Utraque enim lex prius testes dari, deinde uno die atque eodem et ab accusatore et a reo perorari iubebat, ita ut duae horae accusatori, tres reo darentur. His legibus obsistere M. Caelius tr. pl. studiosissimus Milonis conatus est, quod et privilegium diceret in Milonem ferri et iudicia praecipitari.'

cum . . . constituta] Cf. Mil. 13: 'Hanc vero quaestionem, etsi non est iniqua, numquam tamen senatus constituendam putavit. Erant enim leges, erant quaestiones vel de caede vel de vi, nec tantum maerorem ac luctum senatui mors P. Clodi afferebat, ut nova quaestio constitueretur.' Cicero probably refers to the Lex Cornelia de Sicariis and the Lex Plautia de Vi.

In the event, Milo was convicted by thirty-eight votes to thirteen before the special court *de vi*. He then went into voluntary exile at Massilia, without awaiting the verdicts of the special court *de ambitu* and the standing courts *de vi* and *de sodaliciis*, before all of which he was condemned in absence.

23. *The relations between Pompey, Caesar, and Cicero.*

History is adapted for the occasion. Bibulus and Caesar were consuls in 59: the compact between Caesar, Pompey, and Crassus, usually known as the First Triumvirate, had undoubtedly been made in the previous year, probably before the consular elections (Rice Holmes i. 474–6). Its existence, at first a secret, was unmistakably revealed at the passing of Caesar's first agrarian law (probably in April 59), when Pompey and Crassus announced their approval of the measure, and Pompey declared himself ready to support it by force of arms. Letters written by Cicero early in May show that he then regarded Pompey as having recently committed himself more definitely to Caesar's policy. In A. ii. 16, 1–2, discussing Caesar's second agrarian law for distributing Campanian state domains, he observes that Pompey has 'taken the mute off his instrument', since he has been induced to go so far: hitherto he had prevaricated. In A. ii. 17, 1 he mentions with apprehension Pompey's recent engagement to Caesar's daughter Julia. From this epistolary evidence we may fairly conclude that 'postea quam se totum Pompeius Caesari tradidit' points to late April 59, with special, but not exclusive, reference to the betrothal. Hence *impudentis*, the impertinence of trying to come between a man and his son-in-law. In 'Pompeium a mea familiaritate diiunxit' Cicero is thinking of the last months of 59, reviewed in the light of subsequent events. (Actually, he was half inclined to rely on both Pompey's and Caesar's friendship as late as the last week of October (Q. F. i. 2, 16), and it was not till the crash came in early 58 that he was definitely disillusioned. See below, note on 'ipse . . . diiunxit'.) Cicero complains of Antony's chronology, but his own is sufficiently vague. The second half of § 23 will run more clearly if we take 'In quo . . . diiunxit' as a parenthetical anticipation of events, and 'M. Bibulo . . . consule' as referring not only to 'nihil . . . avocarem' (say, January–April), but also to 'postea . . . conarer' (say, April–December).

Did Cicero pursue the clear-cut and logical policy which he ascribes to himself in §§ 23–4? We may readily believe that after the event he expressed himself, in the pluperfect subjunctive, in such words as *Utinam, Cn. Pompei*, etc., below. But when he writes to Caecina in 46 (F. vi. 6, 4): 'Plurimi sunt testes me et initio ne coniungeret se cum Caesare monuisse Pompeium et postea ne seiungeret. Coniunctione frangi senatus opes, diiunctione civile bellum excitari videbam': when he writes thus, his own contemporary letters forbid us to believe him. In fact, Cicero had no policy whatever in 59. In 60 he intermittently deluded himself with the dream of exercising a 'wholesome' influence on Pompey, and perhaps Caesar as well: a dream artfully encouraged by Caesar's judicious flattery. But his real preoccupation in 60, and even more so in 59, was to provide himself with a shelter against Clodius. This consideration forbade him to offend the triumvirs, though shame made him stop short of supporting them. A political cypher, he sat nursing his hatred against the *reges*, the *dynastae*, hoping they might fall out, gloating over any sign of their unpopularity. Nor did he, at any rate during the first half of 59, regard Pompey with any less disfavour than Caesar. In fact Pompey seemed to him, and doubtless to many men, the most dangerous and tyrannical of the three.

M. Bibulo] Bibulus, after the passing of Caesar's first agrarian law, shut himself up in his house for his remaining eight months of office, and announced daily that he had 'observed the heavens', and that therefore no business might be transacted (see App. III). He also posted up furious manifestos against the triumvirs, accusing Caesar in particular of every kind of crime. The wits used afterwards to say that something or other had occurred, 'Caesare et

Iulio (instead of 'Caesare et Bibulo') consulibus'; and a distich was current:

> Non Bibulo quiddam nuper sed Caesare factum est:
> Nam Bibulo fieri consule nil memini.
>
> (Suet. Iul. 20.)

Cicero retorts here by mentioning Bibulus alone.

At the time Cicero expressed great admiration for his strength of mind, but doubted its practical utility (A. ii. 15, 2), and sometimes spoke impatiently of him: 'Bibulus in caelo est, nec qua re scio, sed ita laudatur quasi "Unus homo nobis cunctando restituit rem"' (A. ii. 19, 2). It is customary to speak of Bibulus as a mere fool, and his name has disinclined posterity to take him seriously. But it is difficult to say what he could have done; and it should be remembered to his credit that, when consul, he faced the furious mob without flinching, and that in 48 he carried out his duties as admiral in the Adriatic, though afflicted by severe illness, until he died at his post (Caes. B. C. iii. 18, 1).

Ipse enim . . . diiunxit] In Sest. 133 Cicero attributes Pompey's alienation to the designs of Vatinius; in Pis. 76 he blames Piso and Gabinius. But no doubt Caesar's hidden hand was the moving force. Crassus also threw his weight into the scale (A. ii. 22, 5, Crassus putting pressure on Pompey). The result was that when Cicero, threatened with outlawry, flung himself at the feet of Pompey, who had assured him that he was in no danger, and that Clodius would have to kill him first if he wished to lay a hand on Cicero (A. ii. 20, 2), Pompey left him where he lay and said 'he could do nothing against Caesar's wishes' (A. x. 4, 3). Cf. the account of Plutarch, who says (Cic. 30) that 'Caesar encouraged Clodius and completely alienated Pompey from Cicero'.

24. Cicero now proceeds to review the period 55–50, and contrasts his 'opposition' (sic) to Caesar in 55 and 52 with his 'peace at any price' attitude just before the outbreak of the civil war.

ne . . . prorogaret] By the 'Lex Vatinia' of 59 Caesar received command of Cisalpine Gaul and Illyricum from 1st March 59 to 1st March 54: to these Transalpine Gaul was subsequently added, by a decree of the senate. By the 'Lex Pompeia Licinia', proposed by the consuls Pompey and Crassus in 55, this command was extended until 1st March 49. (The date fixed for the termination of Caesar's Gallic command has been the subject of voluminous controversy. Dr. Rice Holmes, in an exhaustive discussion (ii. 299–307), gives his reasons for adhering to Mommsen's date, 1st March 49. See also Dr. E. G. Hardy, *Some Problems in Roman History*, 150–206. Other suggested dates are 1st March 50 and 1st January 49.)

ne . . . haberetur] This was in the latter half of 52, after Pompey had nominated Metellus Scipio as his colleague in the consulship. It was of paramount importance to Caesar that he should be allowed to stand in absence for the consulship in the summer of 49. Otherwise he would be compelled to abandon the protection of his army, come to Rome as a private individual, and run the risk of prosecution. Accordingly the ten tribunes, led by M. Caelius, proposed that Caesar should be allowed to stand in absence. Cato attempted to talk the proposal out, but it was carried (A. vii. 1, 4; Caes. B.C. i. 32). Subsequently, however, Pompey carried another law, that all candidates should be required to present themselves for election in person; but, after the law had been engraved and deposited in the aerarium, he added, on his own responsibility, the qualification 'except where formal permission has been granted by name' (Suet. Iul. 26–8; Dio, xl. 56). Suetonius attributes the original omission of this clause to 'forgetfulness', and Pompey may conceivably have been naïve enough to urge that excuse. But the real key to his behaviour is his habitual vacillation of purpose: he had to choose now between alliance with Caesar and alliance with the senate; and, as Meyer remarks (p. 243), the shifting fortunes of the war against Vercingetorix made the decision particularly difficult for him.

The permission to stand in absence was nullified by Pompey's 'Lex de iure magistratuum', which enacted that consuls and praetors should succeed to provincial commands not immediately on the expiry of their office, but after an interval of at least five years. By a clause of the 'Lex Pompeia Licinia', the appointment of a successor to Caesar could not be discussed before 1st March 50; and under the 'Lex Sempronia' that successor could only have been one of the consuls or praetors for 49, so that Caesar's tenure would have been secure until the end of that year. Under the new system it was possible to find a successor who would be ready to take over the province on 1st March 49, namely, one of the ex-consuls who had not yet held a province. Had that been done, Caesar would have been in a precarious position, in spite of the privilege of standing in absence; for his security depended on retaining his provincial command until his assumption of the consulship. See Rice Holmes and Hardy, locc. citt.

That Cicero on either of the two occasions 'advised Pompey against Caesar' is highly improbable. As to the former occasion, during 55 he took no part in public life. He was not anxious to repeat his last year's brief but unfortunate excursion into politics. One of his letters (F. i. 8) gives a summary of his views: the triumvirs were omnipotent, and would remain so for a generation; political life, in the old sense, no longer existed; he would follow Pompey with blind loyalty in all things. Certainly he did not venture publicly to oppose the extension of Caesar's command; and it is most unlikely that he ventured to offer Pompey advice on the subject in private. Eleven years after, with Pompey dead, it was easy to pretend that he had done so. Here, as often, we must remember that Cicero wrote his speeches for an audience which did not possess copies of his private correspondence. He could bluff them more easily than he can bluff us.

As to the latter occasion, we have Cicero's own statement in a letter of 50 that he advocated the legalization of Caesar's absent candidature at Caesar's and Pompey's request: 'Nam ut illi hoc liceret adiuvi rogatus ab ipso Ravennae de Caelio tribuno pl. Ab ipso autem? Etiam a Gnaeo nostro in illo divino tertio consulatu' (A. vii. 1, 4). Four years later he attempts to minimize his action: 'Rationem haberi absentis non tam pugnavi ut liceret quam ut, quoniam ipso consule pugnante populus iusserat, haberetur' (F. vi. 6, 5). That Cicero, while supporting the proposal in public, secretly urged Pompey to obstruct it, is not impossible (cf. A. viii. 3, 3: 'nihil actum a Pompeio ... nisi contra consilium auctoritatemque meam ... contendit ut decem tribuni pl. ferrent ut absentis ratio haberetur'). But it is more probable that here again, as so often, he is misrepresenting history.

It may be added that the use of the first person plural in A. vii. 6, 2 would naturally imply that Cicero supported both proposals: 'cum quinquennium prorogabamus aut cum ut absentis ratio haberetur ferebamus.' If Cicero had resisted these measures, could he have abstained from an 'I told you so'?

opes . . . Romani] Grossly exaggerated. In *suas* Cicero is perhaps thinking of the legion which Caesar borrowed from Pompey in the winter of 54–3 (Caes. B. G. vi. 1) to replace his casualties in Gaul. (The loan, however, was repaid in May 50, at Pompey's request: ib. viii. 54, 3.) As to *populi Romani*, from A. viii. 3, 3, where Cicero is discussing the same topic, it would appear that he here has in mind the extension of Caesar's Gallic command, the assignment of Further Gaul to him on Pompey's motion, and the grant of permission to stand in absence.

seroque . . . coepisset] Cf. F. xvi. 11, 3 (12th January 49): 'Pompei nostri, qui Caesarem sero coepit timere.' Also A. viii. 1, 4; 8, 1.

multo ante provideram] For an elaborate account of Cicero's prophetic powers see his letter to Caecina, F. vi. 6.

pacis . . . destiti] Cicero, returning home from his governorship of Cilicia, landed at Brundisium on 24th November 50, by which time things had already gone pretty far. From the very first he had made up his own mind that peace on any terms was better than civil war, and he was still of this opinion even after hostilities had begun. He told Atticus that he meant to exhort Pompey in private to strive for peace (A. vii. 3, 5). But, judging from his own account of a two hours' interview on 10th December, he apparently refrained from pressing his own opinion. Pompey, who seems to have done most of the talking, held out no hope of a peaceful solution (A. vii. 4, 3) either on that occasion, or at another lengthy interview on 25th December (A. vii. 8, 4).

To what extent Cicero made his influence felt in public or semi-public discussion during the last days of December and the first days of January, is a difficult question. In the frequent letters to Atticus from 11th to about 25th December he repeatedly states that, while personally desiring peace at any price, he will follow Pompey in whatever he decides. Nevertheless, at the last he seems to have taken a more independent line. On 4th January he was outside Rome (to enter would have been to give up his hopes of a triumph), and did his best at the eleventh hour to avert the catastrophe by compromise. But, though he made some impression on Pompey, the hotheads on both sides were too much for them (F. xvi. 11, 2; iv. 1, 1; vi. 6, 5; Plut. Pomp. 59; Meyer, pp. 285–6). That he would have succeeded had he acted earlier is most improbable: he can hardly be excused for not making the attempt.

25. *The charge of complicity in Caesar's murder.*

If one may judge by the words attributed to Antony in § 30, he had accused Cicero of being privy to the plot (*conscium fuisse*). Elsewhere Cicero variously represents the charge as that of 'having planned Caesar's death' (*meo consilio*), that of 'having desired' it, and that of 'having suspected' it.

That Cicero was toying with the idea of Caesar's assassination as early as August 45 is proved by the reference to 'Ahalam et Brutum' in A. xiii. 40, 1. (See § 26, note on 'L. Bruti . . . Ahalae'.) That at a later date he was to a considerable extent in Brutus' confidence is proved by a letter of April 43. (Ad Brut. ii. 5; see § 34, note on 'non solum . . . regnum'.) But that in the actual plot of March 44 he was a confederate, or even an accomplice, is unlikely. (To call him the 'intellectual originator' of Caesar's murder, as Meyer does, p. 457, is surely much exaggerated.) Plutarch states, probably with truth, that the conspirators considered him too timid and too old for their purpose (Brut. 12; Cic. 42); and Brutus may have felt, as he felt later: 'death, exile, and poverty—I believe that these are the worst evils in Cicero's eyes, and so long as he has people from whom he can get what he wants, and who will make much of him and flatter him, he has no horror of servitude, provided it is tempered with a show of respect' (Ad Brut. i. 17, 4; see Rice Holmes, iii. 340, whose translation I quote). Ferrero's view (ii. 310) that the conspirators were reluctant to risk Cicero's valuable life, seems to me less likely.

The object of the charge was of course, as Cicero remarks in F. xii. 2, 1, to inflame the veterans against him.

praevaricatorem] In order to secure honesty in prosecution, Roman law recognized as offences *calumnia* (wittingly making a false accusation) and *praevaricatio* (employing collusion with the accused). A third offence, probably included in *praevaricatio* in Cicero's time, but subsequently distinguished from it, was *tergiversatio* (abandoning a prosecution from corrupt motives). Greenidge, Leg. Proc. 468–72.

iactasse se aliquos] Appian (ii. 119) mentions Lentulus

Spinther and Dolabella among those who borrowed daggers after the murder and posed as accomplices. Lentulus boasts in a letter to Cicero (F. xii. 14, 6) that he 'shared in the perilous venture'. Plutarch (Caes. 67) says that Lentulus and C. Octavius were executed by Antony and Octavian although nobody believed that they had really been in the plot.

quam ut quisquam] This curious transition from accusative and infinitive to subjunctive is common in Livy, e.g. iv. 2, 8: 'se miliens morituros potius quam ut . . . patiantur.' Certain instances can hardly be found in earlier Latin. (Planc. 97 and Lig. 34 can be explained on other grounds.) Kühner, ii. 2, 302; Riemann, *Syntaxe Latine*, 401.

26. tot] Over eighty, according to Nic. Dam. 19; over sixty, according to Suet. Iul. 80.

L. Bruti . . . Ahalae] Cicero seems to have been fond of appealing to these two models of republican virtue. In 59 Vettius, giving evidence of a supposed plot to murder Pompey, stated 'consularem disertum' (Cicero) 'vicinum consulis' (Caesar) 'sibi dixisse Ahalam Servilium aliquem aut Brutum opus esse reperiri' (A. ii. 24, 3). The descent of M. Brutus from L. Brutus and, through his mother Servilia, from Ahala, was traced in a genealogical tree which Atticus constructed for Brutus, and which hung in a room named 'the Parthenon'. Hence A. xiii. 40, 1 (August 45): 'ubi φιλοτέχνημα illud tuum quod vidi in Parthenone, Ahalam et Brutum?' can only be a hint at the possibility of Caesar's assassination.

The descent from L. Brutus is certainly fictitious, for L. Brutus extinguished his line by executing both his sons (Dion. Hal., Ant. Rom. v. 18; Dio, xliv. 12, 1). A third son, an infant at that time, was invented by Posidonius to save the situation (Plut. Brut. 1). The genealogy was widely credited at Rome. People wrote on Lucius' statue appeals to his laggard descendant Marcus (Plut. Brut. 9).

imaginem] *Imagines* were wax masks of ancestors who had held curule offices (Verr. II. v, 36; F. ix. 21, 2). They were kept (probably fastened to busts) in wooden cupboards (*armoria*: ξύλινα ναΐδια, Polyb. vi. 53, 4) in the recesses (*alae*) of the atrium, with inscriptions recording the individual's achievements. At funerals, these masks (or, far more probably, copies of them) were worn by persons, resembling the deceased in figure, who marched in the procession, the masks of related and connected families being also included. Many passages imply that the *armoria* were normally kept shut, being only opened on festal occasions, e.g. Polyb. loc. cit: τὰς εἰκόνας ἐν ταῖς δημοτελέσι θυσίαις ἀνοίγοντες: Sull. 88: 'Domus erit, credo, exornata, aperientur maiorum imagines.' *Cotidie videret* in our passage seems inconsistent with such a practice; but the difficulty has apparently not been noticed.

(D. & S., s.v. *Imagines*; Blümner, 36–7, 493–5; Schneider and Meyer in P.-W., s.v. *Imagines maiorum*).

Ahalae] According to Dion. Hal. XII. i–iv, and Liv. iv. 12–15 (the two accounts are in substantial agreement) Spurius Maelius, a rich plebeian (Livy anachronistically calls him an *eques*) in 439, during a famine, collected a quantity of corn, which he sold at a low price, or distributed it gratis, to the populace. He usurped the functions of L. Minucius, the *praefectus annonae*, and openly criticized his inefficiency. Minucius laid information before the senate that Maelius was aiming at tyranny. In alarm they nominated Cincinnatus, an old man of over 80, as *dictator* for the third time, to deal with the emergency. Cincinnatus chose as his *magister equitum* C. Servilius Ahala. Ahala summoned Maelius before the dictator's tribunal, to stand his trial. Maelius attempted to escape, but was pursued by Ahala and cut down. His property was confiscated and his house razed to the ground, the site being still known in Dionysius's day as the Aequimaelium. According to Cicero (Dom. 86) Ahala was exiled, in consequence of popular indignation, but subsequently recalled: Livy and Dionysius, however, know nothing of this.

Dionysius also gives, but does not credit, another version of the story (on the authority of Calpurnius Piso and Cincius), according to which Cincinnatus was not dictator, and Servilius not *magister equitum*, but a private individual charged by the senate with the task of assassinating Maelius: he drew Maelius aside, and killed him with a dagger concealed under his arm-pit (*ala*: hence the name Ala or Ahala). Mommsen (*Röm. Forsch.* ii. 199–220) believes this to be the older version: he attributes the later version to reluctance to credit the senate with organizing assassination. At the same time he rejects the whole story of Maelius as a relatively late invention, a piece of optimate propaganda. Incidentally he points out (p. 210) that the cognomen Ahala appears before the time of the supposed occurrence. See also § 87; Mil. 72.

C. Cassius . . . natus] The reference is to Spurius Cassius Vecellinus (or Vicellinus), who was consul in 502, 493, and 486, and who, after conquering the Hernici in this last year, is said to have proposed a law for the distribution of public land, the terms of which are variously given, in consequence of which he was put to death, on the charge of aiming at tyranny. The tradition of the land-law is rejected by Mommsen (*Röm. Forsch.* ii. 153–79, followed by Münzer in P.-W. iii. 2, 1749–53) as an anachronistic invention of later times, concocted in the light of the careers of C. Gracchus and M. Livius Drusus. The only certain fact about Vecellinus is that he was executed for aiming at tyrrany: Mommsen infers, on inconclusive evidence, that his crime consisted in erecting a statue of himself in public. His father, according to one account, condemned him to death; according to another, bore witness against him at the trial. The latter version of the story is followed by Cicero in Rep. ii. 60.

(Dom. 101; Rep. ii. 49; 60; Lael. 36; Liv. ii. 41; Dion. Hal., Ant. Rom. viii. 69–80; Plin. N. H. xxxiv. 30. A full discussion in Mommsen and Münzer, locc. citt.).

hanc rem . . . confecisset] Before Pharsalus Cassius was operating successfully with his fleet off the south Italian and Sicilian coasts (Caes. B. C. iii. 101). On hearing of the disaster he joined Cato at Corcyra, where the remaining Pompeian forces collected. He took part in the abortive attempt to recover Achaia, but, on hearing of Pompey's death, resolved, like many others, to make his peace with Caesar (Dio, xlii. 13, 5). He and Cicero had agreed to throw up the sponge after the first defeat (F. xv. 15, 1). He did not, however, for whatever reason, go direct to Caesar (A. xi. 13, 1; 15, 2, 14th May 47: 'C. Cassium aiunt consilium Alexandream eundi mutavisse.') Exactly where and when Cassius, through Brutus's good offices (Plut. Brut. 6), received the pardon of Caesar, who afterwards appointed him legate (F. vi. 6, 10), cannot be determined. But it may well have been at Tarsus, the capital of Cilicia, where Caesar spent a few days in July 47, on his way from Syria to Pontus, where he was to defeat Pharnaces at Zela on 2nd August (Bell. Alex. 66).

Meyer (p. 536) is disposed to accept, Rice Holmes (iii. 210) to reject, this story, which rests on Cicero's authority alone. It seems to me unnecessary to doubt it, in view of Cicero's intimacy with Cassius. During Caesar's lifetime, of course, the incident was a dead secret.

(Appian (ii. 88; 111) has confused the Tarsus incident by mixing up C. Cassius with a L. Cassius, otherwise unknown, who surrendered to Caesar in the Hellespont. Dio (xlii. 6, 2) and Suetonius (Iul. 63) correctly give L. Cassius on that occasion. See Groebe-Drumann, ii². 102, n. 6; 543-5; Meyer, loc. cit.; Rice Holmes, iii. 482.)

Cassius took no part in the campaigns of 46 and 45. During the latter he kept out of the way at Brundisium, waiting for news. In F. xv. 19, 4 he writes to Cicero: 'Quid in Hispaniis geratur rescribe. Peream nisi sollicitus sum ac malo veterem et clementem dominum habere quam novum et crudelem experiri. Scis Gnaeus' (Pompeius) 'quam sit fatuus; scis quo modo crudelitatem virtutem putet; scis, quam se semper a nobis derisum putet.'

Cassius is stated by Plutarch (Brut. 8; 10) and Appian (ii. 113) to have been the instigator of the conspiracy against Caesar. This is usually accepted (also by Rice Holmes, iii. 339). Dio (xliv. 14, 1-2) makes Brutus the leading spirit: so Fröhlich in P.-W. iii. 2, 1730.

si . . . appulisset] Below Tarsus the Cydnus spreads out into a marshy lake (Strabo, xiv. 5, 10).

27. Cn. Domitium non patris interitus] The father, L. Domitius Ahenobarbus, was consul in 54. Early in the Civil War he attempted to hold Corfinium against Caesar's advance, disregarding Pompey's repeated and urgent requests to join forces with him at Luceria, in Apulia. The town was captured by Caesar on 21st February, and father and son were immediately released. Lucius governed Massilia during its siege in the summer of 49. Escaping when the town capitulated, he joined Pompey's army in Thessaly. Both father and son fought at Pharsalus, where Lucius was killed in the pursuit by Antony (§ 71). Gnaeus remained in exile till 46, when he received Caesar's pardon, and returned to Italy, though he did not re-enter public life (hence Cicero's exaggerated phrase *spoliatio dignitatis*). He was condemned to death at the time of the proscriptions in 43, with Caesar's other murderers, though it was sometimes stated in later times that he was innocent (perhaps because Nero preferred not to have a tyrannicide for a great-grand-father). Vell. ii. 69, 5; App. v. 62; Suet. Ner. 3. He escaped to Brutus and Cassius, commanded a fleet both before and after Philippi, and finally, seeing that the game was up, went over to Antony, who allowed him to return to Italy and rise to the highest political honours. In the next Civil War he served under Antony, but went over to Octavian, dying shortly afterwards. See Suetonius (Ner. 3), who says he was 'omnibus gentis suae procul dubio praeferendus'. His various allegiances appear to have sat lightly on him.

avunculi mors] M. Cato, whose sister Porcia married Lucius. See further § 12, note on M. Catoni.

C. Trebonio] Trebonius served under Caesar in Gaul and Britain: on Caesar's departure for Spain in the spring of 49 he was put in command of the land forces at the siege of Massilia; he subsequently governed Further Spain; in 45, on Caesar's relinquishing the sole consulship, he was appointed consul. With such a record, it is not surprising that Cicero says he would not even have ventured to approach him. But the argument is spoiled by Cicero's statement in § 34 that Antony and Trebonius had notoriously planned Caesar's death at Narbo in 46 (as to the truth of which see note ad loc.). What then more natural than to invite him to renew the attempt in 44?

Quo etiam] 'For which very reason,' i. e. that he was bound to Caesar by such close ties. *Quo* refers to the thought implicit in the previous sentence.

L. Tillius Cimber] Mentioned as one of Caesar's friends in F. vi. 12, 2, and appointed by him to the province of Bithynia. His part in the murder was to solicit pardon for his exiled brother, and give the signal by plucking Caesar's toga.

Cascas] Publius Servilius Casca, who struck the first blow, and his brother Gaius.

28. Ciceronem nominatim exclamavit . . . gratulatus] This would not of itself, perhaps, necessarily imply Cicero's presence. But he was in fact present. '. . . laetitiam, quam oculis cepi iusto interitu tyranni' (A. xiv. 14, 4).

rebus eis] Cicero will never let us forget Catiline for long at a time.

29. Ecquis est igitur, &c.] For the answer see the noble letter of Matius to Cicero (F. xi. 28). There must have been many others, who, while disapproving Caesar's policy, deeply lamented him on personal grounds. And there must have been many who disliked his absolutism, yet preferred it to a renewal of civil war.

30. pecudis] 'Sheep.' The Romans also used *asinus* as we use 'ass'. 'Beast,' as a term of abuse, is *belua*.

Brutus, quem ego honoris causa nomino] 'Brutus, whose name I mention with all respect.' Commentators misrepresent Cicero as making overmuch of a purely conventional formula, like our 'the honourable gentleman'. But the phrase is something more than a conventional formula, as is proved by Rosc. Com. 18: 'Nonne quotienscumque in causa in nomen huius incidisti, totiens hunc et virum bonum esse dixisti et honoris causa appellasti? quod nemo nisi aut honestissimo aut amicissimo facere consuevit.' See also Rosc. Am. 6: 'L. Sulla, quem honoris causa nomino.' The opposite phrase was 'contumeliae causa nominare'. See Verr. I. 18, and compare also § 113 below, 'quam ego sine contumelia describo'.

31. nego . . . medium] The old dilemma, which was first propounded in the temple of Tellus on 17th March. In spite of logic, the facts of the situation demanded compromise.

patriae parentem] Suetonius mentions 'cognomen Patris Patriae' as one of the honours accorded to Caesar, and says that the words *Parenti Patriae* were inscribed on a twenty-foot column erected in the Forum after Caesar's murder (Iul. 76 and 85). The title is used in Antony's letter quoted in Phil. xiii (§§ 23 and 25). It is found on coins (E. Babelon, *Descr. . . . des monnaies de la république romaine*, i. 497), and in inscriptions (*C.I.L.* i². 789: 'C. Iulio Caesari pont. max. patri patriae'). Cicero writes to Cassius in October 44 (F. xii. 3, 1): 'Auget tuus amicus' (Antony) 'furorem in dies. Primum in statua quam posuit in rostris inscripsit "PARENTI OPTIME MERITO", ut non modo sicarii, sed iam etiam parricidae iudicemini.' This incident would have been fresh in people's memory when the Second Philippic was published. According to Suetonius (Iul. 88), it was decided, he does not say when, that the Ides of March should be called *Parricidium*. Q. Catulus had hailed Cicero as *parentem patriae* after the suppression of the Catilinarian conspiracy.

cur . . . solutus] For Brutus's departure from Rome see i. 6, note on *patriae liberatores*.

The natural assumption is that this dispensation was granted at the time when Brutus and Cassius left Rome, in the second week of April 44. So Ferrero, iii. 37; Heitland, iii. 378. (I cannot understand why some authorities put the decree later, e.g. Sternkopf *Hermes*, xlvii. (1912) 385, who suggests 5th June.) The question was probably discussed at the interview between Antony and Brutus and Cassius, mentioned in A. xiv. 6, 1.

ludi Apollinares] i. 36, note on *Apollinarium ludorum*.

cur . . . datae] App. I.

cur quaestores . . . auctus] Nothing further is known of these measures. 'Cur quaestores additi' must mean, 'why were extra quaestors assigned?' I can find no parallel to this enactment. All provinces had one quaestor each, except Sicily, which had two, one for the western district, one for the eastern (Mommsen, St. R. ii. 1, 563).

The number of *legati* seems to have been fixed by the senate for each command, and to have varied normally from two to five. Cicero had four in Cilicia. Caesar was allowed ten in 56, Pompey twenty-five by the Lex Gabinia of 67 for the Pirate War. Perhaps the extra number of officials was intended as compensation for receiving such unimportant provinces: the provinces to which Cicero refers being Crete and Cyrene, assigned to Brutus and Cassius for 43 (perhaps on 1st August 44: see App. I). That at any rate is the accepted view. But it is possible that Cicero may mean the Corn Commission (which he describes as *provincia* in A. xv. 9, 1). For the purchase of corn over a wide area an extra staff would no doubt be necessary. This would give 5th June as the date of 'cur . . . auctus', and thereby upset the chronological order; but the order may be determined by climax.

32. diiunctius] See note on § 18. The comparative is curious: 'in a sort of dilemma.'

conclusionis] Cicero defines *conclusio* in Acad. ii. 26 as 'ratio, quae ex rebus perceptis ad id quod non percipiebatur adducit'.

retexo] 'Cancel,' lit. 'unweave.' (The sense 'reweave' is poetical and post-classical.) *Orationem*, viz. the disclaimer in § 25.

33. expulsos . . . praedicas] This is rhetorical, and out of keeping with the context. Is it likely that Antony, who, as Cicero has been emphasizing, was anxious to show his respect for the conspirators, would 'openly assert' that he had driven them into exile?

relegatos] *Relegatio* consisted either in forbidding a person to live at, or within a certain distance of, Rome or other specified place: or in commanding him to live in a certain specified place. Unlike exile, it did not involve the forfeiture of citizen rights.

The punishment was a common one under the empire, and not unknown under the republic. Liv. iii. 10, 12 'exilio et relegatione civium': iv. 4, 6; xl. 41 'factum est senatus consultum ut M. Fulvius in Hispaniam relegaretur ultra novam Carthaginem'. When, therefore, Cicero says with reference to the relegation of L. Lamia by Gabinius, 'quod ante id tempus civi Romano Romae contigit nemini' (F. xi. 16, 2), he seems to be speaking inaccurately. Certainly he does not assert lack of precedent in his public utterances on the subject. (Post Red. in Sen. 12, Lamia; Sest. 29, Lamia; Pis. 64, Aelius.)

qui locus . . . videatur] The present tense, 'adfari atque appetere', clearly refers to something which is supposed to be happening at the moment. Brutus left Velia shortly after 17th August (A. xvi.

7, 5). Cassius's fleet followed a few days later (Phil. x. 8). The two met in Athens (Plut. Brut. 28). Cassius then went east, and Cicero was sufficiently in touch with his movements to correspond with him in late September and early October (F. xii. 2; 3), though he knew nothing of his intentions. Brutus stayed in Athens, going to lectures on philosophy, but doubtless preparing in secret for coming events (Plut. Brut. 24). (O. E. Schmidt, *Rh. M.* liii. 235, maintains that Brutus and Cassius did not leave Italy till October. But this is inconsistent with Phil. x. 8. Groebe (Drumann, i². 431) rightly gives the second half of August as the date.) 'Locus desertus . . . inhumanus' and 'homines agrestes' manifestly does not fit Athens: nor does the vagueness of § 113, 'ubicunque terrarum', 'quam volent illi cedant'. But such language fits Cassius's peregrination very well, and that is enough excuse for the purple patch.

34. non solum regem, sed etiam regnum] Cf. F. xii. 1, 1: 'non regno sed rege liberati videmur.' A. xiv. 14, 2: 'sublato tyranno tyrannida manere video.' Ad Brut. ii. 5, 1: 'Scis mihi semper placuisse non rege solum sed regno liberari rem publicam.' In this letter to Brutus, written in April 43, Cicero goes on to say that none of the present troubles would have come to pass 'nisi tum conservatus esset Antonius'. Although wisdom after the event was a foible of Cicero's, he would scarcely have ventured to boast of his prescience to one who could so easily have convicted him. We may therefore infer that Cicero did discuss with Brutus the possibility of assassinating Caesar (see § 25, first note), and that he did recommend the simultaneous assassination of Antony. As to the reasons for sparing Antony see below, note on 'a Trebonio sevocari'.

si meus stilus ille fuisset] Commentators say that there is a double entendre in *stilus* ('pen' and 'dagger') to which *ut dicitur* alludes. But though the word, which usually means 'pen', is occasionally used for other pointed instruments, e.g. a stake or a pointed gardening tool, I can find no passage in which it means 'dagger'. (Obviously that meaning is not attested by the fact that Horace (Sat. ii. 1, 39) talks of 'sheathing his *stilus*', and Cicero (Clu. 123) of 'fearing the censors' *stilus*, whose point our forefathers blunted, as much as the dictator's sword'. One could use 'pen' in English exactly so, but there is no double entendre in 'pen'.)

No doubt the allusion is to the fact that the assassins concealed their daggers in their pen-cases (Dio, xliv. 16, 1). As for 'ut dicitur', it refers, I think, not to 'stilus' but to 'non solum . . . confecissem', and denotes that the metaphor, from play-writing, is a common one. (It is, in fact, a favourite of Cicero's. See L. and S., s.v. *actus*.) For the expression *ut dicitur* Mayor compares De Off. i 80 'de gradu, ut dicitur, deici'; Lael. 101 'ad calcem, ut dicitur, pervenire'.

Several times in his letters Cicero regrets the sparing of Antony. Cf. the disgusting metaphor in a letter to Cassius (F. xii. 4, 1):

'Vellem Idibus Martiis me ad cenam invitasses; reliquiarum nihil fuisset. Nunc me reliquiae vestrae exercent, et quidem praeter ceteros me hercule.'

et Narbone . . . cepisse] The incident occurred during Caesar's return march from Spain. He reached Rome early in September 45: Velleius (ii. 56, 3) gives the date as October, but Caesar made his will on 13th September at a country-house south-east of Rome (Suet. Iul. 83: see Meyer, p. 458). 'All the principal men in Rome went many days' journey to meet Caesar' (Plut. Ant. 11); cf. § 78 below: 'C. Caesari ex Hispania redeunti obviam longissime processisti.' According to Plut. Ant. 13, Trebonius, who was travelling with Antony and sharing his tent, sounded him cautiously on the subject of assassinating Caesar: Antony understood the hint, but did not respond: however, he did not inform Caesar. If this account of the incident is correct (and we have no reason to doubt it) *consilium cepisse* is a characteristic piece of Ciceronian exaggeration.

(In Ant. 10 Plutarch confuses Antony's return from Narbo on this occasion with his previous return from the same place in the early spring of 45. He makes him go to meet Caesar μετὰ τὴν νίκην, viz. Munda, 17th March, and arrive back in Rome before 13th March (A. xii. 18 *a*, 1: see § 77, note on 'urbem . . . perturbasti')! The confusion vitiates § 20 of Halm's Introduction, even in the latest edition.)

Trebonius had been appointed governor of Further Spain in February 47. His history between that date and the time we are considering is a blank. That, like Antony, he had quarrelled with Caesar, is obvious. Hence, in spite of his Spanish experience, he was in Rome during the Munda campaign.

a Trebonio . . . sevocari] Cf. xiii. 22: 'Sceleratum Trebonium? quo scelere, nisi quod te Idibus Martiis a debita tibi peste seduxit?' Trebonius was told off to engage Antony in conversation outside the door of the Senate House (App. ii. 117; Plut. Brut. 17). Cicero represents the sparing of Antony as a reward for his 'complicity' (*sic*) in Trebonius's design. No doubt the true motive was that given by Appian (ii. 114) and Plutarch (Ant. 13): if they killed Antony as well as Caesar they would seem to be actuated by personal animosity, not by abstract hatred of tyranny. In Brut. 18 Plutarch adds that Brutus alone stood out for sparing Antony, partly on grounds of justice, partly because he hoped that he might be won over to the cause of freedom. (I see no reason to doubt, with Ferrero, that Antony was spared mainly on grounds of justice, though, as Plutarch suggests, the republicans may have hoped to win him over to their side. But it is surely going too far to call him a 'recent convert to the party of tyranny' (ii. 311). Ferrero thinks the conspirators were also influenced by 'the reflection that the simultaneous disappearance of the two consuls would have prevented the immediate restoration of the old constitution'.)

35. illud Cassianum] L. Cassius Longinus, as tribune of the plebs in 137, introduced voting by ballot. As president of the court he always urged the jury to consider who had benefited by the crime. Cicero several times refers to this maxim 'cui bono fuerit' (hence our *cui bono*), and also tells us that Cassius was 'ipsa tristitia et severitate popularis'. *Fuerit* must be perfect subjunctive, as it is replaced by *fuisset* when the phrase occurs in historic sequence. The question is therefore indirect. (Mil. 32 and Asconius ad loc.; Rosc. Am. 84; Brut. 97.)

Quamquam . . . regnas] *Quamquam* is often used by Cicero as an adversative connecting particle at the beginning of a sentence (cf. § 34), and Halm[8], who renders *freilich*, seems to be right in taking it so here. The objection introduced by *quamquam* is then brushed aside by *tamen*, 'still after all.'

ut tu dicebas] On 17th March, Halm and King say. But the imperfect tense suggests a general reference. Cicero may be referring to the time immediately after Caesar's murder, Antony's early conciliatory period. But Antony would not then have spoken so strongly. Much more probably Cicero refers to the time between the African and Spanish campaigns, when Antony was on bad terms with Caesar (see §§ 71-5), and might very well, in private of course, have used such words as these.

ad aedem Opis] See note on i. 17.

tabulas] 'Account-books.' See § 103.

tam multa] Caesar's ready money and private papers. See Introd., p. viii.

falsorum . . . vectigalium] See § 97 for details.

37. Castra . . . tempus] When, at the beginning of the Civil War, Italy was divided into recruiting areas, Cicero was put in charge of Capua and the Campanian coast. He was unwilling, he says, to accept a more important post, which would have made it impossible for him to play the part of mediator (F. xvi. 12, 5). One would have thought that the post which he did accept committed him sufficiently, but he exercised his powers with discretion, assuring Pompey of his diligence and Caesar of his complete neutrality (A. viii. 11 *b*; ix. 11 *a*, 2). With the latter he remained on outwardly friendly terms, though he refused repeated invitations to come to Rome. He was a prey to conflicting emotions. He freely criticized Pompey's strategy, and dreaded the Sullan proscriptions which seemed likely to follow his return: also he frankly admitted that he dreaded the hardships of service overseas. At the same time he was losing reputation by his conduct, and Pompey was annoyed with him for ignoring reiterated requests to join him. (Pompey doubtless knew that he was doing nothing whatever in Campania, while his presence at head-quarters would be a political asset: for similar reasons Caesar eagerly desired his presence in Rome.) If Pompey won after all, as seemed not impossible, he would be placed in an awkward position. In his quandary he turned, as usual, to Atticus, whose letters he filed and constantly reread. Atticus advised him, emphatically and repeatedly, if not quite consistently, not to follow, if Pompey left Italy.

Pompey sailed from Brundisium for Dyrrachium on 17th March 49. Before the month was out Cicero had decided to join him, and from this resolve, though Caelius Rufus, Antony, Dolabella, and Caesar himself all endeavoured to dissuade him, he never really looked back. He acted, however, with characteristic dilatoriness, and it was not till 7th June that he finally sailed, from Caieta, for Pompey's camp in Epirus. A complete gap now appears in his hitherto voluminous correspondence, and during the remaining months of 49 no letters either from or to him are extant. A few written from head-quarters early in 48, dealing almost entirely with private affairs, have been preserved. In one of these he writes that he has 'hitherto avoided being entrusted with official duties' (A. xi. 4). We might have conjectured, even if Plutarch had not told us (Cic. 38), that such duties were not thrust upon him, and can imagine that the reception he met with at head-quarters, after his vacillating, not to say treacherous, conduct, was a cool one. His ineradicable habit of harping on what might have been done, and of criticizing strategy, of which he knew nothing, must have proved little short of maddening to an able soldier fighting for existence: especially if he was unable to abstain from irritating sarcasms and ill-seasoned witticisms (see note on *iocis* below: Plut. Cic. 38). His impressions on arriving at head-quarters are recorded in a letter written long afterwards (F. vii. 3, 2, August, 46): 'primum neque magnas copias neque bellicosas; deinde extra ducem paucosque praeterea (de principibus loquor) reliqui primum in ipso bello rapaces, deinde in oratione ita crudeles, ut ipsam victoriam horrerem; maximum autem aes alienum amplissimorum virorum. Quid quaeris? nihil boni praeter causam. Quae cum vidissem, desperans victoriam primum coepi suadere pacem, cuius fueram semper auctor; deinde, cum ab ea sententia Pompeius valde abhorreret, suadere institui ut bellum duceret. Hoc interdum probabat et in ea sententia videbatur fore et fuisset fortasse, nisi quadam ex pugna coepisset suis militibus confidere. Ex eo tempore vir ille summus nullus imperator fuit. Signa tirone et collecticio exercitu cum legionibus robustissimis contulit; victus turpissime amissis etiam castris solus fugit.'

When Pompey, after inflicting a severe reverse on Caesar, and breaking the blockade, marched eastwards to join Scipio, Cicero stayed behind, in poor health, with Cato's garrison at Dyrrachium. When the news of Pharsalus arrived, Cato offered Cicero, as a consular, the command. He refused it, having made up his mind to take no further part in the war, and was nearly killed by Pompey's elder son Gnaeus. But Cato saved him, and he crossed over to Brundisium (§ 3).

What are the limits of 'illud omne tempus?' Antony can hardly have passed over the period from the outbreak of war to Cicero's departure from Italy, the most discreditable portion of his career. Cicero in his reply says nothing of that period, probably because he has nothing to say. (For an attempt at a defence see Strachan-Davidson, *Cicero*, pp. 330 ff., which is refuted by the letters: on the other side see J. D. Duff, *J. Phil.* xxxiii (1914) 154–60.)

si . . . valuisset] The advice was to make peace. See extract from F. vii. 3, quoted in preceding note. *Ut dixi*, which is rather loosely used, must refer to § 24, where Cicero describes himself as taking a similar line on a previous occasion.

tot . . . exercitus] Besides Pompey, the most important superior officers killed, after the time of which Cicero is here speaking, were: L. Domitius Ahenobarbus, at Pharsalus: L. Afranius, after Thapsus, in 46; P. Attius Varus and T. Labienus, at Munda, in 45; Cn. Pompeius, soon after Munda. M. Petreius, M. Cato, and Q. Metellus Scipio, Pompey's father-in-law, died by their own hand after Thapsus.

The armies are those defeated at Pharsalus, Thapsus, and Munda.

vitae cupiditatem] Cicero is speaking of the period before Pharsalus; but I believe he is partly thinking of the period after that battle. It was freely stated after the decisive defeat at Thapsus that he should have killed himself, as Cato and others had done. In F. vii. 3, written to Marius in August 46, he gives a justification of his conduct: he had seen reason to desire death, but not reason to kill himself; the pursuit of learning and the memory of his glorious past were his consolation; his death would not have helped the state; enough were dead already: had they listened to him, they would be living still, honourably, though under unjust terms of peace, inferior in might, not in right.

tot consularis . . . exercitus] Appian (ii. 82) says that ten senators and forty distinguished knights fell on Pompey's side at Pharsalus: he gives the total of Pompeian killed, on the authority of Asinius Pollio, one of Caesar's officers, as 6,000. Caesar himself (B. C. iii. 99) put the Pompeian killed tentatively (*cecidisse videbantur*) at 15,000, and the prisoners at 24,000: his own killed at 30 centurions and 200 rank and file. The republicans lost 10,000 killed at Thapsus (Bell. Afr. 86; Plut. Caes. 53, much exaggerated): 33,000(?) killed at Munda (Bell. Hisp. 31, perhaps exaggerated). Caesar's losses in killed were small at Thapsus, 1,000 at Munda.

mihi . . . videbatur] Cicero had urged this view from the beginning of the war. A. vii. 14, 3 (Jan., 49): 'Equidem ad pacem hortari non desino; quae vel iniusta utilior est quam iustissimum bellum cum civibus'; A. viii. 11 D, 6 (to Pompey, 27th Feb., 49): 'Mea quae semper fuerit sententia de pace vel iniqua condicione retinenda . . . meminisse te arbitror.'

38. Cn. Pompei . . . oratio mea] This is certainly true. See § 37, first note.

Quod autem . . . dissensio] They agreed to differ: and so there was less friction than if they had been perpetually trying to convince one another. A dignified way of saying that Pompey ignored Cicero and did not ask his advice.

39. qui . . . persecuti sunt] Pompey left the battlefield before the action was over, realizing that the rout of his cavalry was decisive. He stayed in the camp till the enemy entered it, then tore off his insignia of rank, seized a horse, and fled at a gallop to Larissa. Joined there by a handful of fugitives from the battle, he rode by night through the vale of Tempe to the mouth of the Peneus. There he boarded a grain-ship and sailed to Amphipolis. Caesar had followed with his cavalry close on his heels, to prevent him from raising new forces and resuming hostilities. Pompey had issued a recruiting proclamation at Amphipolis, and possibly hoped to make a stand there. But hearing of Caesar's approach he embarked again and sailed to Mytilene, and thence to Attalia in Pamphylia, Cilicia, and Cyprus, where he put in at the harbour of Paphus. He intended to cross to Antioch, but, finding that the inhabitants refused to admit him, abandoned this plan and sailed to Pelusium. Here he solicited the aid of the boy king Ptolemy, who was carrying on a war against his sister Cleopatra. The king's guardians, after receiving his envoys with outward friendliness, enticed him into a boat, where he was murdered by Achillas, one of Ptolemy's officers, and L. Septimius, an officer who had served under him as centurion in the war against the pirates (Caes. B. C. iii. 94-104: Plut. Pomp. 72-9).

Pompey was accompanied in his flight by the two Lentuli, Publius and Lucius, the latter of whom shared his fate: also by M. Favonius, who had opposed him at the outset of the war, but now rendered him menial service, and by King Deiotarus (De Div. ii. 79). At Mytilene he was joined by his wife Cornelia and his younger son Sextus, and at Attalia by sixty senators.

sector] Buyer of captured or confiscated goods. The abstract noun is *sectio* (§ 64). *Sectores* were regarded with dislike (Rosc. Am. 124).

iocis] Macrobius devotes a chapter (ii. 3) to Cicero's witticisms. Cf. especially §§ 7-8: 'Pompeius Ciceronis facetiarum impatiens fuit. Cuius haec dicta ferebantur, "ego vero quem fugiam habeo, quem sequar non habeo". Sed et cum ad Pompeium venisset, dicentibus sero eum venisse respondit, "minime sero veni, nam nihil hic paratum video". Deinde interroganti Pompeio ubi gener eius Dolabella esset, respondit "cum socero tuo". Et cum donasset Pompeius transfugam civitate Romana, "o hominem bellum," inquit "Gallis civitatem promittit alienam qui nobis nostram non potest reddere". Propter quae merito videbatur dixisse Pompeius "cupio ad hostes Cicero transeat, ut nos timeat".' Except for the ready, if obvious, retort about Dolabella, these are poor enough. The selection in Plut. Cic. 38 is even worse. But the mots are perhaps genuine (though such things spring up like mushrooms). Meyer (384) points out that Tiro made a collection (which Macrobius knew (ii. 1, 12)), as did Trebonius (F. xv. 21, 2), and also Caesar, who, on his return journey from Africa in 46, had all Cicero's choicest witticisms sent out to him for his collection of ἀποφθέγματα, and could distinguish unerringly the genuine from the spurious (F. ix. 16, 4). Cicero enjoyed a high reputation as a wit, and set considerable store by it (F. vii. 32, 1); Macrobius puts him beside Plautus. Vatinius and other enemies called him a *scurra*. For his power of anecdote see Clu. 58–9; Planc. 64–5; for his power of repartee see the passage at arms with Clodius described in A. i. 16, 10. His letters show much humour, even if the laboriously facetious epistles to Trebatius (F. vii. 6–22) tempt us to echo § 7, 'quam multa ioca', &c. See further the 'Fragmenta facete dictorum' in Müller's Teubner text, Pars iv, vol. 2, 341–50.

plena curae] Depressed the Pompeians doubtless were in spirit. But, according to Caesar's account of the captured camp (B. C. iii. 96), they were well off for material comforts and luxuries, 'summer-houses, quantities of silver plate, huts of fresh-cut turf, with ivy trellises'. One remembers descriptions of captured German dug-outs.

40. in utroque . . . moderatum] A transparent fallacy. It was the alternation of gloom and flippancy that was so trying to strained nerves.

amplius . . . ducentiens]. Tyrrell (*Correspondence of Cicero*, i. 35) thinks this exaggerated. Cicero received legacies from the Stoic Diodotus, from the architect Cyrus, and a very considerable one from his friend Cluvius.

nemo nisi amicus] Tyrrell remarks (loc. cit.) that 'distinguished public characters often became the heirs of men personally quite unknown to them'. The suggestion (repeated by Dio, xlv. 47, 5) that Antony obtained possession of the legacies by illicit means may therefore be unfounded.

41. Nothing is known of Rubrius, Fufius, or Turselius.

qui . . . ignoras] The Latin equivalent of 'don't know him from Adam'. Cf. Catull. 93:

> Nil nimium studeo, Caesar, tibi velle placere,
> Nec scire utrum sis albus an ater homo.

ne nominat quidem] Perhaps the force of this is: 'did not even mention him among the second heirs,' who inherited if the original heirs were debarred from doing so.

Q. Fufi] Sc. *filium*.

42. cum ipse . . . adisses] 'Did not come into your own father's property.' (For *hereditatem adire* cf. Rosc. Com. 55; *obire*, Leg. Agr. i. 8.) Antony's father, M. Antonius, was satirically named Creticus in celebration of his complete failure (74–1 B.C.) against the pirates, whom he attacked in Crete, where he died (Liv. Ep. 97). Sallust (Hist. iii. 65) says he was 'perdundae pecuniae genitus vacuusque curis nisi instantibus'. A harpy in his official capacity

(Verr. II. iii. 213), he was open-handed enough to his friends (Plut. Ant. 1). Hence it is likely that he left an estate heavily encumbered with debt, and that his son could not afford to accept it. This, I think, is the meaning of 'hereditatem non adisses'. Cf. 44, *praetextatum decoxisse*. Some (including Dio, xlv. 47, 3) have inferred from this passage that Antony was disinherited. But there is no evidence that he quarrelled with his father. He was in fact only eight when his father left Rome, and eleven when he died. Cicero unreasonably holds him responsible for a decision which must have been taken by his guardians on his behalf. (Reid, in Peskett's edition, points out that non-acceptance of an inheritance, as casting a slur on the family name, was repugnant to Roman sentiment. He compares Plin. Ep. ii. 4).

tot . . . villa] More specifically in v. 19, 'seventeen days' (i.e. from 2nd to 19th September) 'in the Tiburtine villa of Metellus Scipio' (Pompey's father-in-law, who killed himself after Thapsus).

Cicero writes in a letter to Cassius (F. xii. 2, 1, end of September): 'Caedem enim gladiator quaerit eiusque initium a. d. XIII K. Octobr. a me se facturum putavit; ad quem paratus venerat, cum in villa Metelli complures dies commentatus esset. Quae autem in lustris et in vino commentatio potuit esse? Itaque omnibus est visus, ut ad te antea scripsi, vomere suo more, non dicere.'

vini exhalandi . . . causa] Declamation had its physical side for the Romans, and even, to some extent, took the place of outdoor exercise. Cicero says in F. ix. 18, 3 that it improved his health and enabled him to eat more peacock. In v. 19 another motive is suggested for Antony's oratorical exercises. 'He wanted to raise a thirst.'

magistrum] Sextus Clodius, a Sicilian rhetorician. See §§ 43, 101; iii. 22. Suetonius (de Rhet. 5) says that Clodius was 'male oculatus et dicax', and used to say he had 'worn out a pair of eyes in friendship with M. Antonius the Triumvir'. He was a professor of both Greek and Latin rhetoric. Doubtless on the strength of the permission mentioned here, he ventured to observe that Fulvia, 'cui altera bucca inflatior erat, acumen stili tentare', an ingenious double pun which 'made him more, not less, popular with Antony'. Cicero perhaps refers to him in a letter written to Atticus in 54: 'Vereor ne lepore suo detineat diutius rhetor' (MSS. *praetor*) 'Clodius', *sc.* 'on your way back from Asia' (A. iv. 15, 2).

omnino] 'Under any circumstances,' King. But much more probably concessive in sense: 'a witty man, certainly, but wittiness at your expense is too easy to be taken as a test.' So Halm[8] and Peskett. 'Omnino . . . sed . . .' is common in Cicero in this sense.

dicta] 'Witticisms,' 'mots.' Cicero's definition, quoted by Macrobius (ii. 1, 14), is: 'quae facete et breviter et acute locuti essemus.' This sense of the word was obsolete in Macrobius's day:

'iocos hoc genus veteres nostri dicta dicebant' (ib.). Novius and Pomponius had used *dicteria*, which reappears in Martial.

avum] For M. Antonius the Orator see i. 27 n. For his characteristics see De Orat. iii. 32, where he is described as 'in sua quaque re commorans' (cf. *sensim*), and Brut. 139.

tu . . . aliena] His oratory was of the florid Asiatic type, which Plutarch observes (Ant. 2) suited his temperament.

43. Duo milia iugerum] About 1,250 acres. For the fact cf. § 101 and iii. 22. Sextus Clodius became 'ex oratore arator'.

immunia] Free from the tax of one-tenth of the produce, paid to the state (*decumae*).

alio loco] § 101.

44. praetextatum] The *toga praetexta*, a white garment with a broad purple border, was worn by curule magistrates on all public occasions, and by members of the four great priestly colleges on certain occasions (Mommsen, *St. R.* i. 418-22). It was also worn by all free-born boys until they assumed the plain white *toga virilis* of manhood. The age at which this occurred was apparently left to the discretion of the parent or guardian; but the completion of the fourteenth year seems to have been the *terminus a quo*, and our evidence indicates that some time during the fifteenth or sixteenth year was normally chosen, at any rate in the imperial epoch. The ceremony consisted in laying down the *praetexta* before the altar of the Lares (*praetextam ponere*) and taking up the *toga virilis* (also called *pura* or *libera*): cf. *virilem sumere* below (Blümner, pp. 214, 335-6, following Marquardt, *Privatleben*, 124 ff.).

For the date of Antony's birth see § 16, note on *adulescens*.

lege Roscia] Ascon. in Cornel. 70: '(lege) quam L. Roscius Otho biennio ante confirmavit, in theatro ut equitibus Romanis XIIII ordines spectandi gratia darentur.' Liv. Ep. 99: 'L. Roscius tribunus plebis legem tulit ut equitibus Romanis in theatro quatuordecim gradus proximi adsignarentur.' Hor. Epod. 4, 16. The seats assigned to the Equites by Roscius's law (67 B.C.) were the fourteen front rows of the *theatrum* (the semicircular rows rising in tiers). The senators sat in the 'orchestra'. In Mur. 40, Vell. ii. 32, 3 *restituit* implies that this was an ancient equestrian privilege, abolished, it has been plausibly conjectured, by Sulla. Cf. also Juv. iii. 153-9; xiv. 323 ff. There is no other evidence for Cicero's statement here that the Lex Roscia assigned certain seats to bankrupts.

To sit in the fourteen rows when not qualified to do so was a penal offence. Augustus mitigated the rigour of the law: 'Cum plerique equitum attrito bellis civilibus patrimonio spectare ludos e quattuordecim non auderent metu poenae theatralis, pronuntiavit non teneri ea quibus ipsis parentibusve equester census umquam fuisset.' Suet. Aug. 40.

47. notiora vobis quam mihi] Cicero perhaps refers to his absences from Rome and Italy during the Civil War and after Caesar's death. Cf. § 57.

incidamus media] Cicero only devotes the three following sections to the years 67–49. The whole of the rest of the speech is devoted to the period 49–44.

48. **Intimus . . . Clodio**] Clodius was tribune in 58. Supported by Caesar's army he carried out a violently democratic programme, including laws for the free distribution of corn, the removal of religious checks on legislation, the restoration of political clubs, and the limitation of the censors' power. He then obtained the banishment of Cicero, by means of a bill directed against any one who had executed a Roman citizen without trial.

incendiorum fax] *Fax* is used metaphorically by Cicero: e. g. 'seditionis ista fax' (Dom. 13). But here there is also no doubt a reference to the literal meaning of the word, as Cicero several times charges Clodius with incendiarism (Dom. 62; Cael. 78).

molitus est] No doubt an intrigue with Clodius's wife Fulvia.

Inde] Plutarch (Ant. 2–3) says that, after a brief intimacy with Clodius, Antony left Italy for Greece, where he studied soldiering and oratory. Early in 57 Aulus Gabinius, the new proconsul of Syria (consul with Piso in 58), invited him to join his army, which he did as Praefectus Equitum (at the early age of twenty-five), and served with great distinction against Aristobulus in 57.

iter Alexandream] Ptolemy Auletes, king of Egypt, had been driven out by his subjects in 58. Towards the end of 57 we find him in Rome, scattering bribes broadcast, in true oriental fashion, in the hope of recovering his kingdom. His restoration was the burning question of the hour, and Cicero's letters to his friend P. Lentulus Spinther, governor of Cilicia in 56, give full details of the discussions which took place. The commander charged with reinstating the king would have an excuse for raising a large army for the purpose, and so placing himself in a powerful position. Numerous proposals were made. Some, including Cicero, wanted Lentulus, others Pompey. Crassus suggested three legati selected from persons possessing imperium, Bibulus three from persons not possessing it. Others proposed that the king should not be restored at all. The senate had, indeed, already passed a decree, late in 57, entrusting the operation to Lentulus; but on 13th January 56, on the strength of a prophecy which had been opportunely discovered in the Sibylline books, they cancelled this decree by another, 'cum multitudine eum reduci periculosum rei publicae videri' (Q. F. ii. 2, 3). The discussions dragged on for months, and the restoration was finally carried out by Gabinius, on his own responsibility, in the early spring of 55. Plutarch (Ant. 3) says that Antony's influence decided the hesitating proconsul to undertake the expedition (F. i. 1–7; Q. F. ii. 2; A. iv. 10, 1).

contra . . . religiones] 'Senatus religionis calumniam non religione, sed malevolentia et illius regiae largitionis invidia comprobat'

(F. i. 1, 1). 'Haec tamen opinio est populi Romani, a tuis (sc. Lentuli) invidis atque obtrectatoribus nomen inductum fictae religionis' (F. i. 4, 2).

quicum . . . posset] Contrast with this, and Cicero's general abuse of Gabinius, Josephus' favourable estimate (Ant. xiv. 5, 2-4; 6, 1-2; Bell. Iud. i. 8, 2-7). See Rice Holmes, ii. 149. Cf. also Butler and Cary's *De Provinciis Consularibus*, Appendix II.

Prius . . . Galliam] Gabinius arrived before Rome on 19th September 54 (Q. F. iii. 1, 15). Here, as was to be expected after his insubordination, he found three separate prosecutions awaiting him. Doubtless Antony thought it advisable to keep clear of these and of his creditors. Antony must have found Caesar's army in northern Gaul in winter quarters, after the relief of Quintus Cicero.

Suam . . . tua] In contrast with a later time, when men like Varro (§ 103) were turned out of their homes by Antony.

Misenum] Antony had an estate there. See § 73.

Sisapo] In Hispania Baetica. There were cinnabar (vermilion) mines there. It is conjectured that they were owned by a company; that Antony had made over a portion of his property at Misenum, or conceded certain rights over it, to his creditors; and that consequently he was a mere partner in his own property.

49. Venis e Gallia ad quaesturam petendam . . . (50) Quaestor es factus] The date of Antony's quaestorship. In B. G. vii. 81, 6 (siege of Alesia, 52 B.C.) Caesar describes Antony as *legatus* ('M. Antonius et C. Trebonius legati'). In B. G. viii. 2, 1 (end of December 52); 24, 2; 38, 1 (siege of Uxellodunum, 51) Hirtius refers to him as quaestor. In viii. 46, 4 (Caesar's dispositions for winter quarters at the end of 51) Hirtius writes 'M. Antonio et C. Trebonio et P. Vatinio legatis', and in viii. 50, 1 (early in 50) 'municipia et colonias . . . quibus M. Antoni quaestoris sui (Caesar) commendaverat sacerdoti petitionem'.

The quaestor's term of office commenced on 5th December (In Verr. I. 30, with Schol. Gronov.; Lex Corn. de XX Quaest. *C. I. L.* i. 108), and it has been argued, on the strength of the above references in the *Bellum Gallicum*, that Antony's quaestorship ran from December 52 to December 51 (Mommsen, *St. R.* i. 534 n. 1; Groebe-Drumann, i². 401; iii². 698; cf. Rice Holmes, *De Bell. Gall.*, p. 393). In connexion with viii. 46, 4 it is pointed out that the Roman calendar was in 51 B.C. over a month ahead of the astronomical: *quaestoris sui* in viii. 50 is explained by Groebe as a reference to a 'past relationship'.

This conclusion would be irresistible were it not for 'quo quidem tempore P. Clodium . . . es conatus occidere'. Clodius was killed in January 52, and Antony could not have offered to kill him while standing for the quaestorship towards the end of that year; nor could Cicero venture on such a palpable falsification of facts.

I cannot reconcile the evidence in the *Bellum Gallicum* with Cicero's statement here. Surprisingly enough, the discrepancy has not, as far as I know, been noticed. (In Groebe-Drumann, i². 48 it is stated that Antony came to Rome to canvass for the quaestorship in 53, and was quaestor in 52. But in the margin 5th December 52–5th December 51 is given as his term of office, and this statement is upheld in iii². 698, where, however, 9th December is given.)

parentem] Julia.

satis fieri . . . a te] Intimacy with Clodius (§ 48) required an apology from Antony; and there may have been more, of which we know nothing. On the other side of the account stood Cicero's execution of Lentulus.

P. Clodium . . . occidere]. Cf. § 21.

50. sine senatus consulto . . . cucurristi] Normally the new quaestors drew lots for the various provinces at the *aerarium*, perhaps on the day on which they entered office. 'Apud aerarium sortiri provincias et quaestores solebant et scribae' (Schol. ad Cic. in Clod. et Cur.). The drawing of lots was authorized by a s. c., 'Quaestor ex senatus consulto provinciam sortitus es' (Verr. II. i, 34). But occasionally a special s. c. allowed a governor to choose his own quaestor, or perhaps assigned him an individual at his request. '. . . cuius eo anno quaestoris extra sortem ex s. c. opera utebatur' (Liv. xxx. 33). In A. vi. 6, 4 Cicero couples Caesar's choice of Antony with Pompey's choice of Q. Cassius without suggestion of irregularity. 'Pompeius . . . Q. Cassium sine sorte delegit, Caesar Antonium', and Q. F. i. 1, 11 implies that choice was not infrequently allowed: 'Quaestorem habes non tuo iudicio delectum, sed eum quem sors dedit.' In the present passage Cicero clearly mentions s. c. as an alternative to *sors* (as in Liv. loc. cit.), not as a preliminary to it (as in Verr. loc. cit.).

I can find no instance of a quaestor being assigned *lege* to a particular province. (Mommsen, *St. R.* ii. 1, 532–4; Greenidge *R.P.L.* 213.)

Id enim . . . perfugium] Cicero says in A. vii. 3, 5 (9th December 50) that disgraced and ruined men were flocking to Caesar in great numbers. 'Largitionibus et rapinis' sounds very well, but the ethics of Roman warfare did not forbid looting.

effundas] Opportunities for extravagance were not lacking at Caesar's headquarters. (Q.F. iii. 1, 22; Suet. Iul. 46; 48.)

tribunatum] Antony entered on his office on 10th December, 50 (Mommsen, *St. R.* i. 604), and on 21st December delivered a violent speech attacking Pompey's whole career (A. vii. 8, 5). (Cicero omits to mention Antony's election to the augurate, perhaps because he has already noticed it in § 4.)

51. L. Lentulo C. Marcello consulibus] On 1st January 49 Curio handed to the senate Caesar's ultimatum, in which he said that he was ready to lay down his imperium if Pompey did the same; but that, while Pompey retained his army, he also was compelled to provide for his own safety. The consuls refused to submit these terms specifically to the senate for discussion, but opened a debate on the general political situation. On the following day the senate carried a motion proposed by Scipio, Pompey's father-in-law, that Caesar should be declared a public enemy unless he disbanded his army before 1st March (probably). Two tribunes, Antony and Q. Cassius Longinus, vetoed the resolution: a debate was opened on the validity of the veto, and adjourned at nightfall. On the 5th the debate was resumed: finally, on the 7th, the senate ordered Antony and Cassius to provide for their own safety, and passed the 'senatus consultum ultimum'. The same night the two tribunes left Rome for Caesar's head-quarters (Caes. B. C. 1–5; Rice Holmes, ii. 265–9).

In te . . . senatus] The terms of the 's. c. ultimum' seem to have varied slightly on different occasions (Mommsen, *St. R.* i. 694, n. 6). The formula used on the present occasion is given in F. xvi. 11, 2: 'postea quam senatus consulibus, praetoribus, tribunis plebis et nobis, qui pro consulibus sumus, negotium dederat ut curaremus ne quid res publica detrimenti caperet.' Cf. Caes. B. C. i. 7.

52. unus adulescens] Antony was perhaps thirty-two at the time (see § 16). Strictly speaking, *adulescens* came between *puer* and *iuvenis*, the term covering the years 15 to 25 or 30. But *adulescens* is often used for *iuvenis*. See § 113 (Brutus and Cassius); § 118 (of Cicero in the year 63, aged forty-three). See further L. and S., s.v. *adulescens*. *Unus* ignores the fact that Q. Cassius Longinus also interposed his veto.

53. Quid enim . . . Antonius] Caesar made much of this point in his address to the troops at Ravenna at the beginning of the Civil War (B. C. i. 7): 'Novum in rem publicam introductum exemplum queritur, ut tribunicia intercessio armis vetaretur atque opprimeretur. . . . Sullam nudata omnibus rebus tribunicia potestate tamen intercessionem liberam reliquisse.'

But on this occasion Caesar also 'omnium temporum iniurias inimicorum in se commemorat'. In his subsequent speech to the senate he mentioned as grievances, besides the treatment of the tribunes, the unfriendly way in which Pompey had demanded the return of the borrowed legion, and the senate's refusal to pay any attention to his proposals (B. C. i. 32).

For rhetorical purposes Cicero magnifies the importance of one particular *casus belli*.

circumscriptus] Almost technical in the sense of impeding a magistrate in the exercise of his functions. Cf. Mil. 88; Phil. xiii. 19. In A. vii. 9, 2 and Caes. B. C. i. 32 the word is used in reference to the present occasion.

54. consules . . . Pompeium] The consuls sailed from Brundisium for Dyrrachium on 4th March, 49 (Caes. B. C. i. 25; A. ix. 6, 3). Pompey followed on 17th March (A. ix. 15, 6). Cicero sharply criticized the evacuation of Rome and Italy, failing to appreciate that it was a military necessity (A. vii. 13 a; ix. 9, 2; 10, 2). Probably Cicero's account of the exodus from Italy is not much exaggerated. Dio (xli. 9, 7) says: *Πομπήιος . . . τὸ ἄστυ ἐξέλιπε, συχνοὺς τῶν βουλευτῶν ἐπαγόμενος, ὑπελείφθησαν γάρ τινες*—Caesar carried on government as best he could with the rump. Later on (xli. 43, 2) Dio says that the Pompeian government at Thessalonica included nearly 200 senators. Moreover, probably many who left Rome did not cross the Adriatic. Plutarch's rather vague statement (Pomp. 64) *τῶν ἀπὸ Ῥώμης ἡγεμονικῶν ἀριθμὸς ἦν ἐντελοῦς βουλῆς περὶ αὐτόν* does not help us much.

In the *Pro Rege Deiotaro*, delivered before Caesar in November 45, Cicero draws an entirely different picture: 'Maxime vero perturbatus est, ut audivit consules ex Italia profugisse, omnis consularis—sic enim ei nuntiabatur—cunctum senatum, totam Italiam effusam. Talibus enim nuntiis et rumoribus patebat ad orientem via, nec ulli veri subsequebantur' (§ 11).

omnis . . . potuissent] Yet Cicero himself remained in Italy nearly three months after the departure of the Pompeian forces (§ 37, note on *Castra . . . tempus*).

Among prominent senators who remained in Rome were P. Servilius Isauricus, L. Volcatius, and Serv. Sulpicius Rufus, the last of whom actually supported Caesar.

55. tris exercitus] The armies defeated at Pharsalus, Thapsus, and Munda.

clarissimos civis] See § 37, note on *tot . . . exercitus*.

Vt Helena . . . fuit] Plutarch (Ant. 6) contemptuously dismisses this absurdity.

scelus in scelere] By restoring exiles broadcast, yet not restoring his uncle, Antony made a wicked exception to a wicked rule. For his restoration of exiles cf. A. x. 13, 1 (May, 49): 'exulibus reditum pollicetur.'

patrui] C. Antonius Hybrida, Cicero's colleague in the consulship. On his return from the governorship of Macedonia, 62–60, he was prosecuted for extortion. Cicero defended him, and by an injudicious political observation at the trial precipitated his own banishment (Dom. 41). Hybrida was condemned and exiled. Why Antony did not recall him in 49 we cannot say. But from A. x. 4, 8 and Caes. B.C. iii. 1 it appears that only persons exiled under the 'Lex Pompeia de Ambitu' were recalled at that time. He was recalled subsequently, either in 47 (cf. Dio xliii. 27, 2) or in 45 (cf. App. ii. 107). See Halm's Introd. n. 4: at any rate he returned before 1st January 44, when he was sitting in the senate (§ 99).

56. Licinium Lenticulam de alea condemnatum] Nothing else is known of Lenticula.

Laws against gambling were passed at an early period. Plaut. Mil. Glor. 164 'legi . . . aleariae'; Hor. Od. iii. 24, 58 'vetita legibus alea'; Ov. Trist ii. 472 (alea) 'ad nostros non leve crimen avos'. Pseud.-Asconius (In Div. 24) gives the penalty as *quadruplum*. In later times certain exceptions were allowed, e.g. at the Saturnalia, or in the case of manly sports (P.-W. s. v. *Alea*).

restituit] This must mean 'restored to his civil rights', as the following words show that Lenticula was not in exile.

quasi vero . . . non liceret] An excuse (hence *quasi vero*) attributed to Antony: humorously attributed, of course. What reason Antony in fact urged we do not know.

Nihil . . . ad rem] Because this plea does not, like the rest, affect the legality of the verdict. It could only be a ground for mitigation of sentence.

vel in foro alea ludere] Peskett compares De Off. iii. 75 'in foro saltaret'; ib. i. 145, 'in foro cantet'. Prof. Sihler observes that people appear to have played some game on the floor of the Basilica Iulia, where circles may be seen scratched.

studium suum] 'His predilection for gambling.' Sihler refers to A. xiv. 5, 1, where Antony is perhaps called *aleator* (the reading is doubtful).

57. Caesar in Hispaniam proficiscens] In the spring of 49. (He reached Massilia about 19th April: Rice Holmes, iii. 48.) He left Lepidus behind as governor of Rome, and Antony, with the rank of propraetor, as governor of Italy (App. ii. 41; Plut. Ant. 6; A. x. 8 a).

quae fuit, etc.] For Antony's behaviour in Caesar's absence see Plut. Ant. 6. For an amusing instance of the contempt with which he treated local officials see A. x. 13, 1. 'Attende πρᾶξιν πολιτικοῦ. Evocavit litteris e municipiis decem primos et IIIIviros. Venerunt ad villam eius mane. Primum dormiit ad h. III, deinde, cum esset nuntiatum venisse Neapolitanos et Cumanos (his enim est Caesar iratus), postridie redire iussit; lavari se velle et περὶ κοιλιολυσίαν γίνεσθαι.' Cf. § 106. He was, however, very pleasant to Cicero personally (A. x. 13, 1).

omnibus . . . fuerunt] Yet, according to § 54, everybody who counted had left Italy.

qui non fui] In point of fact, Cicero was in Italy till 7th June (§ 37, first note), and had good opportunities in May for observing Antony's behaviour, as the letters show.

58. essedo] Originally a war-chariot, used in Gallia Belgica and Britain. As Mayor remarks, it furnishes Cicero with several jokes in the letters to Trebatius. F. vii. 6, 2 'ne ab essedariis decipiaris caveto'; 7, 1 '(in Britannia) essedum aliquod capias suadeo et ad nos quam primum recurras'; 10, 2. Subsequently used by the Romans as a carriage. We know little of the *essedum*, or the modifications introduced in it when converted to peaceable purposes. It was a favourite type of vehicle among fashionable ladies, sometimes richly ornamented, and later among the Roman emperors; and apparently it was a particularly noisy one (P.-W., s. v. *Essedum*; Blümner, 460–2). For Antony's equipage in general cf. A. vi. 1, 25: 'Hic Vedius mihi obviam venit cum duobus essedis et raeda equis iuncta et lectica et familia magna'.

lictores] Cicero seems to be objecting to a tribune having lictors; but they accompanied Antony as propraetor. *Laureati*, with laurel leaves on their *fasces*, the privilege of victorious generals. Consuls and proconsuls had twelve *fasces* each: praetors and propraetors six. Cf. A. x. 4, 9 (of Curio, in 49, newly-appointed propraetor of Sicily).

inter . . . portabatur] A. x. 16, 5: 'Antonius cuius inter lictores lectica mima portatur.' The fact that it was an open litter made the shamelessness of the proceeding more flagrant. Cytheris behaved like the lady in Apuleius (Apol. 76): 'improba iuvenum circumspectatrix, immodica sui ostentatrix.' See also A. x. 10, 5.

For *Cytheris* see § 30, note on *uxore*; for *lectica* see § 82, note.

raeda] The *raeda*, which, like the *essedum*, was of Gallic origin, was a large four-wheeled carriage for leisurely, comfortable travelling. Where speed was essential, the *cisium* (§ 77) was employed (Blümner, 460).

lenonibus] Plin. N. H. viii. 55: 'iugo subdidit eos (leones) primusque Romae ad currum iunxit M. Antonius, et quidem civili bello, cum dimicatum esset in Pharsaliis campis . . . ita vectus est cum mima Cytheride . . .' A. x. 13, 1 (May, 49) 'Tu Antoni leones pertimescas cave'. Cf. Plut. Ant. 9; Babelon, I, 168 (coins). These passages, in spite of the discrepancy in dates, lend some support to the variant *leonibus* here (read apparently by Pliny). If *leonibus* is right, *comites nequissimi* must go. But is it conceivable that lions could be so tamed?

fecunditatem calamitosam] I think Prof. Sihler is right in seeing a reference to Antony's brothers Lucius and Gaius, for whom he cites Phil. vi. 10–15; vii. 3; x. 5; xi. 36; xii. 17–18.

municipia, praefecturas, colonias] I am indebted to Mr. H. M. D. Parker for the following note:

'By the end of the Republic there was no difference of legal status between these three groups of states. The enfranchising laws of 90 and 89 B. C. had put all Italy south of the Po on an uniform basis of Roman citizenship, and the Lex Roscia of 49 extended this privilege to Transpadane Gaul. Consequently it was immaterial from the legal standpoint whether a community had started as a colony of Roman citizens or as a town composed, for example, of Etruscans or Umbrians. The words "coloniae, municipia and praefecturae" are used by Cicero merely with reference to the historical origin of different states: in itself the expression means little more than "the country towns of Italy".

The history of the words may be briefly summarized. After the end of the Latin War in 338 B. C. Rome adopted a twofold policy in extending her sovereignty in Italy. Either she admitted the states which she conquered to a share in her citizenship, or she formed treaties with individual communities by which they remained outside her citizenship but were obliged to have the same foreign policy as Rome, and to furnish troops for her army. This latter class had the general title of *Civitates foederatae*, and it was from these states that the political agitation emanated which resulted in the Social War. The former class comprised *coloniae*, *municipia*, and *praefecturae*, and the difference between these three groups was as follows:

1. *Coloniae* were settlements of Roman citizens established by Rome as *praesidia imperii*. They had the full citizenship and probably enjoyed from the beginning local autonomy.

2. *Municipia* has two distinct meanings. To start with, it is a collective term for towns possessing incomplete Roman rights; it finishes by meaning towns with the full Roman franchise. In the initial stage *municipia* had the *civitas sine suffragio*, and a further disability was that they were obliged to submit their lawsuits to a representative of the *Praetor Urbanus* who was called a *praefectus*. From this position of dependence upon Roman officials some states, like Formiae and Fundi, emerged quickly, and became *municipia* in the second sense of the word; other communities, like Anagnia, remained for a longer time without local autonomy, but the transition seems to have been affected in most, if not all, cases, before 90 B.C. Thus in the age of Cicero *municipia* are Italian towns possessing the full franchise, and, while incorporated in the *Civitas Romana*, are *res publicae* with local autonomy. This explains how Cicero can describe himself as 'Civis Romanus et municeps Arpinas', because *Arpinum*, while enjoying the local self-government of a *res publica*, is not a separate *civitas*, but her *municipes* are citizens of Rome.

3. *Praefecturae*, like *municipia*, has two meanings. It may be used to describe towns to which the *Praetor Urbanus* sent his *praefectus* for judicial purposes each year, or it may be applied to the ten Campanian towns which after 211 B.C. were reduced to complete dependence upon Rome for the part they played in the Second Punic War, and to which four *praefecti* elected annually by the *Comitia Tributa* were sent for administrative purposes. In the former definition (which is probably that used by Cicero in this passage) *praefecturae* are equivalent to *municipia* in the sense of towns possessing incomplete Roman rights, and it is probably true to say that all *municipia* in one stage of their history were *praefecturae*. This implies that *praefecturae* disappeared as *municipia* attained complete Roman rights, and they are not found after 90 B.C. except at Reate and Amiturnae, which for some unknown reason seem to have preferred to have their cases tried by a Roman *praefectus* (Dess. 6543 and 3701). In the second sense *praefecturae* survive in Campania till 20 B.C., after which date *praefecti* ceased to be sent from Rome.

(See Festus in Bruns, vol ii. svv. *municipium* and *praefectura*; Liv. xxxviii. 36 for Fundi and Formiae; Liv. ix. 43 for Anagnia; Sest. 32 for similar use of the terms to this passage; Hardy, *Six Roman Laws*.)'

59. Reliquorum factorum] Antony sailed from Dyrrachium with reinforcements towards the end of March, 48, and after a perilous voyage landed at Nymphaeum (San Giovanni di Medua). He then marched south and joined Caesar (Rice Holmes, iii. 129–32). At Pharsalus he commanded the left wing (§ 71 note on *antesignanus*).

veteranis] For the importance of the veterans as a political factor Sihler cites F. xi. 1; Phil. x. 18; xi. 37–8. Cf. also F. xii. 2, 1.

quamquam] Picked up by *tamen*.

tu quaesisti ducem] There may be something in this distinction. But, after all, Antony owed some loyalty to a commander whom he had served for over four years.

Ibi me non occidisti] With characteristic inconsistency Cicero reverts to the admission he made in i, 11, but retracted in § 5.

60. licuitne . . . tuebar] Either (1) stressing 'per tuas contumelias', 'did your insults allow me to regard your kindness as I did regard it', i. e. 'your insults nearly, but not quite, made me forget my gratitude'. So Peskett. Or (2) 'could I go on regarding, as I did at first regard'. So King. I prefer the first rendering. The second reads rather too much into the imperfect.

praesertim cum] 'Referring to "per tuas contumelias", affronts which were the more wanton as you knew that I could retaliate' (Halm-Mayor).

61. tot dierum viam] Halm[a] estimates the journey from Rome to Brundisium at 10–14 days; Peskett at 13–15. The distance is about 370 miles.

62. auri . . . direptio] Meyer, p. 372, explains the confiscation of gold and silver as the carrying out of Caesar's law forbidding any person to possess more than 15,000 denarii in gold or silver coin (Dio, xli. 38, 1).

Accessit . . . constitueretur] The dates of Caesar's second nomination as dictator and Antony's nomination as *Magister Equitum* have been much discussed. See Groebe-Drumann, i². 404–6; Ferrero, ii. 253; Meyer, 370; Rice Holmes, iii. 565. Caesar reached Alexandria on 2nd October 48 (Rice Holmes, iii. 180). If we may trust Dio (xlii. 35, 5: cf. Liv. Ep. 112), Caesar had already heard of his appointment when he gave his award in the dispute between Cleopatra and Ptolemy, probably about the end of October (Rice Holmes, iii. 565). The arguments by which Groebe seeks to prove that Caesar was not nominated till after Antony's return to Rome (second half of October) seem to me insufficient. Still weaker are the grounds on which Meyer puts the nomination as late as the end of November.

Constitutionally, the dictator appointed his own Master of Horse, though there are exceptions: Liv. viii. 17, 3; xxii. 57, 9. But Caesar's inaccessibility made the situation exceptional. No doubt, his friends in Rome knew whom he wished appointed. But *Caesare ignaro*, though some scholars have brushed it aside, contains, I think, this much of truth, that Antony was appointed at the same time as Caesar, without the latter being formally consulted (in spite of Dio, xlii. 21, 1 τὸν Ἀντώνιον μηδ' ἐστρατηγηκότα ἵππαρχον προσελόμενος. That passage is the only evidence that having held the praetorship was a necessary qualification for a *Magister Equitum*).

Tum existimavit . . . tradere] Editors cite four passages:

(1) Liv. xxiv. 18, 10: 'Cum censores ob inopiam aerarii se iam locationibus abstinerent aedium sacrarum tuendarum curuliumque equorum praebendorum ac similium his rerum . . .'

(2) Ascon. in Orat. in Tog. Cand. 83: 'Praeterea Antonius (*sc.* Gaius) redemptas habebat ab aerario vectigales quadrigas, quam redemptionem senatori habere licet per legem.'

(3) Dio, lv. 10, 5: Augustus in arranging the games to Mars Ultor, ordained τὴν παράσχεσιν τῶν ἵππων τῶν ἐς τὴν ἱπποδρομίαν ἀγωνιουμένων καὶ βουλευταῖς ἐργολαβεῖν ἐξεῖναι.

(4) Festus ep., p. 49: 'Curules equi vectigales.'

But *vectigales* is only a conjecture: and the latest editor of Festus (Lindsay, 1913) retains the MSS. *quadrigales* (p. 43).

From (1), (2), and (3) it seems clear that the responsible officials invited contracts for the supply of horses for chariot races at the public games; that (for certain occasions, at any rate) senators were allowed to tender such contracts; and that the teams were called *vectigales quadrigae*. Why the word *vectigalis*, which otherwise means 'in payment of a tax' or 'subject to a tax', is used in this connexion does not appear: the sense 'bringing in profit', given by some editors to the word here, is not attested.

Antony seems to have done one of two things. Either he tendered a contract for supplying horses, nominally on his own account, but actually as the representative of Sergius, whose status did not permit him to tender in person. Or he made Sergius a present of the horses after the games were over. It must be admitted that the difficulty of making *equos vectigalis* equivalent to *redemptionem equorum vectigalium* goes against the former interpretation.

(Abram's explanation, quoted by King, that *equos vectigalis* means horses supplied as tribute by conquered nations, as the Cilicians paid a tribute of horses to Darius (Hdt. 3. 90), gives a natural sense to *vectigalis*, but ignores the technical sense of that word which Asconius clearly implies.)

In either case, the point of the poor pun is that it was natural for the *Magister Equitum* (ἵππαρχος in Greek) to be concerned in shady horse-dealing and to be intimate with Hippias the mimic actor (Plut. Ant. 9): the second half of the joke being improved by the fact that Peisistratus's sons were named Hippias and Hipparchus.

hanc . . . tuetur] Pompey's house, which Antony subsequently purchased (§ 67). Pompey's son Sextus continued desultory hostilities in Spain for some time after Caesar's murder. In negotiating with Antony he made it a *sine qua non* that his father's property should be restored to him (A. xvi. 4, 2). The matter had apparently not yet been settled. Hence *male tuetur*. *Male* is used for the more usual *aegre*.

M. Pisonis] M. Pupius Piso, consul in 61.

L. Rubrio . . . L. Turselio] See § 41.

heres] Sarcastic. 'As he didn't pay, he can't have been a purchaser. Therefore presumably he must have been an heir.'

63. In coetu . . . magister equitum] Quintilian (viii. 4, 8) admires the climax. Each successive word adds fresh force.

64. Caesar Alexandrea se recepit] Caesar left Alexandria on about 7th June, 47 (Rice Holmes, iii. 204). He spent the summer in the conquest of Asia Minor, in spite of his friends' urgent request that he should return to Italy at once. He landed at Tarentum in the last week of September, and was met by Cicero (F. xv. 15, 3). The two returned to Rome together and put up on the way at Cicero's house at Tusculum. Cicero wrote rather a curt note to his wife (F. xiv. 20), asking her to get everything ready in advance, particularly the bath-room.

Hasta posita] A spear was always stuck in the ground at a Roman auction, perhaps because the earliest auctions were sales of booty captured in war.

Iovis Statoris] 'Iuppiter the Stablisher of the battle line.' We hear of other similar cults of Iuppiter in his military aspect: 'Iuppiter Versor', 'Iuppiter Depulsor', 'Iuppiter Territor'. A temple of Iuppiter Stator was consecrated by M. Atilius Regulus in 294, in the Third Samnite War, on the Nova Via. Another tradition ascribes the foundation of this temple to Romulus, at the time of the Sabine War. A second temple to Iuppiter Stator was consecrated by Q. Caecilius Metellus Macedonicus in 146, near the Circus Flaminius (see Wissowa, p. 122).

acerbissimae] Combines, I think, the ideas 'rasping' and 'cruel'.

inventus . . . Antonium] Very probably exaggerated, but Phil. xiii. 11–12 does not disprove Cicero's words, as some commentators maintain. In that passage Cicero is speaking of those into whose hands the property passed, by gift or sale (§ 67). Antony never thought he would have to pay. Cf. Dio, xlii. 50, 5.

praesertim cum] 'And that too, although.'

65. poetam nescio quem] Naevius. See Festus, p. 248, Lindsay; Ribbeck, *Trag. Fragm. Inc. Nom. Rel.* 1.

67. animal] It is impossible to say what animal. Charybdis plays but a slight part in mythology. Homer, who describes Scylla in detail, only says of Charybdis (Od. xii. 104–5):

> *τῷ δ' ὑπὸ δῖα Χάρυβδις ἀναρροιβδεῖ μέλαν ὕδωρ.*
> *τρὶς μὲν γάρ τ' ἀνίησιν ἐπ' ἤματι, τρὶς δ' ἀναροιβδεῖ.*

Ovid in the *Metamorphoses* (xiii. 730–1) is equally vague. Later mythology makes Charybdis the daughter of Poseidon and Ge.

me dius fidius] Originally Iuppiter in his capacity of 'Defender of good faith' (*fides*). Compare the Greek cult of Ζεὺς Πίστιος. Afterwards worshipped as a separate and independent deity. His temple, on the Quirinal hill, was consecrated on 5th June 466. An old etymology, followed by some modern authorities, explains Dius Fidius as = Diovis Filius, 'Son of Iuppiter', and identifies the god with Hercules, and the oath with *mehercle*. (For the interchange of *d* and *l* compare *lacrima* from δάκρυμα, and *lingua* from the old Latin *dingua*.) But a recently discovered statue of Dius Fidius bears no resemblance to extant representations of Hercules. (See Wissowa, pp. 129–31.)

Apothecae] Store rooms for wine, often placed in smoky places, smoke being supposed to assist in maturing wine (Columella, i. 6, 20).

68. rostra] Captured, no doubt, from the pirates in 67. The house-entrance was often used for the display of such trophies. See Blümner, p. 14, n. 4.

69. Fuit . . . domesticis] Apart from rumours of a youthful liaison with one Flora (Plut. Pomp. 2), and the negligible obscenities of Clodius (ib. 48), Pompey's scrupulous chastity is attested by all ancient writers (ib. 1; 2; 18; 36; 53; Vell. ii. 69, 3; A. xi. 6, 5 'integrum et castum'). He married five times. The callousness with which he divorced his first wife, on political grounds, and married his second while pregnant by her first husband, shocked Plutarch (ib. 9). But for Julia and Cornelia, the fourth and fifth, he seems to have felt real affection.

suas res sibi habere iussit] Gaius (Dig. xxiv. 2, 2, 1) gives, as the formula of divorce, 'tuas res tibi habeto', or 'tuas res tibi agito'. Juvenal's *collige sarcinulas* (vi. 146) is a comic variant. *Vade* or *exi foras* seems to have been an alternative formula (Varro ap. Non. 77, 16; Plaut. Cas. 212; Blümner, p. 363, n. 6).

duodecim tabulis] Rome's first legal code, known as the 'Twelve Tables', was drawn up by successive decemvirates in 451 and 450. Schoolboys in Cicero's boyhood had to learn the Tables by heart (De Leg. ii. 59). Gaius' treatise (second century A. D.) was a commentary on them. (Greenidge, *R.P.L.* 102–5).

clavis ademit] Cf. Ambros. Epist. 6, 3: 'mulier offensa clavis remisit, domum revertit.' Apparently the custom was as old as the Twelve Tables. Another piece of ceremonial was the destruction of the marriage bond. 'Rumperet tabulas nuptialis' (Tac. Ann. xi. 30; Juv. ix. 75).

cum mima fecit divortium] The whole application of the technical formulae of divorce to Antony's casting off his mistress is of course sarcastic. Cf. § 20 *mima uxore*.

70. et consul et Antonius] I think Antony used this expression, not as a mere variant of the formal 'M. Antonius consul', but as a grandiloquent phrase 'I, a consul and an Antony' (as Peskett renders it). Cicero, however, affects to regard the expression as a variant of the formula, and asks why M. Antonius the Orator and

C. Antonius Hybrida (i. 27 and § 55) never used it. *Quam crebro* is probably exaggerated.

partium] 'Role,' I think, like *partis* below. I do not think there is any double entendre, 'role' and 'political party', as some have supposed.

timiditatem] A ridiculous charge. Random misinterpretation of this kind, which can have deceived nobody, greatly impairs the effect of the Philippics.

71. antesignanus] The meaning of the term *antesignanus* has been much disputed. See *Dict. Ant.* i. 807–8; ii. 672–3; von Domaszewski in P.-W., s.v. Antesignani; Rice Holmes, iii. 391–7.

There can be no doubt that in the pre-Marian army the *antesignani* were identical with the *hastati*, the first of the three lines in which Roman armies were then normally deployed. Livy's evidence (viii. 11, 7; ix. 39, 7; xxii. 5, 7) is conclusive on this point; and Frontinus, ii. 3, 17 shows that the term *antesignani* bore the same meaning as late as 86 B.C.

But what meaning did it bear in Caesar's time? Rice Holmes maintains that it still meant *prima acies*; or that it meant picked men selected from the *prima acies* (p. 392, ll. 22–4; p. 397, ll. 20–3). Other scholars have held that it meant the front rank, or two front ranks, of each line (a view which Rice Holmes shows to be untenable); or that it denoted a picked body of men who skirmished in front of the front line.

First of all, to what *signa* does the term refer: to the legionary *signa* (five to a legion in the pre-Marian, one to a legion in the post-Marian, army), which were stationed behind the first line: or to the manipular *signa*, which have been variously located in the front, second, last, or behind the last, rank of the various lines? At first sight the simplest view is that of Rice Holmes: that the reference is always, both before and after Marius, to the manipular *signa*; and that these *signa* were always stationed behind the first line. But there are difficulties. (1) Caesar's order at the battle of Ruspina (Bell. Afr. 15, 1), 'ne quis miles ab signis IIII pedes longius procederet', can hardly be understood without supposing the existence of standards in one of the two front ranks. It is true that *signum* (and its Greek equivalent σημαία) is sometimes used in the sense of maniple. But it is scarcely conceivable that a maniple in action would preserve a front regular enough to make intelligible the order that no one was to advance more than four feet 'in front of the maniple'. (Cf. also B. G. v. 34, 4; vi. 40, 1.)

(2) Vegetius (ii. 2) speaks of 'principes, hastatos, triarios, antesignanos', thus distinguishing between the *antesignani* and the first line (*hastati*).

(3) *Antesignani* are mentioned five times in the *Bellum Civile* (i. 43, 3; 44, 5; 57, 1; iii. 75, 5; 84, 3), but never in the *Bellum Gallicum*. And they are mentioned in the *Bellum Civile* in such a manner as to make probable von Domaszewski's suggestion that

they were a picked corps organized by Caesar as a counterpoise to Pompey's cavalry, to operate in advance of, or in detachment from, the legion, frequently dispensing with their heavy equipment. This view is supported by evidence showing that in imperial times they were regularly light-armed: (1) the expression *arma antesignana* in an inscription of the second century A.D.; (2) a sepulchral monument of Tiberius's reign, depicting a Roman legionary in light armour.

We must assume, then, two distinct meanings of *antesignani*, in Livy and in Caesar. And it seems reasonable to conclude that in Caesar's army the manipular *signa* were stationed in the front rank, to give the dressing. (Mr. H. M. D. Parker suggests to me that, after Marius had substituted for the legion's five *signa* a single standard, designated *aquila* in contradistinction to the manipular *signa*, the term *antesignani*, as denoting the front line (troops fighting in front of *legionary signa*), would naturally pass out of use. It could then be reintroduced by Caesar, in a new signification, to denote a flying body of picked troops (fighting in front of *manipular signa*), used for skirmishing or for special duties.)

In describing Antony as an *antesignanus* Cicero is of course speaking figuratively. Antony commanded the left wing at Pharsalus (Plut. Ant. 8). For the metaphorical use of the word cf. Ascon. in Mil. 28, 'antesignanus servorum eius'.

L. Domitium] § 27, note.

in Africam . . . sequerere] Caesar left Rome towards the end of November, 47 (Rice Holmes, iii. 236; about 1st December, Meyer, p. 382: he arrived at Lilybaeum on 17th December and sailed for Africa on 25th, Bell. Afr. 1, 1). He got back to Rome, after the campaign of Thapsus, on 25th July 46 (Bell. Afr. 98, 2).

The breach between Caesar and Antony.

It is credible enough that Antony was indignant at having to pay for Pompey's property. Caesar on his side had reason to be dissatisfied with Antony's conduct in 47. His behaviour had lowered Caesar's prestige in the eyes of moderate men (Plut. Ant. 6); he had failed to suppress a serious mutiny; and he had quelled riots in the capital, consequent upon Dolabella's proposal for the abolition of debt (i. 30, note), with what Caesar may have thought unnecessary bloodshed. (There seems, however, little evidence for Ferrero's view (ii. 263) that Caesar definitely moved to the 'left' at this juncture, and consequently inclined to Dolabella rather than to Antony.)

Whatever the cause of the estrangement, it undoubtedly occurred. Antony did not serve in the African campaign, whether because Caesar did not offer him a command, or because he was unwilling to accept it (Plut. Ant. 10, *καί φησιν αὐτὸς διὰ τοῦτο* (Caesar's request for payment) *μὴ μετασχεῖν Καίσαρι τῆς εἰς Λιβύην στρατείας*, for whatever it may be worth, is in support of the second supposition, which Cicero here adopts). After the campaign, when Caesar was appointed Dictator for the third time, he chose Lepidus, not Antony, as his *Magister Equitum* (Plut. Ant. 10).

testamento . . . filius] As Meyer points out (p. 380, n. 1), Nicolas of Damascus (21, fin.) says that, according to one account, the hope of being adopted by Caesar was Antony's motive for offering him the diadem at the Lupercalia (§§ 84–7). Antony was named in Caesar's will as one of the 'second heirs' (the persons to whom the inheritance passed in the event of the original heirs failing to inherit), Dio, xliv. 35, 2.

72. leges perniciosas] Cf. Dio, xli. 17, 3 (of April 49) διὰ τοῦ Ἀντωνίου τὰ πλείω αὐτῶν ἐσεφέρετο.

73. partem Miseni] § 48.

risus] There was also humour in the fact that Antony was selling Pompey's property in order to pay for it.

74. heredes L. Rubri] See § 41. Cicero appears to use *heredes* somewhat loosely here, for the persons passed over in Rubrius' will. They seem to have contested the legality of Antony's inheritance. Why they interposed on this occasion is not clear. Perhaps Antony included some of Rubrius' property in the sale.

percussor ab isto missus] There is no corroboration of this, but, whether or not Antony was guilty, Cicero would hardly have ventured on the statement 'de quo Caesar in senatu . . . questus est' if Caesar had not acted so.

Proficiscitur in Hispaniam Caesar] Towards the end of 46. The date cannot be exactly fixed (Rice Holmes, iii. 541–2).

rudem tam cito?] *Rudis* was the wooden sword used by gladiators in the training-school. When a gladiator was discharged, he was presented with a *rudis*. Hence the discharged were called *rudiarii* (Hor. Ep. i. 1, 2; Ov. Am. ii. 9, 22; Juv. vii. 171; Mart. iii. 36, 10; Suet. Tib. 7).

For the expression 'gladiator' applied to Antony cf. § 7, note on 'uno gladiatore nequissimo'.

75. tuto . . . pervenire non potuit] He only got as far as Narbo, as the sequel shows. We do not know what the danger was.

Dolabella] Atticus, on reading the speech before publication, seems to have objected to this eulogy of Dolabella. Cicero writes on the 5th November 44 (A. xvi. 11, 2): 'De laudibus Dolabellae deruam cumulum. Ac tamen est isto loco bella, ut mihi videtur, εἰρωνεία, quod eum ter contra cives in acie' (afterwards altered to 'ter depugnavit Caesar cum civibus'). The words 'Si de meo iudicio . . . reprehendendum' may be part of the toning down.

Cn. Pompei liberi] The elder, Gnaeus, commanded the Pompeian forces in Spain until shortly after the battle of Munda, 17th March 45, when he was killed. The younger, Sextus, continued to carry on guerrilla warfare.

larem suum familiarem] See § 62, note on 'hanc . . . tuetur'.

76. Narbone reditus] The anecdote which follows is recounted, with slight additional touches, by Plutarch (Ant. 10).

ante Kalendas Ianuarias] Cf. i. 6-10.

quo modo] A variant for *cur* above, providing an excuse for describing the *circumstances* of Antony's return.

nullis nec Gallicis nec lacerna] The best commentary on this is a passage in Aulus Gellius (xiii. 22), where he describes how a certain T. Castricius, a teacher of rhetoric in Hadrian's reign, rebuked some senatorial pupils of his for appearing on a holiday 'tunicis et lacernis indutos et gallicis calciatos'. Castricius could pardon them for leaving off their togas, a laxity sanctioned by custom, but not for walking about the streets *soleati*: and he took occasion to remind them of our passage. They asked him why he spoke of them as *soleati*, when they were wearing *Gallicae*, not *soleae*. But Castricius spoke correctly, Gellius says: anything covering only the sole and the base of the heel was a *solea* (also styled *crepida* or *crepidula*, after the Greek κρηπίς): *Gallicae* was a new word, just introduced in Cicero's day: Gellius could not find it in any other author of repute. Diocletian, in his edict (ix. 12), mentions several varieties of *gallicae*: 'gallicae viriles rusticanae bisoles; gallicae viriles monosoles; gallicae cursoriae; gallicae muliebres'.

Old-fashioned Romans were conservative in these respects. It was a charge against the elder Scipio that he used 'cum pallio crepidisque inambulare in gymnasio' (Liv. xxix. 19, 12). One of the minor crimes of Verres was that he stood on the shore of Sicily 'soleatus cum pallio purpureo tunicaque talari' (Verr. II. v. 86). The drunken Piso emerged from his hovel 'involuto capite, soleatus' (Pis. 13). And finally Caligula was noted for a catholic taste in foot-wear (Suet. Cal. 52).

Soleae were worn indoors; out of doors, correct Romans wore the *calceus*, a kind of boot covering part of the upper part of the foot. It is remarkable that Antony should have chosen to wear sandals on a long journey in March. Zahn (P.-W., s.v. *Gallicae*) thinks that he wore the shoes in Gallia Narbonensis because of their Gallic origin. The *lacerna* was a cloak probably provided with a hood (*cucullus*), and fastened with a buckle (*fibula*) over the right shoulder. It could be worn over the toga, as a protection against rain. It was probably a novelty in Cicero's day, being first mentioned in our passage, but afterwards became very popular, and Augustus prohibited its use in the Forum (Suet. Aug. 40).

(*Dict. Ant.*, s.vv. *calceus*, *solea*, *lacerna*; P.-W., s.vv. *Gallicae*, *Lacerna*; Blümner, pp. 215, 222-4).

fuisse viderere] A reference, I think, to the supposed irregularity of Antony's appointment (*Caesare ignaro*, § 62), rather than to his degradation of the office by improper behaviour.

peteres] 'Stand for' the consulship: *rogares*, 'ask Caesar for it as a favour'.

Galliae] For the importance of the Gallic vote in the elections King compares A. i. 1, 2: 'quoniam videtur in suffragiis multum posse Gallia.' (The reference is, of course, to *Cisalpine* Gaul.)

77. **Saxa rubra**] On the Via Flaminia, nine miles north of Rome. So called on account of the red volcanic rock found there.

cisio] A light two-wheeled vehicle, used for rapid travelling. Rosc. Am. 19: 'decem horis nocturnis sex et quinquaginta milia passuum cisiis pervolavit.' This does not seem a furious speed, particularly as the plural *cisiis* implies a change of vehicle; but the *raeda* (§ 58) went slower still (twenty-four miles a day, Hor. Sat. i. 5, 86). The drivers, *cisiarii*, had their cabs for hire in ranks at the gates of towns, and were organized in *collegia* (P.-W., s.v. *cisium*; Blümner, 459–60).

urbem . . . perturbasti] Doubtless an exaggeration. But there really was considerable uneasiness. Perhaps people inferred from Antony's return, as Drumann suggests, that the Civil War was over, and that Antony had been sent on in advance, to begin the long-dreaded proscriptions. Plutarch (Ant. 10) says that a rumour was current in Italy that Caesar was dead and the Pompeians marching on Rome. That would have been equally likely to cause a panic, and we need not necessarily reject Plutarch's explanation on the ground that he misdates Antony's return. (See § 34, note on 'et Narbone . . . cepisse'.) Cicero was at Astura when he received a letter from Caesar's friends Balbus and Oppius, informing him of Antony's return, and telling him not to be alarmed, a reflection on his courage which piqued him considerably. (A. xii. 18 a, 1; 19, 2; 20, 1, 13th to 15th March 45).

78. **L. Plancus**] One of the eight (perhaps six) *Praefecti Urbi* (an old title revived for the occasion) to whom Caesar nominally entrusted the home government on his departure for Spain. The real rulers of Rome during his absence were, however, Balbus and Oppius. (Meyer, pp. 429–30.) The duties normally performed by the Praetor Urbanus appear to have devolved upon Plancus.

praedes tuos venderet] This was the theory Cicero favoured at the time. 'Opinor propter praedes suos accucurrisse' (A. xii. 18 a, 1).

productus . . . in contionem] A private citizen could only address a public meeting (*contio*) if introduced by a magistrate (Greenidge, *R. P. L.* 159–60).

rei tuae causa] 'On business.' As *res* also means 'property', the joke may have lain in the fact that Antony had no property. I doubt any side reference to 'love affair' (King).

ex Hispania redeunti] See § 34, with note on *et Narbone . . . cepisse*. A combination of that section with Plut. Ant. 13 shows that *longissime* here = as far as Narbo.

isti, redisti] Editors compare 'irent, redirent' (§ 89) and 'itus, reditus' (A. xv. 5, 3). But what do the words mean? A reference to the speed of Antony's journey to Narbo and back seems rather pointless, particularly as he returned with Caesar (Plut. Ant. 11) and so could not choose his own pace. Perhaps the words mean 'went hither and thither' at head-quarters on errands for Caesar.

nescio quo modo] Probably Caesar, in view of Antony's usefulness, let him off his debts.

79. iussus . . . consul] After the victory of Munda the senate voted Caesar, among other honours, the right to appoint the magistrates. Outwardly he declined the privilege, but by 'recommending' certain persons to the people for election he accepted the substance of it (Dio, xliii. 45, 1; 47, 1; Suet. Iul. 41).

promissum] No doubt as a reward for his services in Spain (§ 75). 'But Antony intended that Caesar, not Dolabella, should be his colleague; for when Caesar set out for the Parthian War he himself would be supreme' (Rice Holmes, iii. 330).

80. prius quam proficisceretur] For the Parthian campaign. Expecting the war to be a long one, Caesar nominated magistrates for two years in advance (A. xiv. 6, 2; Dio, xliii. 51, 2).

Dolabellam . . . iussurum] This, as Rice Holmes points out (iii. 331), was an attempt at compromise. Dolabella was to be consoled for his original disappointment by taking Caesar's place as *consul suffectus*. That Antony should have persisted, perhaps not unsuccessfully, in his opposition, is remarkable. He must have had popular opinion, so far as that counted for anything, behind him. Was it Dolabella's revolutionary behaviour in 47 that told against him? Or was it his youth? Appian (ii. 129) says he was only twenty-five in 44. This cannot be true (see Meyer, 460, n. 3; Rice Holmes, iii. 516), and perhaps, as has been suggested, we should emend κε′ in Appian, loc. cit., to λε′ (35). According to Phil. v. 48 the legal minimum age for the consulship in Cicero's day was forty-three. (Mommsen, *St. R.* i. 568–9.) But Antony was only thirty-eight in 44.

hic bonus augur] On the difficulties connected with §§ 80–4 see, in general, Appendix III. For the sake of clearness I have reserved the discussion of certain points of detail for the notes.

81. si augur . . . esses] 'Had you been only consul, instead of both consul and augur.'

Nos] *Sc.* the augurs.

nuntiationem] 'Qui malam rem nuntiat, obnuntiat, qui bonam, adnuntiat: nam proprie obnuntiare dicuntur augures, qui aliquid mali ominis scaevumque viderint' (Donat. ad Ter. Ad. 547). Donatus's testimony has sometimes, without due reason, been questioned, as by Bouché le Clercq, *Hist. de la Div.* iv. 252–3 and in D. and S. i. 582, n. 20; Mommsen, *St. R.* i. 111, n. 2; Wissowa, 531, n. 8. Mommsen and Wissowa assign *nuntiatio* to the augur, *obnuntiatio* to the magistrate. But 'augur auguri, consul consuli obnuntiasti' in § 84 below implies that an augur had the right of *obnuntiatio*. (Mommsen's attempt to evade this conclusion (loc. cit.) is scarcely convincing.) And Valeton seems to be right in following Donatus, and in holding that the power of *obnuntiatio* was possessed not only by augurs but by private citizens, the only difference being that a private citizen's *obnuntiatio* could be ignored by the presiding magistrate, while the augur's could not. (Greenidge, *C. R.* vii. 159, also accepts Donatus' statement. He cites § 84 and 'dirarum obnuntiatio', De Div. i. 29.)

consules . . . spectionem] The only ancient interpretation of the term *spectio* is in Festus, p. 446, Lindsay. 'Spectio in auguralibus ponitur pro asspectione et nuntiato (*nuntiatio*, Ursinus) quia omne ius sacrorum habent au[x]guribus. Spectio dumtaxat quorum consilio rem gererent magistratus non (*hos*, Mommsen) ut possent impedire nuntiando quae cum (*quaecunque*, Scaliger) vidissent; at is (*at iis*, Scaliger; *satis*, F) spectio sine nuntiatione data est, ut ipsi auspicio rem gererent, non ut alios impedirent nuntiando.' This is obviously corrupt, and scholars have emended in accordance with their various theories. It is, however, generally admitted that *spectio* denotes the magistrate's right of looking for *auspicia impetrativa*, and is thus, in the Ciceronian period, equivalent to 'de caelo servare'. (Valeton thinks that private citizens possessed the right of *spectio* in the sphere of their domestic concerns, and augurs in the religious sphere. But, as he adds that *spectio* was also used, as here, in a limited political sense, his view essentially coincides with that of other scholars (*Mnem.* xvii. 440; xviii. 407).)

It seems clear that the tribunes, as well as the patrician magistrates, possessed the power of *spectio*, at any rate within certain limits. Valeton, on the authority of Zonaras, 7, 19, thinks that they received this power, for obstructive purposes, in 449 B.C. (*Mnem.* xix. 87). Mommsen rejects Zonaras's statement, but thinks that the tribunes obtained the privilege, at some unknown time, 'anomalously' (*St. R.* ii. 283–5). Greenidge, refusing to admit that the tribunes ever possessed the privilege, is driven to supposing ambiguity in the term 'de caelo servare'. (See App. III.)

multis ante] Exaggerated. The reference is to 1st January, 44 (§ 80).

aut prohibiturum . . . fecit] Either stop the *comitia* from assembling, by using the magistrate's power of *spectio*; or dissolve or invalidate it ('vel impedire vel vitiare') by using the augur's power of *obnuntiatio dirarum.* (This interpretation, though not strictly consistent with Antony's declared intention (§ 80) of using augural, not consular, powers, seems preferable to making *prohibiturum* equivalent to *impedire* above, and *id quod fecit* to *vitiare.*

82. Atque . . . petebat] This description of Antony's subservience is rather oddly inserted in an episode which illustrates his recalcitrance.

apparitor] A general term for the free attendants on the Roman magistrates and priests (as distinguished from the *servi publici*); the corresponding verb *apparere* is often found in inscriptions. In its widest sense the term includes *scribae, lictores,* *viatores*, *praecones*, *accensi* and numerous other classes; but it appears also to be used in a more limited sense, as including *viatores* and *praecones* alone; and in a still more limited sense, as denoting, by itself, a particular form of service (P.-W., s.v. *Apparitores*).

lecticam] The normal Roman litter was a sort of portable four-post bedstead with an awning and sides of leather. A sumptuous specimen, reconstructed out of fragments found on the Esquiline, is to be found in the Palazzo dei Conservatori in Rome; illustrations in D. and S., iii. 2, 1005 and Blümner, 447. There were openings in the sides closed by curtains, later by regular window-panes. The litter was *aperta* when the curtains were drawn back, *operta* when they were drawn to. The present passages implies, what is natural enough, that one of the openings was in the back, by the head of the occupant.

Whether or not permanently open litters were also made, without awning and sides, has been much disputed. The latest (1924) authority, Lamer (in P.-W. xii. 1, 1092), holds that such litters were made, arguing from the apparently contrasted terms φορεῖον κατάστεγον, often used by Dio, and κλίνη, and from a passage in Aretaeus, a medical writer of the second century A.D., deprecating the use of open litters as liable to cause sun-stroke. Lamer's conclusion is: 'A *l. operta* always had awning and curtains, but one could *aperire* it.' A. ix. 11, 1, 'cum is paullum lecticam aperuisset'. If this, as appears, is sound, there is some difficulty in determining the meaning of *aperta* and *operta* in any particular passage. *Aperta* in § 58 might refer to a permanently open litter, or to one with the curtains drawn back. *Operta* in § 106 obviously means 'with the curtains drawn to'.

Litters were introduced into Italy, probably from Asia Minor, in the second century B.C. Plautus never mentions them, and we first hear of them in 170 and 168. C. Gracchus' story of a rustic who mistook a litter for a bier suggests that they were still a novelty in his day. They were used principally by women. Caesar restricted their use (Suet. Iul. 43), and, if he employed one himself, his poor health was an excuse, as Peskett remarks. Lamer thinks that Caesar's measure, though often evaded, remained in force long after his death, and that litters first became common in Rome under Nero. (D. and S., s.v. *Lectica*; Blümner, 446-8; Lamer in P.-W., s.v. *Lectica*, exhaustive and full of interest.)

comitiorum] Roman magistrates were elected by the *Comitia Centuriata*. This was originally a military assembly, and was organized into classes on a property basis. (The principal ancient authorities are Cic. De Rep. ii. 39; Dion. Hal. iv. 16 ff.; Liv. i. 43.) In its original form, ascribed by tradition to King Servius Tullius, the *Comitia* consisted of 193 centuries, eighty of the first class, twenty each of the second, third, and fourth, and thirty of the fifth, with five miscellaneous centuries and eighteen centuries of *equites*. Each class contained an equal number of centuries of older and younger men, *seniores* and *iuniores*. The property qualification varied from 100,000–125,000 asses for the first class to 4,000–12,500 for the fifth. (Our authorities differ.) The centuries of *equites* may perhaps have been real centuries, 100 strong; the remaining centuries naturally varied in strength. Perhaps in 241 (possibly later, but in any case before 218) this organization was combined with the tribal organization. Exactly how, is uncertain. The most probable hypothesis is that each of the thirty-five tribes was divided into ten centuries (one *seniorum* and one *iuniorum* from each of the five classes); while the eighteen centuries of *equites* and the five miscellaneous centuries remained unaltered; the total number of centuries being therefore 373. (Mommsen, *St. R.* iii. 274 ff., while accepting this total, holds that the 373 centuries only had 193 votes; an untenable conclusion to which he is led by an attempt to take Cicero's words in De Rep. ii. 39 as referring to the Ciceronian age, whereas Kübler has shown (in P.-W. iii. 2, 1958–9) that they must refer to the earlier organization of the *Comitia*.)

Under the reformed organization the voting was still by classes, not by tribes. The eighteen centuries of *equites* originally possessed the privilege of voting first (*praerogativae*). This privilege they lost at some time between 296 (Liv. x. 22, 1) and 215 (Liv. xxiv 7, 12), probably at the time of the reorganization of the *Comitia*. Hereafter the right of voting first went to a century chosen by lot, either out of all the centuries or perhaps out of those of the first class. (Liv. xxiv. 7, 12, 'cum sors praerogativae Aniensi iuniorum exisset'; xxvii. 6, 3, 'Galeria iuniorum, quae sorte praerogativa esset'.) The importance of the lead given by the *praerogativa* was very great (Mur. 38; Planc. 49, 'una centuria praerogativa tantum habet auctoritatis ut nemo umquam prior eam tulerit quin renuntiatus sit aut eis ipsis comitiis consul aut certe in illum annum'), and had a considerable market value (Q. F. ii.14, 4, 'HS centiens constituunt in praerogativa pronuntiare').

Under the reformed organization twelve of the eighteen equestrian centuries voted with the first class; the remaining six voted after the first class, and were known as the *sex centuriae* or *sex suffragia*. Curious as this division of the equestrian centuries may appear, the ancient authorities leave no doubt as to the fact. De Rep. ii. 39: 'Nunc rationem videtis esse talem ut equitum ⟨centuriae cum sex⟩ suffragiis et prima classis, addita centuria quae ad summum usum urbis fabris tignariis est data ⟨LXXX⟩VIIII centurias ⟨habeat: quibus ex cent. quattuor centuriis⟩, tot enim reliquae sunt, octo solae si accesserunt, confecta est vis populi universa. (The words in brackets, added by a later hand, are almost certainly sound. P.-W. iii. 2, 1959.) Liv. i. 43, 8–9: '(Servius Tullius) equitum ex primoribus civitatis duodecim scripsit centurias: sex item alias centurias, tribus a Romulo institutis, sub iisdem quibus inauguratae erant nominibus fecit'; i. 36, 8: 'quas nunc, quia geminatae sunt, sex vocant centurias.' Festus, p. 452, Lindsay: 'sex suffragia appellantur in equitum centuriis quae sunt adiectae (adfectae cod.) ei numero centuriarum quas Priscus Tarquinius rex constituit.' Liv. xliii. 16, 14: 'cum ex duodecim centuriis equitum octo censorem condemnassent multaeque aliae primae classis.'

(Mommsen, *St. R.* iii. 254-5, thinks that originally the six centuries consisted only of patricians, while the twelve were from the first open to plebeians also; Kübler (P.-W. vi. 1, 275-6) doubts this. In any case Livy seems to be right, as against Festus, in making the six earlier, and the twelve later, in date.)

(Mommsen, *St. R.* iii. 240-99; Greenidge, *R. P. L.* 69-74, 252-3; P.-W., s.v. *Centuria*, iii. 2, 1952-60; s.v. *Equites Romani*, vi. 1, 274-6, 288-9; G. W. Botsford, *The Roman Assemblies*, c. 10.)

Renuntiatur] Viz. the result of balloting for the privilege of *praerogativa* is announced.

suffragia] The *sex suffragia* mentioned by Festus (see above). Niebuhr proposed to add the numeral, but Mommsen points out that the omission is possible in technical language (*St. R.* iii. 292, n. 2).

83. Confecto negotio] Not necessarily much exaggerated. If the eighteen equestrian centuries and the first two classes voted solid for Dolabella, he had 158 votes. To get a majority out of 373 he needed 187.

C. Laelium] C. Laelius Sapiens: born about 190; his intimate friendship with the younger Scipio Africanus portrayed in Cicero's *Laelius sive de Amicitia*; also a friend of the historian Polybius and the satirist Lucilius; philosopher and orator; one of the characters in the *De Senectute*, the *De Re Publica*, and the *De Natura Deorum*, where Cicero says of him (iii. 5): 'habeo C. Laelium augurem eundemque sapientem, quem potius audiam dicentem de religione in illa oratióne nobili quam quemquam principem Stoicorum.'

Alio die] For the formula cf. De Leg. ii. 31: 'Quid gravius quam rem susceptam dirimi, si unus augur "alio die" dixerit?'

Neque . . . dicis] Therefore Antony's *obnuntiatio* could only be justified on the basis of a real *auspicium oblativum*, actually observed during the meeting.

Ergo . . . auspicia] Because the Roman religious conscience, while permitting the manufacture of *auspicia impetrativa*, demanded that *auspicia oblativa* should be genuine. See App. III and Valeton, *Mnem.* xviii. 440-3.

Ementitus is technical. Liv. xxi. 63, 5: 'auspiciis ementiendis'. De Div. i. 29 (a valuable commentary on this passage): 'M. Crasso quid acciderit, videmus, dirarum obnuntiatione neglecta. In quo Appius, conlega tuus, bonus augur, ut ex te audire soleo, non satis scienter virum bonum et civem egregium censor C. Ateium notavit, quod ementitum auspicia subscriberet. Esto; fuerit hoc censoris, si iudicabat ementitum; at illud minime auguris, quod adscripsit ob eam causam populum Romanum calamitatem maximam cepisse. Si enim ea causa calamitatis fuit, non in eo est culpa qui obnuntiavit, sed in eo qui non paruit. Veram enim fuisse obnuntiationem, ut ait idem augur et censor, exitus adprobavit; quae si falsa fuisset, nullam adferre potuisset causam calamitatis.' Cicero there maintains the more reasonable religious view; but here, with Appius, he allows the possibility of the state suffering the consequences of the individual's mendacity. (Valeton's explanation, loc. cit., seems to me over-subtle.) The latter view is also expressed in De Orat. ii. 268, where the phrase 'religione civitatem obstrinxisse' occurs; but the passage is generally admitted to be spurious.

ad nostrum conlegium deferantur] It rested with the college of augurs to decide whether or not a magistrate's action had been 'vitiated' by neglect of the auspices. Cf. Liv. iv. 7, 3, 'augurum decreto perinde ac vitio creati honore abiere'; viii. 23, 14, 'consulti augures vitiosum videri dictatorem pronuntiaverunt'; xlv. 12, 10, 'vitio diem dictam esse augures, cum ad eos relatum est, decreverunt'. § 88 below, 'de quibus . . . fuit in senatu Caesar acturus', suggests that the referring authority was the senate. (Mommsen, *St. R.* i. 115, says the senate or an individual magistrate.)

Cicero speaks of Dolabella's acts being referred to the augural college, because the validity of his acts rested on the invalidity of Antony's *obnuntiatio* to his election, and the question of the validity of the *obnuntiatio* would be referred to the college.

The upshot of Antony's interference.

Modern historians agree in holding that Caesar bowed to Antony's *obnuntiatio*, and that the assembly was forthwith dissolved. On the other hand Halm[8] (Introd., p. 19) states that 'the election was apparently carried out, though its validity was questioned'. Plutarch, our only ancient authority for the incident, except Cicero, says definitely (Ant. 11) that Caesar yielded (*εἶξε καὶ προήκατο Δολοβέλλαν ἀχθόμενον*).

There are grounds for agreeing with Halm, in spite of Plutarch.

(1) It seems unlikely that Caesar, imperious as his temper was towards the end of his life, would have tolerated such open defiance of his authority.

(2) Cicero's words 'vitiosus consul Dolabella', 'salvis auspiciis creatus', suggest that the election was carried through; so also does the assumption of the consulship by Dolabella after Caesar's murder.

(3) That Cicero should omit to describe the conclusion of the election is not surprising; he is concerned here with Antony's mendacity, not with Caesar's arbitrariness. Nor can we conclude from Caesar's intention to initiate proceedings (§ 88 'in senatu acturus') that the election had ended in a manner contrary to his wish. If Dolabella had been elected, but elected in circumstances which might be impugned, it was clearly to Caesar's interest to have the validity of the election formally vindicated before his departure from Italy.

84. rem unam pulcherrimam] This famous episode, which is recorded in essentially the same form by all our authorities, must be regarded in the light of other events which happened at about the same time. An unknown hand adorned Caesar's statue on the Rostra with a diadem, which was removed by the tribunes Flavus and Marullus. A street crowd hailed Caesar as king: he answered 'my name is Caesar, not Rex'. When the same tribunes arrested the ringleader, Caesar was furious and had them deposed. Then came the Lupercalia. Later still it was rumoured that one of the custodians of the Sibylline books intended to produce an oracle that the Parthians would only submit to a Roman king, and to propose that Caesar be given the royal title outside of Italy.

The facts, which are in outline so well attested as to be beyond dispute, admit of two interpretations. Either Caesar was feeling his way towards monarchy, and sending up a series of kites to test popular opinion; or he did not aim at monarchy, and his enemies were trying to discredit him. Among recent historians, Meyer (526–8) takes the former, Heitland (iii. 364–5) the latter, view. Ferrero (ii. 294) is doubtful.

The two first incidents suggest at first sight the malice of enemies. But why then did Caesar play into those enemies' hands by his treatment of the tribunes (unless irritation overcame policy)? The rumour regarding the Sibylline books, though only a rumour, is significant; if Caesar wanted to be king, but found public opinion hostile, it would be not unnatural that he should content himself, as a *pis aller*, with the acquisition of the royal title abroad (as Meyer points out, he had the precedent of Alexander and the Seleucidae in making such a distinction). It must further be admitted that, if Caesar did not aim at kingship, he showed surprising rashness in accepting at any rate partial deification (see § 110) and various insignia of royalty (Dio, xliii. 43, 2; xliv. 6, 1).

To return to the Lupercalia. On main points, our other authorities agree with each other and with Cicero, except that Nicolas of Damascus associates several other persons with Antony in the occurrence. Other points of detail will be noticed as they occur. The incident may be motivated in several ways. Either it was stage-managed by Caesar, whose object may have been either to provide the people with an opportunity for a monarchist demonstration, or himself with one for repudiating monarchical ambitions once and for all. Or it was designed by Antony, who may have wished to press the monarchy upon Caesar, or to bring unpopularity upon him. Meyer rejects out of hand the idea that Antony acted on his own initiative. But Antony was no cypher, as his recent defiance of Caesar shows. It is likely that this defiance, at a time when Caesar was growing more and more autocratic and irritable, had reopened the old breach. Caesar intended to complain in the senate of Antony's behaviour (§ 88); and it seems improbable that, if he had arranged the Lupercalia incident, he would have chosen Antony to bring it about. It is worth noting that, of the three persons whom Nicolas associates with Antony on this occasion, two, Casca and Cassius, were among Caesar's murderers. And it is by no means impossible that the whole affair was a deliberate device to discredit Caesar.

(On the whole of the above cf. Nic. Dam. 20–1; Liv. Ep. 116; Plut. Caes. 60–1; 64; Ant. 12; Suet. Iul. 79; App. ii. 108–10; Vell. ii. 56, 4; Val. Max. i. 6, 13; Dio, xliv. 9–11; 15, 3; Meyer, 526–30; Rice Holmes, iii. 334–8.)

Lupercalia] This feast was held annually on 15th February. The ceremonies began at the Lupercal, the cave at the bottom of the Palatine Hill in which, according to tradition, Romulus and Remus were suckled by the she-wolf. Here goats were sacrificed, and young men called Luperci had their foreheads smeared with the bloody knife. The stains were then wiped off with wool dipped in milk, and the Luperci had to laugh. Then, after a feast, they ran round the foot of the Palatine, girt with the skins of the sacrificed goats, and hitting any women they met with strips of the same skins, as a fertility charm. The thongs were called *februa*, an old Latin word meaning 'instruments of purification'; hence the verb *februare*, *dies Februarius*, and the month *Februarius*.

For a full account of the festival see Warde Fowler, *Roman Festivals*, pp. 310–21. It is difficult to determine in whose honour it was celebrated. Warde Fowler (312–13) thinks that possibly the Romans themselves did not know. Wissowa, on Ovid's authority (Fast. ii. 268), decides for Faunus. Justin (xliii. 1, 7) speaks of 'Faunus Lupercus'; and W. F. Otto (*Phil.* lxxii (1913), 161–95), pointing out that Varro (Arnob. iv. 3) knew of a Luperca, sees evidence for a pair of deities, Faunus Lupercus and Fauna Luperca, like Faunus Fatuus and Fauna Fatua, Liber and Libera.

The ceremonial seems to be the result of a fusion of rituals. L. Deubner (*Archiv. f. Religionswiss.* xiii (1910), 481 ff.), with whom Wissowa (209–10) and Warde Fowler (*Rel. Exp.* 478–80) substantially agree, recognizes three elements: (1) men running round the bounds of a pastoral community in a magic circle to keep off wolves, hence the name Luperci = 'qui lupos arcent'; (2) a sacrifice of goats to the rustic god Faunus; (3) a ceremony of fructification connected with Juno, hence the striking of women; (4) a ceremony of purification, hence the wiping away of blood-stains. On the other hand, Otto (loc. cit.) holds that the ceremonial had nothing to do with keeping off wolves, but was apotropaic and purificatory in origin; that it was a commemoration of the wolf which suckled Romulus and Remus (Arnob. iv. 3; Fabius Pictor ap. Serv. ad Aen. viii. 630); and that the Luperci originally represented wolves. Otto connects *Lupercus* with *lupus* as *noverca* with *novus*.

porticu Minucia] This was a portico (or, rather, two porticoes) situated west of the Capitoline Hill (the exact locality cannot be determined: O. Richter, *Topographie der Stadt Rom*, 217) built by M. Minucius Rufus, consul in 110, after his victory over the Thracian tribe Scordisci. Cicero is probably here referring to the episode mentioned in § 63.

85. **rostris**] The stone platform in the Forum from which speakers addressed the assembly was called *rostra*, because it was decorated with the beaked prows of the ships captured from the Antiates in 338. From its height and commanding position it formed a suitable view point on spectacular occasions. Hence Caesar was sitting there watching the runners at the Lupercalia.

amictus toga purpurea] This was the purple toga ('habet tamen album aliquid', Serv. ad Aen. vii. 612), worn by the Roman kings, and apparently retained in Republican times as a triumphal robe. Caesar was granted the right, first, of wearing it ἐν πάσαις ταῖς πανηγύρεσι (Dio, xliii. 43, 1), subsequently, of wearing it on all occasions (xliv. 4, 2). Dio, who regards the regal and triumphal robes as distinct (cf. xliv. 6, 1), seems to have conflated two sources and duplicated the granting of the privilege (Mommsen, St. R. i. 416, n. 2; Groebe-Drumann, iii. 2, 596, n. 5.

in sella aurea] Θρόνων ἐλεφαντίνων τε καὶ χρυσῶν (App. ii. 106; δίφρος ἐπίχρυσος (Dio, xliv. 6, 1); *sedem auream* (Suet. Iul. 76).

coronatus] Suetonius (Iul. 45) says that Caesar used freely the permission to wear on all occasions a wreath of bay, with which he concealed his incipient baldness. στέφανος δάφνινος (Dio, xliii. 43, 1). In xliv. 6, 3 Dio says that Caesar was allowed to bring into the theatre τὸν δίφρον τὸν ἐπίχρυσον καὶ τὸν στέφανον τὸν διάλιθον καὶ διάχρυσον: and on the present occasion Dio describes him as τῷ στεφάνῳ τῷ διαχρύσῳ λαμπρυνόμενος (xliv. 11, 2). But surely such a crown would have proved as objectionable as the diadem?

Escendis] By the steps at the back of the rostra. Nicolas (21) gives the most detailed account of the crowning. First of all Licinius (? Calvus) approaches with the crown. He is lifted up on to the rostra by friends (cf. Plutarch, Ant. 12, συνεξαρθείς, viz. from the front, where there were no steps). He places the diadem at Caesar's feet. The crowd shout for Lepidus to put it on Caesar's head, but he hesitates. Cassius, with Publius Casca, sets it on his knees. He pushes it away, amidst applause. Antony runs up and sets it on his head. Caesar throws it into the crowd. Antony again places it on his head. Caesar directs that it be taken to the temple of Capitoline Jupiter.

Lupercus] To the two old guilds of Luperci, Quinctiales and Fabiani, a third, Iulii, had recently been added (Wissowa, 559). Antony belonged to the third, and was *Magister* either of that guild or of the whole body of Luperci. (Dio, xlv. 30, 2, ἐπὶ τοῦ ἑταιρικοῦ τοῦ Ἰουλίου ἐτέτακτο; xlvi. 5, 2, ἡγεμόνα τῶν συνιερέων. In inscriptions we find both 'magister lupercorum' and 'magister collegii lupercorum': Wissowa, loc. cit.) Cicero clearly thought it *infra dig.* for Antony to be a Lupercus. As Wissowa points out (560), he speaks contemptuously of the Luperci in Cael. 26; and that the prestige of this priesthood was low is attested by the fact that even freedmen were eligible for admission (id. 491, n. 6).

diadema] Nicolas (21) describes it as *δάφνινον στέφανον, ἐντὸς δὲ διάδημα περιφαινόμενον*: and Plutarch (Ant. 12) says *διάδημα δάφνης στεφάνῳ περιελίξας*. The object, I suppose, was to conceal the nature of the thing until the last moment.

reiciebat] Nicolas, Plutarch, Suetonius, and Appian all speak of repeated attempts. In *imponebas* the imperfect is perhaps both iterative and conative. In Appian and Nicolas, Caesar throws the diadem into the crowd. Finally he has it sent to the temple of Iuppiter Capitolinus (Nic. Dam., Suet., Dio).

unus] Inaccurate, if Nicolas's account (see note on *escendis* above) is correct. But such inaccuracies are common enough in Cicero's speeches. (Lepidus did not conceal his disapproval: v. 38: xiii. 17.)

86. supplex . . . abiciebas] Our other authorities say nothing of this. If Antony stooped to pick up the crown from the ground, his attitude might have been mistaken for prostration. If he really did prostrate himself, in oriental fashion, he can hardly have done so except with the intention of making Caesar odious. Perhaps, however, the statement is 'merely corroborative detail'.

peteres] Best taken as = *petere debebas*. Mayor quotes many parallels. But = *petere potuisti* is possible. Cf. Verr. II. v. 168.

a nobis . . . habebas] In Dio's account, Antony presents the diadem with the words, *τοῦτό σοι ὁ δῆμος δι' ἐμοῦ δίδωσι* (xliv. 11, 3). Cf. Nic. Dam. 21, *μὴ διωθεῖσθαι τὴν τοῦ δήμου χάριν*. Hence 'populi iussu' in § 87.

nudus contionatus] Naked except for the goatskin apron. In iii. 12 Cicero reinforces *nudus* with *unctus* (*ἀληλιμμένος* in the Greek accounts) and *ebrius* (as a result of the feast). xiii. 31 'obrutus vino, unguentis oblitus'. The other authorities do not mention anything in the nature of an oration.

stimulis fodiamus] A way of punishing slaves. Sihler quotes Plaut. Aul. 45, 'stimulorum seges'; Cas. 447, 'stimulorum loculi'; Most. 57, 'ita te forabunt patibulatum per vias stimulis'. The sequence of thought is: 'Does not your conduct merit the most degrading punishment? Do you wait momentarily for such punishment? Why, unless you are dead to all feeling, *I* am punishing you now, with these words.'

imminuam . . . gloriam] By suggesting that the 'heroes' left their task unfinished. Cf. § 34.

Quid indignius] Atticus (see Introd., p. xvii) suggested 'indignissimum est hunc vivere'. Cicero approved the alteration, but did not adopt it.

87. fastis] The *Fasti* included dates of historical events as well as of festivals, exactly as our almanacs contain, say, the date of Waterloo. Other incidents in Caesar's life are found in extant remains of the *Fasti*.

de die] 'Beginning early in the day' (cf. § 104, 'ab hora tertia'). The ninth hour was the normal time for dinner (*cena*). Elaborate banquets began earlier (cf. Catull. 47, 5, 'Vos convivia lauta sumptuose de die facitis'; Ter. Ad. 965, 'apparare de die convivium.'

in diem] 'Till dawn.' Antony starts drinking in the morning, and goes on the whole evening and night. So Halm[8]. It must be admitted, however, that this use of *in* for *usque ad* can scarcely be paralleled in Ciceronian or pre-Ciceronian Latin. 'Dormiet in lucem' (Hor. Ep. i. 18, 34) and 'Romani . . . in multum diei stetere in acie' (Liv. xxvii. 2, 9) are parallel; but 'sermonem in multam noctem produximus' (Cic. De Rep. vi. 10) is differentiated by its verb of motion. King renders 'more each day'; but that use of *in* requires a comparative, or a verb denoting increase, like *crescere* or *senescere*.

Perhaps, however, 'de die' = 'on the proceeds of the day' (living from hand to mouth). So Kühner, ii. 1, 499. If so, there is a sort of pun, *diem* meaning 'daylight', and *die* 'a period of 24 hours'. (The conjecture *bibere* for *vivere* seems by no means certain, in view of the complications it involves. With *vivere* all is simple: 'not only (in act) live on what the day brings in, but also (in thought) disregard the morrow!' Cf. F. ix. 17, 1, 'de lucro vivimus'; De Orat. ii. 169, 'barbarorum est in diem vivere'.

in legibus et in iudiciis] See i. 19–26.

L. Tarquinius, Sp. Cassius, Sp. Maelius] See § 26, notes.

M. Manlius] See note on i. 32.

88. tuum de auspiciis iudicium] Antony withdrew his opposition to Dolabella's tenure of the consulship on 17th March. See i. 31, § 84.

id tempus] The events after Caesar's murder. *Eis rebus*, Antony's intentions before the murder.

Quae tua fuga] He fled to his house, *ἐσθῆτα θεράποντος μεταλαβών* (Plut. Ant. 14), *μεταβαλὼν ἐσθῆτα δημοτικήν* (id. Brut. 18), *τὴν ἐσθῆτα τὴν ἀρχικήν, ὅπως διαλάθῃ, ῥίψας* (Dio, xliv. 22, 2), and fortified it (App. ii. 118).

beneficio] For the decision to spare Antony see § 34.

89. Dicebam illis] Cf. A. xiv. 10, 1: 'Meministine me clamare illo ipso primo Capitolino die senatum in Capitòlium a praetoribus vocari debere? Di immortales, quae tum opera effici potuerunt laetantibus omnibus bonis, etiam sat bonis, fractis latronibus! Liberalia tu accusas. Quid fieri tum potuit? iam pridem perieramus.' A. xiv. 14, 2: 'Illam sessionem Capitolinam mihi non placuisse tu testis es. Quid ergo? ista culpa Brutorum? Minime illorum quidem, sed aliorum brutorum qui se cautos ac sapientis putant.'

in aedem Telluris] See i. 1.

90. M. Bambalionis nepotem] See i. 2, 'liberos eius'. *Bambalio* (stammerer) was the *cognomen* of M. Fulvius, the father of Antony's third wife Fulvia. The boy cannot have been more than eighteen months old, as Antony did not marry Fulvia till 46.

iii. 16: 'Tuae coniugis, bonae feminae, locupletis quidem certe, Bambalio quidam pater, homo nullo numero. Nihil illo contemptius, qui propter haesitantiam linguae stuporemque cordis cognomen ex contumelia traxerit.'

si illud funus fuit] Cf. i. 5, 'insepultam sepulturam' and note.

91. laudatio . . . cohortatio] Suetonius (Iul. 84) says: 'Laudationis loco consul Antonius per praeconem pronuntiavit senatus consultum, quo omnia simul ei divina atque humana decreverat, item ius iurandum, quo se cuncti pro salute unius astrinxerant; quibus perpauca a se verba addidit.' Appian's account begins in the same way (ii. 144-5), except that he makes Antony recite the decree himself, and intersperse a brief running commentary on the several points (ἐπεφθέγγετο δέ πού τι καὶ βραχὺ ἑκάστῳ). But in the following chapters (146-7) Antony goes on to make a regular oration, displaying to the crowd Caesar's tattered raiment and a wax image of his body, showing the wounds. Plutarch's brief description in Ant. 14 is in general agreement with Appian. Dio (xliv. 36-49) inflicts on us a speech covering twelve Teubner pages.

It is unlikely that Antony neglected the opportunity to inflame the populace: that it was inflamed, the ensuing disorder proves. It seems clear that Suetonius is holding back facts. 'Laudatus miserabiliter', in a private letter of Cicero (A. xiv. 10, 1), is sufficient to show that Antony went further than Suetonius admits.

semustilatus] Sihler compares 'huius ambusti tribuni plebis' (Mil. 12) of Clodius' corpse. Plutarch (Brut. 20) notes the similarity of the two funerals, and the parallel must have been present to all minds.

L. Bellieni] Perhaps, but not certainly, the Pompeian mentioned in A. viii 15, 2.

in nostras domos] Suet. Iul. 85, 'Plebs statim a funere ad domum Bruti et Cassi cum facibus tetendit atque aegre repulsa'; A. xiv. 10, 1 'servique et egentes in tecta nostra cum facibus immissi'.

Idem . . . tolleres] See i. 3.

92. Inspectantibus . . . dabatur] See i. 24.

immunitates] Cicero's objection to the extension of the franchise was economic rather than political. Under the republic, *libertas* normally carried *immunitas* with it. But even then there were exceptions: at Pompey's Asiatic settlement the former was in certain cases conferred without the latter; and under the empire the dissociation of the two privileges became complete. (Mommsen, *St. R.* iii. 681-6; Greenidge, *R. P. L.* 318, 428-9; P.-W., s. v. *Immunitas*.)

93. Vbi est septiens miliens] See i. 17, note on *pecunia . . . maneret.*

Funestae] Because much of it was the confiscated property of men killed in the Civil War. So in i. 17 it is called *cruenta.*

tributis] A levy on capital, raised when required to meet war expenditure, amounting usually to one-tenth per cent., but sometimes to as much as three-tenths per cent. The money was occasionally refunded by the state. In 167, after the Third Macedonian War, *tributum* ceased to be levied, the influx of revenue from conquered territories having rendered it unnecessary (De Off. ii. 76). Its reimposition was regarded as a possibility in 59 (Flacc. 80). In 43 something known as *tributum* was levied, but its nature is obscure (Ad Brut. i. 18, 5; Dio, xlvi. 31, 3). Greenidge, *R. P. L.*, p. 137; *Dict. Ant.*, s. v. *Tributum.*

Deiotaro] One of the tetrarchs, eventually sole tetrarch, of Galatia: assisted many Roman commanders, including Sulla, Lucullus, and Pompey, in their Asiatic campaigns; at Pompey's settlement of Asia Minor received, as a reward for his services, the title of king and considerable accessions of territory on the south shore of the Black Sea, advantages which were confirmed by the senate in 59, and increased by the addition of Armenia Minor; in 51 offered Cicero, then governor of Cilicia, help against the Parthians; in the Civil War fought for Pompey and escaped with him after Pharsalus. In 47, nevertheless, he applied to Caesar's general, Domitius Calvinus, for aid against Pharnaces of Pontus; this was granted, but the combined forces were defeated at Nicopolis. At about this time, apparently, Deiotarus murdered Castor Tarcondarius, tetrarch of the Tectosages, and possessed himself of this tetrarchy, and of that of the Trocmi as well. On Caesar's arrival, later in the year, to retrieve the disaster of Nicopolis, he abjectly begged pardon for past offences. Caesar left him his crown, but after the battle of Zela deprived him of the tetrarchy of the Trocmi, which now went to Mithradates of Pergamum, and of Armenia Minor, which went to Ariobarzanes, King of Cappadocia. The death of Mithradates in 46 or 45 gave him a chance of recovering part of what he had lost: he sent an embassy to Caesar in 45; a counter-embassy from his Galatian rivals accused him of having attempted to assassinate Caesar in 47, and of having raised troops to support the Syrian revolt of Caecilius Bassus. He was defended by Cicero in an extant speech delivered in Caesar's house, and apparently acquitted. (There is no record of the result of the trial.) After Caesar's murder, in April 44, a member of Deiotarus' mission, Hieras by name, managed to obtain, through Fulvia, the restitution of his kingdom at a price of ten million sesterces. The way in which the transaction was carried out aroused the indignation of Pansa (A. xiv. 19, 2) as well as of Cicero, who writes on 22nd April: 'Deiotari nostri causa non similis? Dignus ille quidem omni regno, sed non per Fulviam' (A. xiv. 12, 1). Meanwhile, however, Deiotarus had taken the law into his own hands, and himself recovered his lost possessions, thereby rendering the contract, Cicero maintains, null and void.

94. Massiliensibus] Massilia sided with Pompey in the Civil War. Defended by L. Domitius, the town was besieged by Trebonius and D. Brutus in 49. Reduced to great straits, the inhabitants obtained an armistice from Trebonius, but treacherously violated it (Caes. B.C. ii. 14). Compelled to surrender shortly after, they were deprived by Caesar of a great part of their territory (exactly how much cannot be determined), a considerable proportion of which was included in the new colony of Arelate (P.-W., iv. 1, 528).

In De Off. ii. 27 Cicero cites the treatment of Massilia as an example of how Caesar 'universas provincias regionesque uno calamitatis iure comprehenderet'. Both that and our present passage are scarcely consistent with his statement in Phil. viii. 19: 'Caesar ipse, qui illis fuerat iratissimus, tamen propter singularem eius civitatis gravitatem et fidem cotidie aliquid iracundiae remittebat.' In view of these words, Dio's statement that it was Caesar's men who broke the truce, and that he 'subsequently deprived the Massiliots of everything save freedom', cannot be maintained (Rice Holmes, iii. 93, 420; Meyer, 487, 500 n. 2).

In xiii. 32 Antony is represented as saying to the senatorial party, 'Massiliensibus iure belli adempta reddituros vos pollicemini'.

nec praesens nec absens] Neither in his interviews with Caesar before and after Zela, nor subsequently through his embassy.

quicquam aequi boni] The admitted facts show that Caesar treated Deiotarus with his usual clemency. This is freely conceded in the fulsome 'Pro rege Deiotaro'. See especially §§ 10–15.

Compellarat] After the battle of Zela, when Caesar was staying with Deiotarus. It was during this visit that Deiotarus was supposed to have attempted to assassinate him.

computarat pecuniam] Deiotarus, like other Pompeians who turned their coats after Pharsalus, had to buy his pardon. (Dio, xii. 63, 2; Bell. Alex. 34, 1; Reg. Deiot. 14, 24. In the Reg. Deiot., Cicero, for his own purposes, speaks as if the contributions had been spontaneous.)

in eius tetrarchia . . . conlocarat] For the Galatian tetrarchies cf. Strab. xii. 5, 1–2; Niese, *Rh. M.* xxxviii. 583–600. There were three Galatian tribes, Tolistobogii, Tectosages, and Trocmi, each originally divided into four tetrarchies. Subsequently (Niese thinks, at Pompey's settlement of Asia) each of the three tribes was united under a single tetrarch. Deiotarus acquired the westernmost tetrarchy, the Tolistobogii (Strab. xii. 3, 13). He afterwards ('a few years' before 47: Bell. Alex. 78, 3) annexed the other two (see note on *Deiotaro* above), though his sovereignty was neither complete nor undisputed. 'Deiotarus, tetrarches Gallograeciae tum quidem paene totius, quod ei neque legibus neque moribus concessum esse ceteri tetrarchae contendebant' (Bell. Alex. 67, 1). At the settlement after Zela Caesar deprived him of the tetrarchy of the Trocmi, but seems to have left him the other two.

'In eius tetrarchia' is therefore vague and somewhat misleading. In De Div. ii. 79 Cicero is more explicit: 'is (Caesar) cum ei (Deiotaro) Trocmorum tetrarchiam eripuisset et adseculae suo Pergameno nescio cui dedisset.'

The 'Graecus comes', 'adsecula Pergamenus' was Mithradates Pergamenus. He was the son of one Menodotus and Adobogiona, a mistress, as rumour had it, of Mithradates the Great: on the strength of which his relations gave him the name Mithradates, hoping to pass him off as a son of his namesake (Strab. xiii. 4, 3). Mithradates took him from Pergamum in boyhood, to accompany him on his campaigns. As a reward for brilliant service in the Egyptian campaign Caesar gave him the tetrarchy of the Trocmi, to which he had some claim, his maternal uncle, Brogitarus, having been tetrarch of the Trocmi before Deiotarus (Bell. Alex. 26-8; 78; G. Hirschfeld in *Hermes*, xiv (1879), 474-5.

Armeniam . . . a senatu datam] Cf. De Div. ii. 79, 'Armeniam a senatu datam'; Bell. Alex. 67, 'rex Armeniae minoris ab senatu appellatus'. Eutropius (vi. 14) says that Deiotarus received Armenia from Pompey. But his evidence cannot stand against that of Cicero and Hirtius. Moreover, Strabo (xii. 3, 13) expressly says that Pompey gave Deiotarus *τὰ περὶ Φαρνακίαν καὶ τὴν Τραπεζουσίαν μέχρι Κολχίδος καὶ τῆς μικρᾶς Ἀρμενίας*, where *μέχρι* proves that Deiotarus did not receive Armenia Minor from Pompey (Rice Holmes, i. 435).

Armenia Minor now went to Ariobarzanes, King of Cappadocia (Niese (loc. cit. and in P.-W.) says, to Mithradates Pergamenus. But I find no evidence for this statement). Dio (xli. 63, 3; xlii. 48, 3) says that a part of this territory was left in Deiotarus' possession.

Abstulerat needs some qualification. As Dio observes in the former of the passages quoted above, Deiotarus had already lost the whole of his Armenian territory to Pharnaces of Pontus. Caesar's action in this respect was refusal to restore, rather than deprivation.

95. modo aequum . . . modo non iniquum] An odd phrase, certainly. Perhaps a half-humorous *παρὰ προσδοκίαν*. 'Sometimes reasonable . . . sometimes—not unreasonable.'

quod nos pro illo postularemus] Besides Cicero, and doubtless others too, there was M. Brutus, who spoke on Deiotarus's behalf before Caesar at Nicaea in Bithynia, in 47. 'De quo quidem (*sc.* Bruto) ille, ad quem deverti (*sc.* Matius), Caesarem solitum dicere: "Magni refert, hic quid velit, sed, quicquid volt, valde volt"; idque eum animadvertisse, cum pro Deiotaro Nicaeae dixerit; valde vehementer eum visum et libere dicere' (A. xiv. 1, 2).

legatos] The names are given in Reg. Deiot. 41: Hieras, Blesamius, Antigonus, Dorylaus. Doubtless because of their *imperitia* of Roman manners and customs, they had been instructed to do nothing without consulting one Sextus, and Cicero was at the time annoyed at their ignoring this injunction and acting on their own responsibility (A. xvi. 3, 6).

in gynaecio] Fulvia's boudoir. 'Deiotari nostri causa non similis? Dignus ille quidem omni regno, sed non per Fulviam' (A. xiv. 12, 1).

96. iste . . . consultus] The reference may be to Sextus Clodius, the restored exile (see i. 3), whom Publius Clodius had employed as a drafter of bills. Cf. Dom. 25; 47; 83; De Har. Resp. 11; Sest. 133. But, as we hear nothing elsewhere of Antony's using this man's services, it may be more natural to suppose a reference to the other Sextus Clodius, the Sicilian rhetorician (§§ 42–3).

97. gladiatorum libellos] 'Programmes at the gladiatorial shows'.

ne post M. Brutum . . . provincia] The date on which Crete was assigned to M. Brutus cannot be determined with certainty. See App. I. It is difficult to credit Antony with this astonishing anachronism.

98. eorum . . . inquinatos] Appian (ii. 107) says that Caesar (in 45) κατεκάλει τοὺς φεύγοντας, πλὴν εἴ τις ἐπὶ ἀνηκέστοις ἔφευγε. The subsequent return of these jail-birds brought discredit on the respectable persons whom Caesar had restored.

in loco patrui] The position of having to remain in banishment when other exiles had been recalled. Cf. § 55, note on *patrui*.

risus . . . moveret] Expelled from the senate himself in 70, he was ill qualified for the task, as censor, of purging that body of undesirables. However, in 42 he was elected censor with P. Sulpicius Rufus (*C. I. L.* xiv. 2611). Cf., for a precedent, Clu. 119.

99. sinistrum fulmen] There is great difficulty in *sinistrum*. Apart from this passage, our authorities are unanimous in stating that lightning on the left was in general a good omen, but that all lightning was unfavourable for holding the *comitia*. E.g. De Div. ii. 42: 'Iove tonante fulgurante comitia populi habere nefas. . . . Itaque comitiorum solum vitium est fulmen, quod idem omnibus rebus optimum auspicium habemus, si sinistrum fuit'; ib. ii. 74, 'fulmen sinistrum auspicium optimum habemus ad omnis res praeterquam ad comitia'; Vat. 20; Phil. v. 7; Tac. Hist. i. 18; Dio, xxxviii. 13, 4: Mommsen, *St. R.* i. 80; Wissowa, 533. Why then does Cicero add *sinistrum*, which has no effect on the significance of the omen, and would have a favourable effect if it had any? I find only two scholars who have asked the question, and their answers to it are not convincing. Peskett says that 'Cicero is here clearly adopting the Greek usage, whereby *sinistrum* means unlucky'. Valeton (*Mnem.* xix. 80) thinks that it was only 'fulmina quaesita' that were universally unlucky for the *comitia*, whether they appeared on the right or on the left: 'fulmina fortuito conspecta' were, he thinks, favourable to the person who saw them if they appeared on his left, unfavourable to him if they appeared on his right: hence a 'fulmen fortuito conspectum' would be adverse to the holding of the *comitia*, if it appeared, on his left, to a person who wished the *comitia* not to be held. In the present passage, Valeton thinks, Cicero chooses to ignore the tribunes' right of *spectio*: he therefore talks of the 'fulmen quaesitum' in terms strictly applicable to a 'fulmen fortuito conspectum' only.

Cum . . . sunt] For this and 'VII viratu' below see v. 7–8 and § 6 above, with notes.

intervenit . . . non posses] Sarcastic, hence *credo*. A sneer at Nucula and Lento, and the other figure-heads on the commission.

Filiam] Antony's second wife, Antonia. (*Sororem* here = 'first cousin'.) The date of her marriage with Antony cannot be determined. Plutarch also (Ant. 9) mentions Antonia's supposed infidelity as the cause of the quarrel between Antony and Dolabella in 47. The occurrence of the divorce in this year explains Antony's refusal to recall his uncle.

alia . . . perspecta] The intrigue with Fulvia began as early as 58. See § 48.

Kalendis Ianuariis] 1st January 44, when Antony declared his intention of obstructing Dolabella's election to the consulship. See § 79.

an improbior . . . Dolabellam] An amazing statement. Dolabella's profligacy was notorious. He married Cicero's daughter Tullia in 50, and was divorced from her in 46. Caelius, writing to Cicero at the time of the engagement, and trying to make the best of things, expresses the hope that Dolabella has grown out of his youthful follies, and that the influence of Cicero and Tullia will complete his conversion (F. viii. 13, 1). Cicero usually refers to his irregularities in guarded and deprecatory language, but is more explicit about his intrigue with Metella (A. xi. 23, 3). In Phil. xi. 9 he says: 'Alteri (*sc.* Dolabellae) a puero pro deliciis crudelitas fuit; deinde ea libidinum turpitudo ut in hoc sit semper ipse laetatus, quod ea faceret quae sibi obici ne ab inimico quidem possent verecundo. Et hic, di immortales! aliquando fuit meus. Occulta enim erant vitia non inquirenti.'

100. Quae . . . cognitio] On the whole of § 100 cf. A. xvi. 16 c, 11: 'Cum consules oporteret ex senatus consulto de actis Caesaris cognoscere, res ab iis in Kal. Iun. dilata est. Accessit ad senatus consultum lex quae lata est a. d. IIII Non., quae lex earum rerum quas Caesar statuisset, decrevisset, egisset, consulibus cognitionem dedit. Causa Buthrotiorum delata est ad consules. Decretum Caesaris recitatum est et multi praeterea libelli Caesaris prolati. Consules de consili sententia decreverunt secundum Buthrotios.'

This s. c. can be explained in two ways. Either (1) it was a concession extorted by Antony from the senate, by which he regained, in a limited form, the power to examine and execute Caesar's acts which he had possessed after the murder, but had forfeited by the s. c. 'ne qua tabula post Idus Martias ullius decreti Caesaris aut benefici figeretur' (i. 3: see, however, note ad loc.). Or (2) the s. c. 'ne qua tabula', etc. had been repealed, or had lapsed in practice, or possibly had never been passed in the form in which Cicero gives it, in which case the s. c. we are considering was a conservative measure designed to check Antony.

If we adopt (1), with Groebe (Drumann, i². 422-4), we must necessarily date this s. c. before mid-April, when Antony had already begun to use the *acta*: though why Groebe puts it as early as March I cannot see (nor can Ferrero, iii. 44). Dio's account (xliv. 53, 2-4) certainly favours (1), especially *τῆς βουλῆς τὸ μὲν πρῶτον ψηφισαμένης μηδεμίαν στήλην ὡς καὶ τοῦ Καίσαρος συγγεγραφότος τι ἀνατεθῆναι . . . ἔπειτα δέ, ὡς ἐκεῖνος ἐνέκειτο λέγων πολλὰ καὶ ἀναγκαῖα ὑπ' αὐτοῦ προβεβουλεῦσθαι, κελευσάσης πάντας τοὺς πρώτους κοινῇ αὐτὰ διακρῖναι.*

If we adopt (2), with Ferrero (iii. 44), we should naturally date the s. c. about 20th April, just after the first forgeries. On this hypothesis, the postponement of the commission's operations until 1st June is adequately explained by Antony's departure from Rome on about 25th April; whereas a postponement from late March till 1st June is not easily accounted for. I therefore believe (2) to be correct. We need not attach too much importance to Dio's account, which looks like an attempt to combine into a connected whole several different statements in Cicero.

Quod . . . convocasti] That the commission did meet at least once, is proved by A. xvi. 16 c, 11 (note on *Quae . . . cognitio*).

peragratis . . . coloniis] 'Antoni consilia (*sc.* Balbus) narrabat: illum circumire veteranos, ut acta Caesaris sancirent idque se facturos esse iurarent, ut arma omnes haberent, eaque duoviri omnibus mensibus inspicerent' (A. xiv. 21, 2). 'Dicuntur enim occulte milites ad eam diem (*sc.* Kal. Iun.) comparari, et quidem in istos, qui mihi videntur ubivis tutius quam in senatu fore' (A. xiv. 22, 2). 'Novi conventus habitatores sane movent; in magnis enim versamur angustiis' (A. xv. 3, 1). For further references to the concentration of veterans at Rome during the last days of May, see notes on i. 6.

praeclaram . . . percursationem] *Antony's agrarian legislation.* There were no doubt two laws, as has been pointed out by Lange (*Röm. Alt.* iii². 499, 503; ii³. 690), whom modern historians almost universally follow: (1) 'Lex Antonia Cornelia de coloniis in agros deducendis', proposed by the two consuls on, or about, 24th April: (2) 'Lex Antonia Cornelia agraria', also proposed by the two consuls, in June. (Lange's view, that this measure was proposed by L. Antonius, is disposed of by Sternkopf, *Herm.* xlvii. (1912) 146-51, who relies mainly on v. 9, 'cum eo conlega tulit.') (1) was the necessary consequence of the ratification of the 'acta Caesaris'. It dealt with the assignment of the lands promised by Caesar to his veterans. Cicero could not therefore object to the measure as such: in fact, in v. 10, 'si quam . . . placet', he expressly excludes this law from his general condemnation of Antony's legislation. He confines himself to censuring the manner in which Antony carried the law out. (2) was a more comprehensive measure, designed to secure still further the allegiance of the veterans. Perhaps, as Sternkopf thinks, it provided for the distribution of all available 'ager publicus' in Italy (cf. v. 7, 'omnem Italiam dividendam'). The date of (2) is uncertain. Groebe (Drumann, i². 425) says 'the second half of June'; Sternkopf, 'June'. The language of v. 7-10 seems to me to imply that this law was passed simultaneously with the provincial law, i. e. probably on 2nd June (see App. I). For the personnel of the commission which administered it see § 6 note.

The main references to the land-laws are: i. 6; ii. 6; 100-7; iii. 9; v. 7-10; vi. 14; viii. 26; xi. 13; A. xv. 2, 2; 12, 2; 15, 1; 17, 1; 19, 2; F. xi. 2, 3.

mense . . . Maio] Antony left Rome between 22nd and 27th April, probably on 25th: he returned between 18th and 21st May (Groebe-Drumann, i². 428).

Capuam] 'Non arbitrantur eu (*sc.* Antonium) a Capua declinaturum; quo quidem metuo ne magno rei publicae malo venerit' (A. xiv. 17, 2).

paene non abieris] The advent of the new colonists, whom Cicero describes in viii. 26 as 'mimis, aleatoribus, lenonibus', was resented by the old inhabitants, and it seems that Antony was roughly handled. 'Illa (*sc.* Capua) impios civis iudicavit, eiecit, exclusit. Illi, inquam, urbi fortissime conanti e manibus est ereptus Antonius' (xii. 7).

101. minitaris] Clearly in reprisal for the rough treatment he had received.

de vectigalibus . . . daretur] By Caesar. The first distribution was during his consulship in 59. Cicero read the news at Formiae, in a letter from Atticus, which spoiled an after-dinner nap (A. ii. 16, 1). In his reply he points out that the new measure left the state no single source of internal revenue, except the 5 per cent. tax on manumitted slaves: though Pompey, he admits, could argue that the revenue from the newly conquered territories in Asia might be set off against the domestic loss. He consoles himself, however, with the reflection that, at ten jugera apiece, the Campanian land would only provide for 5,000 holders. Suetonius (Iul. 20) says that

Caesar made it accommodate 20,000. Cicero says nothing of the social consequences of dispossessing the original holders: on this subject see Rice Holmes, i. 316.

A further distribution of Campanian land was made by Caesar in 45 (§ 102; A. xvi. 8, 1; Nic. Dam. 31; Suet. Iul. 81; Vell. ii. 61, 2; App. iii. 40).

agro Leontino] The territory of Leontini was leased out to other Sicilians and to Romans. In 70 B.C. only a single family of Leontini occupied any land there (Verr. II. iii. 109, 114). (On the status of the Ager Campanus and Ager Leontinus see Hardy, *Roman Laws and Charters*, 86–90.)

quoniam] Rightly taken by King as explaining the reason for associating Campania with Leontini. Other editors have taken the connexion to be: 'and yet I might justly complain, since . . .'

grandiferae et fructuosae] 'Annonae perfugia', viii. 26. Mayor cites App. ii. 10 for the fertility of Campania.

Medico] We know nothing of him. For *rhetori* (Sextus Clodius) see note on § 43.

tria . . . duo] In Verr. II. iii. 113 Cicero gives the total area of the 'ager Leontinus' as 30,000 jugera. At that rate, doctor and rhetorician received between them one-sixth of the whole.

102. Casilinum] 'C. Caesar (*sc.* Octavianus) . . . a Casilino veteranos excivit paternos' (Vell. ii. 61, 2).

per litteras] There is no trace of this in the extant correspondence.

ut . . . circumduceres] Cf. 'illud vexillum Campanae coloniae' (Leg. Agr. ii. 86). Mayor remarks that both flag and plough are found on Roman colonial coins. The flag was a token of the military origin of colonial settlements. For *aratrum* cf. Verg. Aen. v. 755, 'Aeneas urbem designat aratro'. Sihler cites Festus, p. 392, Lindsay: 'sulci appellantur qua aratrum ducitur, vel sationis faciendae causa, vel urbis condendae' (cf. id. p. 271, 'primigenius sulcus'); and Pomponius, Dig. I. 16, 239, 'urbare est aratro definire'.

103. M. Varronis] M. Terentius Varro, 116–27 B.C.: held various magistracies, including the praetorship; served under Pompey in 67 against the pirates; also in Spain in the Civil War in 49, where he was captured by Caesar, who pardoned him, and afterwards designated him public librarian; proscribed by Antony in 43, but saved by Fufius Calenus. He wrote some 620 volumes, of widely differing character, including the treatises *De Lingua Latina*, *De Re Rustica* (these two are extant, the former in a mutilated form), *Antiquitates*, *De Iure Civili*, *De Forma Philosophiae*, and *Satirae Menippeae*. A remarkable combination of student and man of affairs.

sanctissimi . . . viri] In a letter written in 59 (A. ii. 25, 1) Cicero describes Varro as 'mirabiliter moratus, sicut nosti, ἑλικτὰ καὶ οὐδὲν —'. But he was anxious at that time to be on good terms with

Varro, in order to please Pompey. And in the same letter he naïvely asks Atticus to repeat to Varro anything complimentary he may say of him. See also A. xiii. 18 and 19.

fundum Casinatem] Varro himself describes the farm in his *De Re Rustica*, iii. 5, 9.

Eodem . . . Rubri] Another passage altered by Cicero on Atticus' advice. He originally wrote 'quo Scipionis' (Scipio's villa at Tibur, to which Antony retired after the delivery of the First Philippic. See § 42). Atticus suggested 'eodem iure quo Rubriana', an alteration which Cicero adopted, with a slight change of wording. For Rubrius and Turselius see note on § 41.

Et si ab hasta . . . liberavisti] For the spear as the sign of an auction see § 64.

The words 'modo Caesaris . . . liberavisti' are a parenthetical digression. The logic of the rest is: 'If you bought Varro's property at an auction, well and good: let the validity of the auction stand unquestioned. But as a matter of fact, no auction of Varro's property was ever held' *Tabulae* means here the bills of sale at an auction; but the mention of the word suggests one of its other meanings, 'accounts', and Cicero goes off at a tangent: 'When I uphold the validity of "tabulae", I mean Caesar's accounts, in which you are entered as owing money for the property of Pompey which you bought and never paid for; not the accounts which you falsified at the temple of Ops, in order to get money to free yourself from debt'. (For a similar play on *tabulae* cf. Cat. ii. 18.)

Varronis quidem] Mayor brings out the force of the particle by italics: 'As for *Varro's* estate at Casinum, who affirms that that was sold?' The connexion ('but') is omitted, as often.

ipsum . . . fuit] But no one could possibly tell when Caesar would be back in Italy. As a matter of fact he arrived back towards the end of September 47, after his campaign in Asia Minor.

104. nullius . . . fuit] So that nothing which happened with regard to Varro's property could pass unnoticed.

aliam . . . tuae] Peskett paraphrases: 'If Caesar chooses to sell confiscated property (as he did Pompey's), well and good, but your audacity in seizing Varro's property is unjustifiable.'

Ab hora tertia] Cf. § 87, 'de die'.

'quam dispari domino'] From an unknown tragedy. The whole line is quoted in De Off. i. 139 (written in 44): 'Odiosum est enim, cum a praetereuntibus dicitur: "o domus antiqua, heu quam dispari dominare domino!" quod quidem his temporibus in multis licet dicere.'

105. inquilino] 'Tenant,' 'lodger.' Catiline called Cicero an *inquilinus* of Rome, because he came from Arpinum (Sall. Cat. 31, 7).

Aquino, Interamna] Respectively seven miles west and six miles south of Casinum.

admissus est nemo] So Cicero writes to Atticus at the end of May 44 (A. xv. 8, 1): 'aditus ad eum difficilior esse dicitur.'

Iure id quidem] 'You were right to prevent strangers from witnessing your degradation of the dignity of office.' According to Mayor, Cicero sarcastically remarks that Antony was quite right to avoid the honour of the *salutatio*, to which he had no claim after his disgraceful behaviour. This seems to me a less natural explanation.

106. sed] Madvig suggests *sed sum vicinus* for the corrupt variants in the MSS. If this is right, Cicero calls himself a 'neighbour' because he had a villa at Anagnia (A. xii. 1, 1), or perhaps in reference to the proximity of his birthplace, Arpinum.

Mustelam et Laconem] In the rough copy of the speech which Cicero sent to Atticus the names were lacking. Atticus was puzzled, so Cicero added them. 'Anagnini sunt Mustela ταξιάρχης et Laco, qui plurimum bibit' (A. xvi. 11, 3).

107. patronos] *Patroni* (in this sense) were distinguished Romans, elected by municipal and provincial towns, sometimes even by whole provinces, with the general duty of looking after their interests. Their names were entered at the head of the 'album' of the municipal senate. The numbers varied greatly: in A.D. 223 Canusium had as many as thirty-nine *patroni*. The honour was conferred for various reasons: the conqueror of a new province, the founder of a colony, an orator who had pleaded on behalf of a town, or an influential person with no special claim, might be chosen. The appointment was engraved upon a bronze tablet, which the *patronus* hung in his hall. The distinction was an hereditary one: Antony, for example, was hereditary patron of Bononia. Cicero himself was adopted sole patron of Capua 'propter salutem illius urbis consulatu conservatam meo' (Sest. 9).

See Mayor, ad loc., and the fully documented account in D. and S. iii. 1, 299–300; iv. 1, 358–9; J. S. Reid, *Municipalities of the Roman Empire*, 442–3.

Magno . . . armis] 'On account of their great zeal, &c., not . . . under compulsion.' The ablatives are rather curious. But Peskett's interpretation cannot possibly be right: 'they (treated them) with great zeal, &c., not as they did you and Basilus with violence.'

non modo] Curiously used for *nedum*. Parallels in Mayor's note.

qui dies . . . evertit] Cf. i. 5, where 'quae, nisi conlega afuisset, credo eis futura fuisse communia' is startlingly inconsistent with *concidisti* here.

Quid . . . nescio] History is adapted for the occasion. Before the end of April Cicero had already reason to believe that Antony and Dolabella were hand in glove (A. xiv. 14, 4 : rumour of an extended provincial command for both consuls). And on 9th May, in the very midst of his rhapsodies about the overturned pillar, he accuses Dolabella of sharing with Antony the spoils from the temple of Ops (A. xiv. 18, 1). Cicero's unbalanced and volatile temperament is strikingly illustrated by the correspondence of the first half of May, which shows clearly that he did not know what to make of Dolabella.

108. reditus Romam] Between 18th and 21st May (Groebe-Drumann, i². 428).

Cinnam nimis potentem] From 87, when he rebelled against the constitution of Sulla, to 84, when he was killed in a mutiny at Ancona.

Sullam postea dominantem] From 83, when he returned from the Mithradatic War, until 79, when he voluntarily resigned the dictatorship. It was under the Sullan regime, in 80 B.C., that Cicero delivered his first speech in a public case, in defence of Sextus Roscius Amerinus, whose father was a victim of the proscriptions.

Erant fortasse . . . barbaria est] Cicero repeats and embellishes the fantastic comparison in Phil. v. 17–18.

Agmine quadrato] 'Varro . . . duo genera agminum dicit: quadratum, quod inmixtis etiam iumentis incedit, ut ubivis possit consistere: pilatum alterum, quod sine iumentis incedit, sed inter se densum est, quo facilius per iniquiora loca tramittatur' (Servius, ad Aen. xii. 121).

This description is borne out by Hirtius, *B.G.* viii. 8, 4–5 ('paene quadrato agmine'), and Tac. Ann. i. 51, 5 ; 64, 8 ; xiii. 40, 2–3. The first recorded instance of the formation is in 151 B.C.: τετράγωνον ἐν πλινθίῳ τὸν στρατὸν ἄγων (Appian, Iberica 55). It was intended to protect the baggage train, and its employment, when a sudden attack was to be expected, is often mentioned by Livy.

Cavalry and light-armed troops were frequently stationed in van and rear, and on the flanks (Sall. Iug. 46 ; 100). (There is no evidence to connect this formation with the march order in three parallel columns described by Polybius, vi. 40, 10–14, in spite of Marquardt, *Römische Staatsverwaltung*, ii. 409–11 ; Masquelez in D. and S. i. 1, 145. On the whole question see, in addition to these authorities, *Dict. Ant.* i. 806–7.)

By the metaphorical use of the term here, Cicero wishes to give the impression of something more than mere active-service conditions. Troops marching with loaded rifles is a modern parallel.

scutorum lecticas] Cf. Phil. v. 18 : 'lecticae conlocabantur, non quo ille scuta occulta esse vellet, sed ne familiares, si scuta ipsi ferrent, laborarent.' The use of litters for the conveyance of material is unparalleled, except possibly by Mart. vii. 53, 10 (P.-W., xii. 1, 1081).

Kalendis . . . vellemus] Cicero speaks for others. He himself was at his Tusculan house, and had no intention of attending (i. 6, and notes).

109. Numerum . . . prorogavit] See App. I. The bill was actually proposed by tribunes (v. 7), but they acted as Antony's tools.

promulgavit] *Sc.* 'novas leges'.

Signa . . . legavit] The other ancient authorities say that Caesar left the people his gardens beyond the Tiber, and a money largesse to each individual citizen. None of them mention *signa* or *tabulas* (Suet. Iul. 83; App. ii. 143; Dio, xliv. 35, 3; Plut. Brut. 20, 2; Tac. Ann. ii. 41).

Cicero might have mentioned here Antony's refusal to hand over Octavian's legacy (App. iii. 14 ff.; Plut. Ant. 16).

110. Et tu . . . diligens] In § 110 Cicero charges Antony with disloyalty to Caesar on two counts. (1) Although appointed his *flamen*, he had never been consecrated. (2) Although he had himself proposed the law enjoining that an extra day, in Caesar's honour, should be added to the 'Ludi Romani', here was the day actually arrived, and yet Antony had made no arrangement for its celebration. This, the general meaning of the passage, is clear enough. The detailed interpretation of it involves some difficulties.

Quem . . . flaminem] Our main authority for the divine honours conferred on Caesar is Dio (xliii. 14, 45; xliv. 4–6), supplemented by a brief enumeration in Suetonius (Iul. 76), by various references in Cicero, and by archaeological evidence. Suetonius's list is: 'tensam et ferculum circensi pompa, templa, aras, simulacra iuxta deos, pulvinar, flaminem, lupercos, appellationem mensis a suo nomine.' Warde Fowler (*Roman Ideas of Deity*, 107–20) thinks that Dio is in some respects inaccurate, that earlier attempts at deification (in 46 and 45) were of no great importance, but that a serious attempt was made by Antony early in 44, with the object of discrediting Caesar. Warde Fowler's reasoning is scarcely conclusive, and both Meyer (447–8, 512–14) and Rice Holmes (iii. 316, 332) accept Dio's account. As Meyer points out, there are two stages in the deification: (1) the preliminary steps after Munda (statue in temple of Quirinus and ivory image in the *pompa*); (2) complete deification early in 44.

pulvinar] At the rite of *lectisternium* (the laying out of couches) images of the gods were placed on cushioned couches (*pulvinaria*) and tables of food were set before them. The rite, which was probably of Greek origin and represents an anthropomorphic view of the gods foreign to Roman ideas, dates from the plague of 399. It was closely connected with the *supplicationes*, though in the case of certain deities it appears to have been practically a standing ceremony. Cf. Liv. xxxvi. 1, 2: 'in omnibus fanis, in quibus lectisternium maiorem partem anni fieri solet'. (Warde Fowler, *Rel. Exp.* 261–6; Wissowa, 421–6.)

simulacrum] 'Image.' 'Simulacra deorum . . . et statuae veterum hominum' (Cat. iii. 19).

(1) A statue of Caesar was placed in the temple of Quirinus (Romulus) on the Quirinal Hill. Cicero twice alludes to it satirically in the letters: 'σύνναον Quirini' (A. xii. 45, 2; 17th May 45); 'Quirini contubernalem' (A. xiii. 28, 3; 26th May 45). Warde Fowler (*Roman Ideas of Deity*, 116) asserts that this does not of itself imply deification, and that after the death of Scipio Africanus Maior his statue was placed in the Capitoline temple, opposite Jupiter's. I find no evidence for the latter statement. The honour was offered to Scipio during his lifetime, but refused by him (Liv. xxxviii. 56, 12: Val. Max. iv. 1, 6). But that it was offered is significant. Dio (xliii. 45, 3) says Caesar's statue was inscribed 'Deo Invicto'. 'But Dio may be wrong', says Warde Fowler, 'or the inscription may have been added later.'

(2) Dio also mentions (xliii. 45, 2) an ἀνδριάντα ἐλεφάντινον . . . ἐν ταῖς ἱπποδρομίαις (viz. carried in the procession before the races). Cicero several times mentions this with displeasure (A. xiii. 44, 1 'etsi acerba pompa'; ib. 'sed pompa deterret'. Cf. A. xiii. 28, 3).

(3) Dio mentions (xliv. 4, 4) 'statues in all the cities and all the temples of Rome'.

What is the reference of *simulacrum* here? (3), if we may believe Dio, must have put (1) in the shade, whereas (2), the public display of Caesar's effigy on festival occasions, would have retained its importance. I believe that *simulacrum* refers generically to all representations of Caesar as superhuman. The use of the singular is certainly curious, and is perhaps due to a desire for symmetry.

fastigium] The gable was a characteristic mark of a Roman temple. As Cicero explains in the *De Oratore* (iii. 180), its original purpose was to let the rainwater run off. But had a temple been built in heaven, where no rain falls, it would have been given a gable all the same.

Caesar 'habitavit primo in Subura modicis aedibus: post autem pontificatum maximum in Sacra via domo publica' (Suet. Iul. 46). Dio (xliii. 44, 6) says: τότε τῷ Καίσαρι οἰκίαν, ὥστε ἐν τῷ δημοσίῳ οἰκεῖν ... ἔδοσαν. The locality of this new house cannot be defined. (Meyer, 447, supposes it to have been on the Quirinal. But the expression 'vicino Caesare' in A. xii. 45, 2; 48, on which he relies, is perhaps a humorous reference to Caesar's statue in the temple of Quirinus. Drumann, iii. 2, 599, n. 6, thinks that Dio's chronology is wrong, and that he refers to the house in the Via Sacra.

For the gable cf. Plut. Caes. 63: ἀλλ' ἦν γάρ τι τῇ Καίσαρος οἰκίᾳ προσκείμενον, οἷον ἐπὶ κόσμῳ καὶ σεμνότητι τῆς βουλῆς ψηφισαμένης ἀκρωτήριον ὡς Λίβιος ἱστορεῖ; Flor. ii. 13, 91 'fastigium in domo'. The night before Caesar's murder Calpurnia dreamed 'conlabi fastigium domus' (Suet. Iul. 81; cf. Plut. loc. cit.).

flaminem] Priests attached to individual deities were so designated. 'Divisque . . . omnibus pontifices, singulis flamines sunto'

(Cic. De Leg. ii. 20). Varro's derivation (L. L. v. 84) from *filum* is rejected by modern authorities, who connect the word with 'flare', or with *flagrare*, *flamma* (the blowing up of the sacrificial fire), or with the Sanskrit *brahman*. The *flamines maiores* (attached to Jupiter, Mars, and Quirinus) were patricians: the remainder, *flamines minores*, were plebeians. The number of flamens rose to fifteen, but many were already obsolete in Cicero's day (Samter in P.-W., s. v. *Flamines*; Wissowa, 504 ff.).

For Antony as Caesar's flamen, cf. xiii. 41, 47; Dio, xliv. 6, 4; Suet. Iul. 76. Plutarch (Ant. 33) states that in 40 he actually assumed the flaminate which in 44 he had avoided: αὐτὸς δὲ Καίσαρι (Octavian) χαριζόμενος ἱερεὺς ἀπεδείχθη τοῦ προτέρου Καίσαρος.

divo] The first occurrence of an appellation conferred, after their death, on most, though not all, of the Roman emperors. Dio (xliv. 6, 4) states that Caesar let himself be styled Iuppiter Iulius, a statement rejected by Warde Fowler (*Roman Ideas of Deity*, 119), but accepted by Meyer (513) and, with some reserve, by Rice Holmes (iii. 332). G. Herzog-Hauser, in P.-W., s. v. *Kaiserkult*, Suppl. iv. 818, rejects Dio's assertion, pointing out that Caesar's assumption of a Mithraistic title such as 'Deus Invictus' was a very different matter from allowing himself to be identified with the greatest of Roman divinities.

As contemporary evidence of the deification of Caesar, Meyer cites *C. I. L.* i². 1611 = Dessau, 6343: 'M. Salvio Q. f. Venusto decurioni [be]neficio Dei Caesaris.'

inaugurarie] The new Flamen was chosen by the Pontifex Maximus from three candidates nominated by the Collegium Pontificum. He was then 'inducted' (*inauguratus*) by an augur at the *comitia calata* (Gell. i. 12, 15; xv. 27, 1; Liv. xxvii. 8, 5; Tac. Ann. iv. 16; Samter in P.-W. vi. 2, 2486).

conlegae] Cf. §§ 4, 84.

quartum . . . Romanorum] The *Ludi Romani* originated in the games promised to the gods, in the event of victory, by Roman commanders in the field (*ludi votivi*). Gradually such games became *sollemnes*, 'customary', and finally fixed annual performances (*annui*). Liv. i. 35, 1c. Similar games continued to be celebrated on extraordinary occasions (e. g. by Pompey in 70), but were then styled *magni* or *votivi* instead of *Romani*. The duration of the *Ludi Romani* was gradually extended, and in the Augustan calendar they occupy sixteen days, 4th–19th September. The earlier days were taken up with *ludi scaenici*, on the 13th was the *Epulum Iovis* (probably the kernel of the whole festival), and on the 14th the *equorum probatio*. On the remaining five days, 15th–19th, took place the 'Ludi Romani in Circo', contests in riding and chariot-driving, beginning, on 15th, with the *pompa*, a procession to the Capitol and thence to the Circus. It appears from the present passage that at the time of the supposed delivery of the

Second Philippic (19th September), the 'Ludi Romani in Circo' only lasted from 15th to 18th September. The proposal which Antony had made on some unknown occasion, but afterwards dropped, to add a fifth day, the 19th, in honour of Caesar, appears to have been carried out by Augustus.

(Mommsen, *Röm. Forsch.* ii. 42–57; Marquardt, *Staatsverw.* iii. 497–8; Warde Fowler, *Rom. Fest.* 216 ff.; Wissowa, 127–8, 452–4.)

praetextati] § 44, note.

an supplicationes . . . noluisti] Cicero contrasts Antony's past conduct in proposing the addition of a day in honour of Caesar to the *supplicationes* (i. 13) with his present reluctance to carry out another proposal, for adding a day, in honour of Caesar, to the 'Ludi Romani in Circo'. But he expresses himself obscurely.

(1) How could Antony defile the *supplicationes* without also defiling the *pulvinaria*? For the rite of *supplicatio* was performed *at* the *pulvinaria*; cf. Cat. iii. 23, 'ad omnia pulvinaria supplicatio decreta est'; Phil. xiv. 37, 'supplicationes . . . ad omnia pulvinaria'; Liv. xxi. 62, 9, 'supplicatio . . . circa omnia pulvinaria indicta'; xxii. 1, 15, 'decretum uti supplicatio . . . ad omnia pulvinaria haberetur'; and in i. 13, 'ut ei (Caesari) publice supplicetur' cannot mean anything else than worship accorded to Caesar before the *pulvinar* on which his image rested.

(2) What had the *pulvinaria* to do with the extra day at the end of the 'Ludi in Circo'? Reid, on p. 138 of Peskett's edition, quotes *Festus*, p. 364: 'tensam ait vocari Sinnius Capito vehiculum quo exuviae deorum ludicris Circensibus in Circum ad pulvinar vehuntur'. (And Caesar was allowed a *tensa*, Suet. Iul. 76.) This is certainly evidence for the use of *pulvinaria* in the ceremonial of the 'Ludi in Circo'. But, as Reid observes (p. 140), the 'pompa' *opened* the 'Ludi in Circo', and, fifth day or no fifth day, the *pulvinaria* must have been 'defiled' already. 'Perhaps it was intended', Reid concludes, 'that there should be some very special celebration of the *pompa* in Caesar's honour on the fifth day.' Yes, or at any rate something particularly involving the *pulvinaria*: knowing nothing of the ritual contemplated for the fifth day, we cannot say anything more definite.

(Halm[a] curiously explains *supplicationes* as 'the institution of the *supplicationes*', *pulvinaria* as the practical performance of the *supplicatio* to Caesar. But (1) this cannot be got out of the Latin; (2) where do the 'Ludi in Circo' come in?)

111. apertiorem] Cf. §§ 84–7. '*Apertum pectus* was proverbial. Lael. 97, "ut dicitur".' (Mayor.)

112. cur valvae . . . patent] The senate met in the temple of Concord on 19th September, when Antony made the speech to which the Second Philippic was a reply (v. 20). The gates were presumably shut in order to complete the helplessness of the senate, and obviate any chance of succour from outside.

Ituraeos] Cf. § 19.

113. sine contumelia describo] Cf. Pis. 68, 'non contumeliae causa describam'; § 31, note on *honoris causa.*

tertiam pensionem] Fulvia's three instalments were her three husbands, Clodius, Curio, and Antony. Cf. § 11, n. on *id.* Cicero describes her in v. 11 as 'sibi felicior quam viris'.

ad quos] The reference is exclusively to Brutus and Cassius, I feel sure.

ubicumque terrarum sunt] Cf. § 33, note on *qui locus . . . videatur*, for the whereabouts of Brutus and Cassius.

tantum modo . . . recuperavit] Very similar language is used in a letter to Cassius (F. xii. 1, 2): 'Adhuc ulta suas iniurias est per vos interitu tyranni, nihil amplius; ornamenta vero sua quae reciperavit?'

adulescentis] See § 52, note.

114. Tarquinium . . . Sp. Cassius, Sp. Maelius] § 26, notes.

M. Manlius] i. 32, note.

115. dictaturam sustulisti] i. 3.

116. Quae est...suis] Cicero may have been thinking of Caesar's remark ὡς βέλτιον ἐστιν ἅπαξ ἀποθανεῖν ἢ ἀεὶ προσδοκᾶν (Plut. Caes. 57).

quosdam] As Halm observes, the reference is both to Caesarians who joined the conspiracy, such as P. and C. Servilius Casca, L. Tillius Cimber, C. Trebonius, L. Minucius Basilus, Servius Sulpicius Galba, and to those who, though Pompeians from the first, had been pardoned by Caesar, such as M. Brutus and C. Cassius.

litterae] Besides his historical works, Caesar wrote treatises on grammar, astronomy, and augury.

muneribus . . . epulis] At his triumphs in 46 and 45 Caesar 'edidit spectacula varii generis; munus gladiatorium, ludos etiam regionatim urbe tota et quidem per omnium linguarum histriones, item circenses, athletas, naumachiam'. The entertainments were so much appreciated that people were frequently crushed to death in the crowds. He made each citizen a present of money, corn, and oil, besides gratuities for his veterans. He also distributed land, and fixed a maximum for house rent. He gave a public banquet and free distribution of meat in 46, and two banquets in 45 (Suet. Iul. 37–9). On the other hand, by reducing the number of recipients of the corn-dole from 320,000 to 150,000 (id. ib. 41), he showed clearly that he realized the danger of pauperizing the masses.

monumentis] Such as the Forum Iulium, the Basilica Iulia, and the extension of the Circus Maximus.

clementiae] This was the quality for which Caesar most desired to be known. A temple was voted to him in common with 'Clementia' (Dio. xliv. 6, 4). 'Et ceteros quidem omnis victores bellorum civilium iam antea aequitate et misericordia viceras: hodierno vero die te ipse vicisti' (Marcell. 12).

'O clementiam admirabilem atque omnium laude, praedicatione, litteris monumentisque decorandam' (Lig. 6).

Cicero wrote to Caesar in 49, praising his generosity in releasing Domitius from Corfinium. Caesar's reply is contained in A. ix. 16.

Cicero had cause enough himself to be grateful for Caesar's clemency, which he acknowledged readily enough, even in confidential letters. E.g. 'In Caesare haec sunt : mitis clemensque natura . . .' (F. vi. 6, 8, Sept. 46; A. xiv. 17, 6). Cf. the words of Matius, 'Clementiam illi malo fuisse' (A. xiv. 22, 1); and Cassius, 'veterem et clementem dominum' (F. xv. 19, 4).

118. non pertimescam tuos] Juvenal's taunt is well known (x. 122-6):

> 'O fortunatam natam me consule Romam!'
> Antoni gladios potuit contemnere, si sic
> Omnia dixisset. Ridenda poemata malo
> Quam te conspicuae, divina Philippica, famae
> Volveris a prima quae proxima.

119. negavi . . . consulari] 'Si quid obtigerit, aequo animo paratoque moriar. Nam neque turpis mors forti viro potest accidere neque immatura consulari' (Cat. iv. 3).

APPENDIX I

NOTE ON THE PROVINCES

THE assignment of provincial commands during the period preceding the First Philippic is an intricate and obscure subject, and it may be helpful to discuss it in a separate note.

Recent historians agree in rejecting Appian's statement (iii. 2) that Macedonia and Syria were assigned by Caesar to Brutus and Cassius.[1] This erroneous notion, which is inconsistent with Phil. xi. 27–30 and A. xv. 9, 1, probably arose from the fact that Brutus and Cassius did in fact subsequently take possession of these two provinces. Some historians consider that Macedonia and Syria were assigned to Antony and Dolabella by Caesar; but Sternkopf (*Hermes*, xlvii (1912), 321–401) gives strong reasons for believing that Caesar had made no provincial arrangements for 43, and that Antony and Dolabella obtained Macedonia and Syria in the normal constitutional way, viz. by drawing lots for the consular provinces after these had been nominated by the senate. Sternkopf conjectures mid-April as the date of the proceeding. (18th April is the *terminus ante quem*; for A. xiv. 9 of that date, 'sed Dolabella et Nicias viderint' (in reference to Parthia), implies that Dolabella had already had Syria assigned to him.)

The exchange of provinces. The historians speak of an exchange (Liv. Ep. 117; App. iii. 7); Cicero does not mention an exchange, but speaks of a prolonged tenure (Phil. ii. 109; v. 7; A. xiv. 14, 4). Sternkopf concludes that the 'Lex tribunicia de provinciis' (Phil. v. 7) and the 'Lex de permutatione provinciarum' (Liv. Ep. 117) are two parts of one and the same law; the historians emphasize the *permutatio* because in fact it led to the Mutinensian War, and ignore the *prorogatio*, which, owing to the turn of events, never materialized: Cicero, on the other hand, was less perturbed by the *permutatio*, for which there were unobjectionable precedents, than by the *prorogatio*. That the two measures were embraced in one law is not certain; but it is *a priori* probable that Antony should have taken both steps at once, and that was without doubt his original intention (A. xiv. 14, 4).

The date of the 'Lex tribunicia de provinciis' is fixed by Phil. ii. 109, where it is described as being passed immediately (*statim*) after the meeting of the senate which took place on 1st June. This points to 2nd June as the date of the Lex Tribunicia, and it cannot have been later, as Dolabella on that day appointed Cicero his

[1] F. xii. 4, 2 does not, I think (though Mr. C. Hignett disagrees), support Appian. The joke seems equally apposite, whether Dolabella was the usurper or the lawful governor.

legate for five years (A. xv. 11, 4).[1] Historians differ as to the date of the 'Lex de Permutatione'. On Sternkopf's view it must, of course, be the same as the date of the 'Lex de Provinciis'. Groebe, on slender grounds, puts it just before 14th June (Drumann, i². 435-6, comparing A. xv. 17, 1); Ferrero puts it in July, but it can scarcely have been passed much later than the middle of June, as the transference of troops from Macedonia, which resulted from it, is spoken of as imminent on 10th July.

Sternkopf proves that by the Lex de Permutatione Antony received Transalpine as well as Cisalpine Gaul. The historians speak either of Gaul without qualification, or of Cisalpine Gaul: Cicero too speaks sometimes of Cisalpine Gaul alone (A. xv. 4, 1). But this is because Cisalpine Gaul was the important province and the eventual *casus belli*. When he is speaking precisely, Cicero always uses, or implies, the plural (Phil. i. 8; iii. 38; v. 37; A. xiv. 14, 4). Groebe (Drumann, i². 436) was misled by supposing that Phil. v. 5, vii. 3, and viii. 27 refer to the supposed willingness of Antony at a later stage to accept Transalpine in lieu of Cisalpine Gaul. As Sternkopf points out, the possibility there mooted is not that of accepting one province instead of the other, but that of accepting one instead of both.

Groebe and Sternkopf consider that the Lex de Permutatione contained a clause assigning the Macedonian legions to Antony. (The Lex Vatinia of 59 embodied a similar provision.) Schwartz, on the other hand, is of opinion that Antony transferred the legions in virtue of his imperium. If this is so, arguments as to the date of the Lex de Permutatione based on troop movements of course break down. The number of legions transferred is uncertain. Appian (iii. 24) speaks of six. Cicero (F. xii. 23, 2) mentions four as shipped to Italy.

The provinces of Brutus and Cassius. It was anticipated that Brutus and Cassius and the remaining praetors would have provinces assigned to them on 5th June (A. xv. 9, 1). In point of fact the remaining praetors drew lots for their provinces on 28th November (Phil. iii. 20; 24-6): Brutus and Cassius received theirs at an earlier, but unknown, date. The *terminus ad quem* is 19th September, the dramatic date of the Second Philippic; for ii. 97 implies that Crete had by then been assigned to Brutus. It is possible that the provinces were assigned on 5th June (the day on which Brutus and Cassius were appointed to the *curatio frumenti* as a stop-gap employment which would keep them out of Italy until the end of the year). If Phil. ii. 31 is in chronological order, as Sternkopf thinks (though it may equally well be in order of climax), the assignment must have been later than the Ludi Apollinares (6th–13th July). 1st August has been conjectured both by Groebe and by Ferrero, but it remains a conjecture.

[1] Unless 'a. d. III Nonas' is the right meaning.

APPENDIX II

THE EQUITES AND THE JURIES

I. *The terms 'eques' and 'eques Romanus'.*

THE term *eques*, in its military and in its political sense, has been the subject of much discussion. Reference may be made to Mommsen, *St. R.* iii. 459–569; Greenidge, *R.P.L.* 73–4, 224–5; Kübler in P.-W. s.v. *Equites Romani.* The Servian organization provided eighteen centuries of Equites, serving on horses found by the state (*equo publico*). To supplement these, at the siege of Veii in 403 B.C., volunteers offered to serve *suis equis* (Liv. v. 7, 13). Subsequently the meaning of *eques* is modified, politically and militarily.

(1) Politically. At a date which cannot be determined, a property qualification seems to have been introduced for the Equites, whether serving *equo publico* or *suo*. And, as not all qualified persons were required for service, the term came to be used in a wider sense, as denoting all persons possessing the requisite property. This class was first given political importance by Gaius Gracchus. In 67 B.C., when the Lex Roscia (see ii. 44) was passed, and under the empire, the equestrian census was 400,000 sesterces, and it is probable that the same census was required in earlier times.

(2) Militarily. The Roman burgess cavalry gradually disappeared, and towards the end of the second century B.C. it had been entirely replaced by allied cavalry. The term *eques Romanus* now denoted, not 'cavalry trooper', but something like 'officer' (the Romans, as Mommsen points out, *St. R.* iii. 539, had no precise term for officer), and *equo merere* meant officer service.

In the Ciceronian period, then, we find, on the one hand, the wider political term *eques* or *equester ordo*, denoting all persons possessing 400,000 sesterces; on the other hand, the narrower military term *eques Romanus*, denoting those of such persons actually serving as officers, the full designation being 'eques Romanus equo publico' (vi. 13). (What happened to the Equites serving *suis equis* is obscure. Mommsen (*St. R.* iii. 489) thinks they disappeared during Caesar's dictatorship. We hear nothing of them in the Ciceronian period.) But the distinction between the terms is not always rigidly observed, *Equites Romani* being frequently used in the political sense, and *Equites* (less frequently) in the military sense (though Mommsen, *St. R.* iii. 481, n. 1, is inclined to doubt the latter use).

II. *The composition of the juries.*

The jurymen of the *quaestiones perpetuae*, the first of which was established in 149 B.C., were at first drawn exclusively from the senate (Dio, Fr. 88; Plut. Tib. Gracch. 16). In 122 Gaius Gracchus transferred the courts to the Equites (Vell. ii. 6, 3; 13, 2; 32, 3; Tac

Ann. xii. 60; Varr. ap Non., p. 454; App. i. 22). This system, in spite of repeated attempts at reaction and compromise, lasted until 81, when Sulla restored the courts to a senate doubled by the inclusion of some 300 Equites (Liv. Ep. 89; App. i. 100; Vell. ii. 32, 3; Tac. Ann. xi. 22; Cic. Verr. I, 37). This was perhaps a reasonable adjustment of senatorial and equestrian claims. But probably, as Greenidge observes (*Leg. Proc.* 442), the new senators quickly assimilated themselves to their new surroundings. In 70 B. C. the leaders of the democratic reaction perhaps at first contemplated the wholesale restitution of the courts to the Equites; in the event they contented themselves, by a Lex Aurelia of L. Aurelius Cotta, with juries drawn in equal proportion from Senators, Equites, and Tribuni Aerarii. (Verr. II. ii. 174; 223; Ascon. in Pis. 15: in Corn. 59: ib. 70; Schol. Bob., p. 229. Liv. Ep. 97, Vell. ii. 32, 3, and Plut. Pomp. 22 are inaccurate.) The next change was made by a Lex Pompeia of 55, which compelled the Praetor Urbanus, in drawing up his annual *album iudicum*, to select the richest, and therefore presumably least venal, of the Equites and Tribuni Aerarii, instead of exercising free choice, as hitherto. 'Pompeius . . . promulgavit ut amplissimo ex censu ex centuriis aliter atque antea lecti iudices, aeque tamen ex illis tribus ordinibus, res iudicarent' (Ascon. in Pis. 15). Cicero expressed strong approval of the measure: 'Ecquid vides, ecquid sentis, lege iudiciaria lata, quos posthac iudices simus habituri? Neque legetur quisquis voluerit, nec quisquis noluerit non legetur; nulli conicientur in illum ordinem, nulli eximentur; non ambitio ad gratiam, non iniquitas ad aemulationem conitetur; iudices iudicabunt ii quos lex ipsa, non quos hominum libido delegerit' (Pis. 94). Next, in 46, a Lex Iulia excluded the Tribuni Aerarii from the juries (Suet. Iul. 41; Dio, xliii. 25, 1). We find, then, in 44, two classes (*decuriae*) of jurymen, Senators and Equites. To these Antony proposed to add a third, the exact composition of which is hard to determine. According to Cicero, it consisted of centurions and of the privates of the *Alauda* legion, together with a mixed riff-raff of Greeks, exiles, gamblers, danseurs, and harpists (v. 12; 15). As to how far Cicero is exaggerating, see § 20, note on *addo . . . Alaudarum*. The measure was carried (v. 12–15; viii. 27), but by March 43 it had been repealed (Phil. xiii. 5), and was not revived.

III. *The Equites and Tribuni Aerarii of the juries.*

We now enter upon controversial ground. It has been pointed out in I above that our authorities use the terms Equites and Equites Romani in a narrower military and in a wider political sense. In which sense, then, are we to understand them when applied to the jurymen? (Cicero usually speaks of Equites Romani: in Verr. I. 38, II. iii. 223–4 of 'equester ordo': in A. i. 16, 3 of 'equites': the historians usually speak of ἱππεῖς or 'equites'.) Up to Mommsen, most authorities understood the terms in the wider sense; and so, at first, did Mommsen himself (in his monograph on the Lex Acilia). But he subsequently changed his mind, and in his later writings (*St. R.* iii. 530, n. 2, 531, n. 1, *Strafrecht*, 209–11) maintained that the Equites who monopolized the courts under the Gracchan law, and shared them under later laws, were not the whole Equester Ordo, but the *Equites Romani equo publico* or *Centuriae Equitum Romanorum*, possibly including those who had completed their service.

The Tribuni Aerarii had originally been responsible for collecting the war-tax (*tributum*) and paying the army out of it. But these functions had lapsed; *tributum* was not levied after 167 B.C., and the troops were paid by the quaestor. Many authorities (including Lange, Zumpt, Bélot, and Greenidge) understand the title as denoting the possessors of 300,000 sesterces, standing midway between the Equites and the fourth decury added by Augustus, consisting of possessors of 200,000. (This theory is supported by a fragment from Cicero's In Clodium et Curionem: 'ut posthac lege Aurelia iudex esse non possit'; with the *scholium*: 'amissis *trecenis* vel quadragenis milibus quae a reo acceperant in egestatem revolverentur ac propterea in iudicum numero non essent.') Mommsen, on the other hand, assigns the equestrian census to the Tribuni Aerarii (after 55 B.C.; see i. 20, note on *Pompeia*), and thus explains the fact that Cicero often ignores their separate existence, and speaks of the juries as consisting of Senators and Equites alone. (Font. 36; Clu. 121 and 130; Flacc. 4, with Schol. Bob., and 96; Rab. Post. 14. On the other hand, the Tribuni Aerarii are mentioned as distinct from the Equites in Planc. 21; Rab. Perd. 27; Cat. iv. 15; A. i. 16, 3.)

Mommsen's view is adopted by Kübler (P.-W. vi. 1, 290) and Strachan-Davidson (*Problems of the Roman Criminal Law*, ii. 84–95), who, however, lays greater stress than Mommsen on the admission to the juries of Equites who had completed their service. 'According to the theory which I advocate', he says, 'all persons who had ever served, all past and present members of the equestrian centuries, so far as they were not disqualified by age, by office, or by loss of property, might be called to act as jurors. This body of persons . . . gradually won their way to the equestrian title, and constituted an *equester ordo* in a sense intermediate between the widest and the narrowest interpretation of the phrase. In a similar way the *ordo* of *tribuni aerarii* is to be taken to include all those who have ever held that annual office.' (For Strachan-Davidson holds that, even after 167 B.C., the term *tribuni aerarii* implies the holding of an office, of uncertain nature, in addition to, and presupposing, the possession of a certain property.)

Mommsen's view has been contested by M. Gelzer (*Regimentsfähigkeit und Nobilität der römischen Republik*, 1912), who points out the difficulty of getting the requisite number of jurymen (see below) out of the eighteen equestrian centuries, after making all the deductions prescribed by the 'Lex Acilia Repetundarum'. (This difficulty is, however, minimized if we increase the numbers available by admitting the ex-members of the centuries.) He further points to Cicero's use of the term *equester ordo* in Verr. II. iii. 223-4, which implies that equestrian census, not membership of the eighteen centuries, constituted the qualification for the equestrian jurymen.

To sum up. Several passages (notably Flacc. 4), in which Cicero includes the Tribuni Aerarii under the designation Equites Romani, at first sight seem to imply that they possessed the equestrian census; and that consequently when, in other passages, Cicero distinguishes the Equites Romani from the Tribuni Aerarii, he means, not the equestrian order, but a category within that order, either the present or the past and present *Equites Romani equo publico*. On the other hand, Verr. I. 38: II. iii. 223-4 and the testimony of the historians imply that the sole qualification needed by equestrian jurymen was the possession of the equestrian census. (Tac. Ann. xii. 60; Vell. ii. 6, 13 and 32; App. i. 22, 35; Plin. N. H. xxxiii. 34; Diod. xxxv. 25. These references, and others relating to the judiciary laws between 133 and 70 B. C., can be conveniently consulted in Greenidge and Clay's *Sources for Roman History*, pp. 26–7, 176, 221–2.)

A possible line of reconciliation might be found as follows. 'The equestrian decury was drawn from the entire equestrian order: the third decury was drawn from the Tribuni Aerarii, a body of men included in the equestrian order, but distinguished from the rest of the order by the possession of certain unknown functions or qualifications (just as the Hebdomadal Council of Oxford University formerly contained Masters of Arts elected as such, and Masters of Arts elected as Heads of Houses): thus, under the Lex Aurelia, there were virtually two equestrian decuries, though, in strict parlance, the second was distinguished by a special name.'

This is, however, not a very natural explanation; and, moreover, the scholium on the fragment from the *In Clodium et Curionem* definitely assigns to the Tribuni Aerarii a lower census of 300,000. I should therefore be inclined, following a hint thrown out by Mommsen (*St. R.* iii. 193, n. 2), to attribute the occasional inclusion of the Tribuni Aerarii among the equestrian jurors to a desire to flatter them by giving them a social status superior to that which of right belonged to them. This consideration reinforces Greenidge's argument (*Leg. Proc.* 444–5): 'As owners of a moderate capital they would thus be inferior only to the knights, and the small interval that separated the qualifications of the two orders would account for their frequent identification.'

IV. *The interpretation of i. 20, 'sed equiti etiam Romano', and 'At si ferretis quicumque equo meruisset, quod est lautius, nemini probaretis; in iudice enim spectari et fortuna debet et dignitas'.*

The equestrian jurymen were drawn either (1) from the whole

equester ordo, or (2) from a part of that *ordo*, viz. either (*a*) the serving *equites equo publico*, or (*b*) the serving and retired *equites equo publico*. (See III above.) Now as, on the accepted view, the *equites equo publico* all belonged to the *equester ordo*, and all therefore possessed the *census equester* of 400,000 sesterces, they would all *ipso facto* possess the right to sit on juries. Why then does Cicero say that to give them all that right would be 'approved by no one'? First of all, perhaps, because many of them (most, in fact, of those actually serving) would be below the age limit. (See § 20, note on *dignitas*.) Hence they lack the *dignitas* of mature manhood. (The centurions lack the *dignitas* of social position.) But why are they also said to lack *fortuna*,[1] since, *ex hypothesi*, they possess the equestrian census? Because, it may be answered, some of them, by loss of property, had fallen short of the equestrian census. But surely, though such cases would doubtless occur, they would not occur very frequently. And Cicero seems to be making a point of general principle.

I would suggest an alternative explanation. While it is indisputable that a property qualification was a condition for membership of the political *ordo equester* under the later republic, and for service in the burgess cavalry as long as burgess cavalry continued to exist, is it equally certain that it was required from all officers in the Ciceronian age? An affirmative answer has been generally assumed, without, I believe, direct evidence. But is it not, on the face of it, improbable that all young officers would have 400,000 sesterces of their own? In fact, the words 'Census praefiniebatur . . . equiti etiam Romano' seem, at first sight at any rate, to imply that the census was *not* a qualification necessary for being an *eques Romanus*. (But Cicero does not always express himself with lucid accuracy, and he may be regarding the *eques Romanus* exclusively from the military standpoint, and therefore representing a monetary qualification which was, strictly speaking, presupposed by the military position, as superadded to it, and as forming a qualification only for the performance of the civil duties of a juryman. Or we may take the datives *centurioni* and *equiti* as standing in different relations to *census praefiniebatur*. 'A census was laid down, not only *for* a centurion who wished to serve as a juror, but *for being* an *eques Romanus*. Or, lastly, with Strachan-Davidson (91–2), we may take the *census* mentioned here as being, not the *census equester* of 400,000 sesterces, but a higher census demanded from the three categories of jurors by the Lex Pompeia of 55: in which case we must construe Asconius's words in the sense that a definite higher census was so imposed on each category; and not in the far more natural sense that a merely general preference was given under that

[1] I think this is clearly what Cicero means. It would be very unnatural, though perhaps just possible, to take 'et fortuna et dignitas' as = 'non modo fortuna sed etiam dignitas'.

law to the richer men in each category, without the superimposition of any such definite higher census.)

It is, however, perhaps safer to maintain, particularly in view of the system prevailing under Augustus, that the *census equester* must have been required for mounted service, even during the republic. But there are grounds for believing that in practice it was frequently dispensed with under the stress of the Civil War. Caesar's head-quarters were a rendezvous for the impecunious (A. vii. 3, 5), and it is improbable that he would refuse commissions to able men who fell short of the required census. We know (ib.) that some of them were made *tribuni militum*, and were therefore mounted (Caes. B. G. vii. 65). Among those of his officers whose circumstances are known to us, Antony, who entered on manhood as a bankrupt (ii. 44), went to Gaul in 54 still in highly embarrassed circumstances (ii. 48), and was at once appointed legatus (probably a *militia equestris*), can scarcely have been the possessor of 400,000 sesterces. Nor can the younger Curio, whose debts Caesar paid. I feel sure that it is young ex-officers of this type to whom Cicero here refers.

(An entirely different explanation of the words 'quicumque equo meruisset' has been propounded by Madvig, *Die Verfassung und Verwaltung des römischen Staates*, i. 165, note. He thinks that Cicero means, not the Roman mounted officer, but the allied cavalry trooper (the burgess cavalry being now extinct. See I above). But, even if the position of such men could be described as *lautius* compared with that of the centurions, it is surely inconceivable that Cicero should represent their admission to the juries as a less violent innovation than the admission of the centurions. Most of them would not even be Roman citizens.)

APPENDIX III

THE ROMAN AUSPICES

THE whole problem of the Roman use of auspices, whether regarded from the religious or from the political point of view, is extremely complicated. Phil. ii, §§ 80–4 forms one of the most important, but most debatable, pieces of evidence on the subject.

By far the most elaborate treatment of the question with which I am acquainted is contained in a masterly series of articles by I. M. J. Valeton in *Mnemosyne*, 1889–91. Other modern authorities are Mommsen, *Staatsrecht*, i. 76–116; A. Bouché-Leclercq, *Histoire de la divination*, iv. 180 ff., and in Daremberg et Saglio, i. 580–5; Greenidge, *Classical Review*, vii. 158–61, *Roman Public Life*, 162–7, 172–3; Wissowa, *Religion und Kultus der Römer*, 523–34.

I. The Romans divided auspices into *auguria impetrativa*, omens requested by man, and *auguria oblativa*, omens sent by heaven unasked.[1] In theory, omens were of many kinds; in practice, only 'omens from the sky' were used for political purposes in the Ciceronian age (though omens from the feeding of chickens continued to be employed by commanders in the field). These *auspicia de caelo*, by which the Romans understood specifically thunder and lightning, were regarded as invariably unfavourable[2] to the holding of the *comitia* (though not invariably to other activities); and, with few exceptions, the political use of auspices in the Ciceronian age is the use of *auspicia de caelo* for obstructing the legislative and electoral functions of the *comitia*. These omens might appear either, on request, as *auspicia impetrativa*, or, without request, as *auspicia oblativa*; and this distinction is the main theme of §§ 80–4.

A. *Auspicia Impetrativa.*

(1) The right of looking for *auspicia impetrativa* was known as *spectio*;[3] and (*signa de caelo* being the only omens employed politically in Cicero's day) the exercise of that right was termed *servare de caelo*. (This identification is probable, and is universally accepted, though not explicitly attested by any ancient authority.)

(2) Strictly speaking, the unfavourable omen, after being seen, had to be announced to the magistrate who was about to preside over the assembly. This announcement was termed *nuntiatio*, or, more usually and more specifically, *obnuntiatio*[4] (*nuntiatio* being the announcement of any omen, *obnuntiatio* the announcement of an adverse omen). But in practice the *obnuntiatio* was only carried out on the rare occasions when the magistrate persisted in his determination to hold the assembly.[5] Usually the announcement by a duly qualified person that he had 'watched the heavens', or merely that he intended to watch them, was in itself sufficient to deter the magistrate from holding the assembly. Nevertheless,

[1] 'Auguria aut oblativa sunt, quae non poscuntur, sed casu eveniunt, aut impetrativa, quae optata veniunt' (Serv. ad Aen. vi. 190). For this Valeton (*Mnem.* xvii. 423) substitutes a tripartite classification: I. *Auguria impetrativa*: you ask the gods for a particular sign; II. *Auguria oblativa quaesita*: you ask the gods for any sign they choose to give; III. *Auguria oblativa fortuito conspecta*: they send a sign without your asking for one. This classification is difficult to reconcile with Servius's words, and is inadequately attested. The point is, however, of little importance for the present discussion. For practical purposes, Valeton's *oblativa quaesita* coincide with the *impetrativa* of other scholars (whom I follow): his *oblativa fortuito conspecta* with their *oblativa*.

[2] See note on § 99 *sinistrum fulmen*.

[3] § 81 *consules . . . spectionem*, and note

[4] § 81 note on *nuntiationem*.

[5] A. iv. 3. 3–5 gives an instructive (and amusing) instance of this. See Valeton, *Mnem.* xix. 101–2.

the term *obnuntiare* was popularly used of the obstructionist's action, as being its formally necessary completion.

(3) The 'watching of the heavens' had to take place before the assembly of the *comitia*. This is expressly stated by Cicero (§ 81 'priusquam habeantur') and is attested by practice.

(4) Popular opinion allowed the 'watcher of the heavens' to fabricate the required omen. Perhaps, as Valeton suggests (*Mnem.* xviii. 253), the pretence was originally assisted by the fact that the assembly met early in the day, and the watching therefore took place during the night or small hours; summer lightning, he observes, is frequent during the night in southern Europe, and the general mass of citizens would not be in a position to deny that it had occurred on a particular night. However this may be, it is difficult to believe that in the Ciceronian age *de caelo servare* was anything else than a fiction. Cicero himself mentions, as a matter of course (§ 81), that a man who has decided to watch the heavens can tell in advance what defect there will be in the auspices; and the general acceptance of the warning 'de caelo aliquem servaturum esse' as implying the certainty that the required omen will be seen is incompatible with a serious belief in such methods of divination.

B. *Auspicia Oblativa.*

(1) The right of announcing an unfavourable *auspicium oblativum* was not a magisterial prerogative, but belonged to all citizens. Whereas, however, the announcement of a private individual could be respected or ignored at will by the presiding magistrate, the announcement of an augur had, of itself, power to dismiss the assembly with the words 'alio die'[1] (§§ 83-4; De Leg. ii. 31). We have, then, in addition to the magistrate's *obnuntiatio* of *auspicia impetrativa* based on the *spectio*, the augur's and private citizen's *obnuntiatio* of *auspicia oblativa*.

(2) It seems to be *prima facie* probable that the announcement of *auspicia oblativa* could only be made *during* the meeting. Otherwise there was nothing to indicate that the omen had reference to the meeting; whereas in the case of an *auspicium impetrativum* the magistrate asked for an omen with regard to a particular event, and the reference could not be ambiguous. At any rate, the recorded instances are all of the announcement of *auspicia oblativa* during the meeting.

[1] The distinction is drawn thus sharply (and rightly, I think) by Valeton, who speaks (*Mnem.* xviii. 420-2, 449) of the 'obnuntiatio cogens augurum' as opposed to the 'obnuntiatio non cogens privatorum'; and by Mommsen, who speaks (*St. R.* i. 109) of the augur's 'Nuntiation mit rechtsverbindlicher Kraft': less sharply by Greenidge, *C. R.* vii. 160. On the precise significance of the terms *nuntiatio* and *obnuntiatio* see § 81, note on *nuntiationem*.

II. Such, in outline, appears to have been the theory and practice of auspices in the Ciceronian age. But complication is introduced by the passing, in 58 B.C., of a Lex Clodia, which abrogated, in whole or in part, the provisions of the Lex Aelia Fufia[1] of 154. Great uncertainty prevails as to the provisions of the earlier and of the later measure. In 59 the consul Bibulus obstructed all Caesar's political actions by 'watching the heavens'. In the following year, to prevent the employment of these tactics in future, Clodius proposed and carried a law which certainly forbade the use of this proceeding against legislation, thereby abrogating the corresponding clause of the Lex Aelia Fufia. What is uncertain is whether the Lex Clodia forbade 'watching the heavens' in the case of electoral *comitia* also. Our authorities nowhere directly state that a distinction was drawn between legislative and electoral *comitia*; but, where they descend to detail, they invariably mention the former and never the latter.[2] Moreover, precisely in the years immediately following 58 B.C., electoral *comitia* were repeatedly obstructed by 'watching the heavens', and it nowhere appears that such obstruction was challenged as illegal; whereas we know of no single certain instance in which legislative *comitia* were so obstructed.[3] There is thus considerable indirect, though no direct, evidence for Valeton's view that, after 58 B.C., 'watching the heavens' was legal in the case of electoral, illegal in the case of legislative, *comitia*.[4] Most scholars, however, hold that it was illegal in both cases during this period.[5] If so, how are we to account for the frequent, successful, and unchallenged use of the privilege in the years following 58? Two solutions have been offered. Mommsen (*St. R.* i. 112) suggests

[1] The designation is convenient; but there appear in fact to have been two laws, one possibly supplementing the other. (Pis. 9; Prov. Cons. 46; Vat. 18; Sest. 33; Greenidge *C. R.* vii. 158).

[2] Prov. Cons. 46; Sest. 33; Post. Red. in Sen. 11; Ascon. in Pis. 7-8. Dio (xxxviii. 13. 5) appears to bring electoral comitia under the Lex Clodia (cf. ἀρχόντων καταστάσεις), but Valeton is probably right (*Mnem.* xix. 255) in restricting the reference to legislative comitia. In any case, Dio is a secondary authority, and may have misunderstood his sources.

[3] Sest. 79 is an uncertain case. Mommsen (*St. R.* 113, n. 3) thinks that the occasion was electoral, Valeton (*Mnem.* xix. 248) that it was legislative, and that this explains the ignoring of the *obnuntiatio* by the consul. For a case of contemplated obstruction, see note 5.

[4] J. S. Reid makes the same suggestion in his addition to Peskett's note (p. 111). Valeton holds that the Lex Aelia Fufia allowed *de caelo servare* against legislative *comitia*, but disallowed it against electoral *comitia*; and that the Lex Clodia reversed both provisions. He argues ingeniously that the obstruction of legislation was disadvantageous to the revolutionaries, while the obstruction of elections suited them, as leading to anarchy and creating the need for constitutional innovations (*Mnem.* xix. 253-4).

[5] Either because, while the Lex Aelia Fufia had allowed *de caelo servare* against either kind of *comitia*, the Lex Clodia disallowed it against

that the Lex Clodia was frequently ignored.[1] But this is not very convincing. Why, as Valeton rejoins (*Mnem.* xix. 266-8), did not the other side impugn the ignoring of the law?

An alternative explanation has been put forward by Greenidge (*C. R.* vii. 158-61), who believes that all instances of obstruction at the *comitia* after 58 are based on the observation of *auguria oblativa* (which, Valeton agrees, was not touched by the Lex Clodia). *De caelo servare* is used, Greenidge holds, in two senses: in the technical sense, of the observation of *auspicia impetrativa*, and in the non-technical sense, of the observation of *auspicia oblativa*: a tribune who threatens *de caelo servare* does not 'do so in the same sense which the magistrates with *imperium* did. He merely asserts the likelihood of his seeing something (*oblativum*).' It appears to me, however, extremely improbable that a stereotyped formula like *de caelo servare* could ever be used in a non-technical sense; moreover, some of the recorded cases of obstruction after 58 B.C. (notably the incident described in A. iv. 3) cannot be explained on the basis of *auspicia oblativa*.

To sum up. Valeton appears to be right in his account of the state of the law of auspices in the period after 58 B.C. (whether he is also right in his account of the successive stages through which the law had passed, is a more debatable point which may happily be left undecided for our present purpose).

III. It remains to attempt the interpretation of §§ 80-4 on these lines.

Antony had a choice between two methods of procedure. As consul he could, by use of the magistrate's power of *spectio*, prevent the *comitia* from assembling for the election of Dolabella: as augur he could, by *obnuntiatio oblativorum*, 'comitia vel impedire vel vitiare', i.e. compel the dissolution of the assembly, *re infecta*, or, if Caesar refused to dissolve it, arraign the election of Dolabella as invalid, 'vitio esse factum'. Why did he reject the first method, which Cicero characterizes as *etiam facilius*, in favour of the second? Clearly not on account of 'incredible stupidity', for Antony was no fool. If Mommsen is to be believed, he acted so

either (as Mommsen maintains); or because the Lex Clodia left unrepealed a clause of the Lex Aelia Fufia forbidding *de caelo servare* against electoral *comitia*, but abrogated a clause allowing it against legislative *comitia*, (as Lange holds). (*Mnem.* xix. 261-2.)

[1] Cicero's language in Prov. Cons. 46 perhaps implies the possibility of ignoring the Lex Clodia: 'aut vobis statuendum est legem Aeliam manere, legem Fufiam non esse abrogatam.' So, more certainly, does the s. c. passed in 57 B.C. 'ne quis de caelo servaret, ne quis moram ullam adferret', in connexion with the proposal for Cicero's recall (Sest. 129); cf. Rice Holmes, ii. 60, n. 5. It is worth noting in this connexion that another clause of the Lex Clodia, forbidding *intercessio*, appears to have been ignored. See i. 25, note on *intercedant*.

because he had no choice in the matter: magisterial *spectio* had been abolished by the Lex Clodia (hence 'quod neque licet comitiis per leges', which appears, however, to be inconsistent with the following words, 'et . . . nuntiare', and with 'neque . . . dicis' in § 83) and could only be employed by some one prepared to ignore the Lex Clodia. But I have given reason above for supposing that magisterial *spectio* had not been entirely abolished by the Lex Clodia, but was (in spite of, or even because of, that law) still permissible in the case of electoral *comitia*. If so, we must seek another explanation of Antony's conduct; and Valeton supplies one (*Mnem.* xix. 96) by pointing out that the use of *auspicia oblativa* had this advantage over the alternative method, that it enabled Antony to wait until the last possible moment, and see whether Caesar really meant to persist in carrying through the election of a man under the legal age.[1] This is ingenious, and may be correct, though it is possible that Antony had some other reason which is beyond our guessing. But how are we to reconcile the words 'quod neque licet comitiis per leges', which appear at first sight to rule out 'watching the heavens' in connexion with the *comitia*, with the assumption that 'watching the heavens' *was* allowed in the case of electoral *comitia*? According to Valeton (*Mnem.* xviii. 449), *comitiis* = 'inter comitia': Cicero's point is that 'obnuntiatio ex spectione' must take place *before* the *comitia*, unlike 'obnuntiatio oblativorum', which must take place *during* the *comitia*; and he makes his meaning clearer by the words which follow, 'et . . . nuntiare'. I confess there appears to be something dubious in the Latinity of this. One would surely expect 'inter comitia' (or the equivalent), and 'non . . . sed' for 'neque . . . et'. I am disposed, however, to accept Valeton's explanation as the least of evils.

It seems probable, then, that Antony could, if he chose, have employed *obnuntiatio ex spectione* as consul; but that he preferred to employ *obnuntiatio oblativorum* as augur. Valeton points out (*Mnem.* xix. 97) that few cases of augural *obnuntiatio* are recorded,[2] for the reason that this method of procedure involved the open and flagrant fabrication of an imaginary omen. *Obnuntiatio ex spectione* was, at any rate originally, on a different footing.[3] The observing magistrate could invent his lightning undetected. And even if it was, towards the end of the republican era, so generally recognized that he did invent it, that Cicero can say 'qui de caelo servare con-

[1] Pompey was perhaps influenced by such a consideration on a similar occasion. See note 2 below.

[2] Valeton thinks (*Mnem.* xix. 95) that Pompey was acting as augur, not as consul, when, in 55 B.C., he dissolved the *comitia* after the *centuria praerogativa* had voted for Cato's election as praetor, βροντῆς ἀκηκοέναι ψευσάμενος (Plut. Cat. Min. 42). That incident supplies the nearest parallel to Antony's action.

[3] See I. A. 4 above.

stituit, divinare potest quid viti in auspiciis futurum sit', it is nevertheless intelligible, if a trifle singular, that popular opinion drew a fairly sharp line between the making of such a forecast and the assertion that an occurrence had just taken place in the presence of a number of persons who knew perfectly well that it had not taken place. Such a lie could be stigmatized, at any rate for rhetorical purposes, as *impudentia*,[1] and the *impudentia* was heightened if a man announced in advance 'multis ante mensibus' that he meant to tell the lie.

[1] Cf. αἴσχιστα διέλυσε τὴν ἐκκλησίαν, in the passage from Plutarch cited in note a above.